Hysterical Psychosis

Katrien Libbrecht

Hysterical Psychosis

a historical survey

Routledge
Taylor & Francis Group
LONDON AND NEW YORK

First published 1995 by Transaction Publishers

Published 2017 by Routledge
2 Park Square, Milton Park, Abingdon, Oxon OX14 4RN
711 Third Avenue, New York, NY 10017, USA

First issued in paperback 2018

Routledge is an imprint of the Taylor & Francis Group, an informa business

Library of Congress Catalog Number: 94-8720

Library of Congress Cataloging-in-Publication Data

Libbrecht, Katrien.
Hysterical psychosis: a historical survey/Katrien Libbrecht.
p. cm.
Includes bibliographical references and index.
ISBN 1-56000-181-X
1. Hysteria—Research—History. I. Title
RC532.L49 1994
616.85'24'009—dc20 94-8720
CIP

ISBN 13: 978-1-138-51072-2 (pbk)
ISBN 13: 978-1-56000-181-2 (hbk)

Contents

Foreword

This book, *Hysterical Psychosis: A Historical Survey* by Katrien Libbrecht, is the only publication to date on the history of mad or seemingly psychotic hysteria. In case there are some reservations as to its completeness, one should recognize the fact that it excels in readability and that it is built upon a number of exceptional and original theses.

Ms. Libbrecht holds the view that someone should review the history of clinical psychiatry at a time when psychiatry itself no longer seems capable of doing so. Should clinical psychology assume this task? Or will the responsibility be a mere hobby for a handful of rare psychiatrists with an interest in the past? Since psychoanalytic curiosity has instilled in the author a sense of history, she has chosen to accept the seemingly paradoxical mission of not letting the historical past of clinical psychiatry go to waste, while also engaging in establishing psychoanalysis as a radically different clinical field.

Her intent is not merely based in science-historical motives. For she believes that historical perspectives can be made meaningful for everyday reality too, i.e., the clinical approach the suffering individual can benefit when one acknowledges how new wine acquires its flavor from old casks. One can interpret the great underlying structural questions in their current ways when they represent themselves to us in the different stages of the psychiatric past. A differential diagnosis and a suitably modulated treatment are more closely connected with the problem of differences with regard to structure than they are with the conspicuous symptomatology and with the phenomenology with which a person announces himself.

The further particularization of the above thesis brings Ms. Libbrecht to the hypothesis that the deep study of this clinical past is a necessary step—at least it should be for every theoretical position taken by the clinical therapist. The fact that—in this sense—this is generally neglected applies not only to all those who are devoted to the Brief Reactive Psychosis (D.S.M.-III-R) but also to Freudo-Lacanian circles.

Considering the consequences for treatment, it is no small feat on her part that she has been able to illustrate this quite convincingly by means of her study of the so-called hysterical psychosis. Either theory categorizes the seemingly psychotic phenomena as psychotic—in which case one is at the mercy of a form of therapy that offers no prospects. Or if one neglects these phenomena —sticking to the tried and tested standard—treatment of this seemingly psychotic hysteria causes the therapist to get stuck in a rut because of a lack of suitable modulation of the treatment. History already warns us to guard us against these two major difficulties of the clinical practice with such patients.

The next link in the cascade of theses connects the historical concern with what is characteristic of psychoanalysis. The analytical treatment is to verbalize the past to make it a "past" suffering. This may turn out to be a far-reaching process. In accordance with this vision the author studies psychiatry's history. In the same manner a patient puts his or her suffering into words, the writing down of the past should be a rewriting of the problems as they reveal themselves in the clinical field.

The next logical and ultimate link is made up of a frame theory from which the whole text is constructed. It is not solely a return to the writings of Freud and to the Prefreudian clinical field of the seemingly psychotic hysteria. Rather it deals with the construction of this history along the three axes that Freud acknowledged in the way in which the hysteric introduces material into the treatment. First there is the linear-chronological axis. Then there is the concentrical-thematical organization of the material around a nucleus which—in this case—is the fascination with the object of examination, that can only be approached through resistance. Finally, there is the logical-dynamical order that reveals itself through the intercutting lines branching out to make up a type of tree structure.

What makes this study, a truly analytically-inspired history, so intriguing is the fact that this frame theory is actually followed throughout and developed in its three aspects. It proves that the scientific-historical dimension can indeed be compatible with an approach that respects both what is characteristic of the material as well as what is specific to the clinical formation.

JULIEN QUACKELBEEN

Introduction and Acknowledgements

Sigmund Freud and Jacques Lacan are the two basic authors who delineated the field of operation from which we take our bearings. They deviated from traditional practice because of impasses they encountered in contemporary psychiatric practice in the years 1895 and 1932. They did so in order to found a different practice. Their respective points of departure are the clinical field of hysteria and that of psychosis. These undertakings—each in its own way—have turned a troublesome encounter with psychiatry into a fruitful development for both psychoanalytic theory and praxis.

Our study proceeds from a clinical standpoint, that includes the current impasse on both sides of the Atlantic, concerning the bounds of hysteria that present themselves within the psychiatric as well as within the psychoanalytic clinical field. Within the psychiatric field this deadlock is rooted in the questions with regard to the reality of a certain clinical entity. We refer to the so-called hysterical psychosis, generally described as a mixture of hysterical and psychotic features or as a hysterical personality manifesting distinct psychotic features. This description indicates that this notion of hysterical psychosis takes on a different meaning than what is given under the formal diagnostic category of Brief Reactive Psychosis (DSM-III-R). As this "hysterical psychosis" rears its head with a certain regularity in psychiatric contributions of diverse tendencies, it demands recognition. It also requires a more distinct diagnosis, i.e., in what way does this so-called hysterical psychosis distinguish itself from other psychoses and more specifically from schizophrenia? Its sporadic mention in literature might at the very least indicate a more than exceptional clinical-psychiatric reality. Hysterical psychosis: acknowledged but unloved?

Within the psychoanalytic practice delineated above, our point of departure, the clinical impasse announces itself in a different manner. In spite of a radical theoretical distinction between hysteria and psychosis, differentiation between the two clinical structures remains neither self-evident nor simple. The radical element in this distinction does not allow itself to be translated gratuitously into clinical practice, so it would seem. It is from this perspective that Jean-Claude Maleval has founded his pioneering work in the psychoanalytic renewal of "hysterical madness."[1]

In order to legitimize the use of "hysterical psychosis" (typified as a distinct psychosis) and the rehabilitation of "hysterical madness" (categorized under the structure of hysteria), one appeals to the clinical richness of psychiatry during the *fin de siècle*—a period in which psychiatry had its greatest flourishing. This period constitutes a direct invitation to investigate this particular domain more thoroughly.

Two concepts, hysteria and madness, make up the *fil rouge* that leads to a return to the basic texts or configurations of signifiers within which so-called hysterical psychosis surfaces, under the heading of this or another signifier.[2] From this initial point in time—1860, the year in which "hysterical madness" sees the light of day as a phrase—we shall review the past one hundred and thirty years. We appeal first to the original texts and their respective contexts. The crucial historical transformations of the initial phrase, hysterical madness, that brought about the contemporary notions of hysteria and madness, are reconstructed. The end result of this historical analysis is a narrative structure that relates the vicissitudes of a pair of signifiers: hysterical madness.[3]

What arguments can justify the resolve to record the history of hysterical psychosis or psychotic hysteria?[4] There is the widely known claim of exhaustiveness. Within the scope of our study the need for completeness can only be met in a limited way and gets the following minimal definition. The field of our object of research is clinical psychiatry and psychoanalysis. We would like to make a strict distinction between them, for their respective clinical realities are not the same. This is determined by the perspective from which one looks at the clinical field. More specifically, it is theory, the symbolical grid, that defines this reality. An exhaustive analysis of the differentiation between hysteria and psychosis therefore requires—beyond the present-day clinical situation—that the history of the psychoanalytic and the psychiatric clinical practice be scrutinized. Only then can we properly gauge the full extent of the problem.

The above investigation becomes even more essential in light of an observation which simultaneously becomes the second aspect of our inquiry. Current psychiatric and psychoanalytic literature on the problematic relationship between the clinical entities of hysteria and psychosis far too often ignores the historical differences—a history which actually dates back to psychiatry's earliest days and beyond the conception of psychoanalysis. More specifically, the fruits of this historical past have not been reaped. Historical monographs and studies of hysterical madness are not put in their original context, which in our opinion is the prerequisite for a reference in order to reveal its value. Nor is the context introduced into the process of decision making. In this way, history remains unattended or even bended.

A third and final argument constitutes our drawing of conclusions. We found that our return to early psychiatry—prior to the conception of psychoanalysis—led to the thesis that digging into the psychiatric and psychoanalytic past and the writing of that history bore fruits that amply reward the amount of energy such a design demands. We observed a sustained methodical strictness in sorting out the facts and the prevalence of theory where the material, articulated in that way, can be constructed and be understood. These marginal conditions, which are ostensibly disconnected from each other, allow the focusing on what is problematic in the relationship between hysteria and madness.

Along the same lines—and adding to these premises—these conditions create the possibility of analyzing and purifying the current rank growth of diagnostic categories which, paradoxically, is both a result and a cause of diagnostic confusion.

Let us first of all explain our basic thesis which grounds itself in the above statements. The history of psychopathology divulges a problematic relationship between hysteria on the one hand and psychosis on the other. At distinct moments the matter is posed acutely and—contrary to popular belief—is not self-evident, and attempts are made to give possible solutions.

The usefulness of each historical reference is determined by the extent we succeed in placing it back into its proper context. We consider this background minimally as the aggregate of concepts a particular author uses. Our theory comes from the position and the meaning of the ideas presented. This means that no concept can be isolated and transposed to a contemporary context without bringing about significant shifts in meaning. The same applies to the mere substitution of a concept by what is commonly prevalent within present terminology. Current terminology, too, only acquires meaning within its pertinent context.

This brings us to the next basic assumption; the relationship between hysteria and psychosis is a problem that has posed itself implicitly and explicitly for over a century and which also asserts itself in the modern-day clinic. The ways in which the relationship is articulated are both diachronically and synchronically extremely diverse and only acquire their significance within the respective frames of reference. Not taking the above statement into account is synonymous with depriving the history of hysterical madness of significance. The past remains without meaning or is crammed with meaning that violates the original configurations.

How can we learn from the history of this relationship? Which method must we rigidly adhere to?

We have written this history along a set of coordinates that maps out the examined material in a way that emphasizes the diversity in articulating the problem mentioned above. We have already introduced this prerequisite by allowing history a right of speech and meaning by placing the signifiers back in their respective chains. In this way we avoid an all too easy *nachträglich* interpretative understanding of earlier works.

Which set of coordinates do we use? Here we are indebted to Michel Foucault. Everyone who is familiar with his work on the history of madness is aware of its complexity, a complexity that does not allow for summarization without gross reduction. This philosopher reconstructs the path of the signifier, madness, with regard to the one of reason. He does so for the period from the Middle Ages up to the nineteenth century. He examines madness, successively in time and in all its possible facets, and how it is allocated within the prevailing discourses, particularly the social, the political, and the philosophical discourse. Through these coordinates of time and of position within discourse he sketches the complex interweaving of madness within the diverse literary products of the distinct epochs.[5]

Though basically following the same pattern, our aim is more modest. Rather than continuing in Foucault's footsteps and writing a sequel to his work, we focus our attention specifically on hysterical madness and concentrate our work on the position of these two signifiers within clinical-diagnostic discourses and theories. Here, too, these are restricted to the field of psychiatry and psychoanalysis.

The signifier, madness, we have derived from Foucault's work—considering the fact that it is used within a certain frame of reference, his position of departure is determined by his philosophical formation. This is our frame of reference, and the position which madness is conferred in it needs further explanation. Our study is based on psychoanalytic theory, more specifically psychoanalysis in the way it has been given shape by Lacan in his rereading of Freud's theory of the unconscious. Lacan's theory essentially emphasizes the linguistic dimension of the unconscious of the subject and of psychoanalytic treatment. This implies that we do not study madness in its dynamical relation with regard to reason, but instead take it as a general reference—as a signifier which is void by definition and which only acquires meaning within distinct historical references. Madness can also be researched in its reference to other signifiers, be it in its position within various chains of signifiers or in its substitution by other signifiers. Our study comprises psychiatric, i.e., nosological and nosographical entities, diagnostic categories rather than concepts such as truth, reason and liberty and it is supported by psychoanalytical formalizations.

This historical method, with consideration for the two fundamental axes of language, being the condensation or metaphor and the displacement or metonymy, permits the designation of a certain structure in what initially seems to be magmatic material. In this respect a passage from Freud's work is highly instructive. In his first elaborate study on hysteria, a piece of work which he published jointly with Breuer in 1895, Freud arrives at a representation of the way in which the psychic material arranges itself around a pathological nucleus, constituted by reminiscences or chains of thought in which the traumatic factor culminates or in which the pathogenic idea finds its purest manifestation. The psychic material—the memories the patient commits to the physician—according to Freud, presents itself as a multi-dimensional structure and is stratified in at least three distinct ways. The first is the linear-chronological ordering of each separate theme, that is, an ordering in time. The second is the concentrical stratification of constituent themes around a pathological nucleus. The contents of each stratum are characterized by the same degree of resistance that rises as the nucleus is approached. The third and, according to Freud irrefutably the most important arrangement, has a dynamic nature, contrary to the two preceding ones which were morphological. It takes the shape of a logical chain and is comparable to the zigzag line from and to the nucleus. A tree-like structure of lines, with various intersections where two or more lines converge seems to Freud an even more accurate simile for this third stratification.[6]

The above multi-layered structure (chronological, thematical and logical) in our opinion not only applies to the material with which a hysterical subject writes his or her history or even for the way in which a hysterical symptom is determined, but we also find it in the material we use to write the history of hysterical madness.

We are using the historical method as the first layer, the chronological ordering of each theme. The concentrically arranged themes that materialize from the material are characterized by a certain degree of resistance and constitute a second layer. These are the various typifications of hysterical madness, whether or not they be cast into a theoretical mold. Only in retrospect, once the history of hysterical madness has been verbalized and written, is it possible to integrally recover and render the most important and fertile layeredness, the logical chain. This appears in the summaries preceding each chapter and is resumed in the conclusions.

Finally, the nucleus, we determine, is that which drives the writing about hysterical madness and which is unequivocally linked with the fascination it exudes. This nucleus is never absent, though it often seems at great distance and intangible.

The inherent presence of this enigmatic nucleus also applies to our writing of this book, which also has a history of its own. The person who takes a special place in this is Professor Julien Quackelbeen. As a supervisor, but every bit as much as the engine behind this and other work, he is owed much appreciation. In the path that we have walked he has achieved an eminence which can hardly be overstated. Any extension of gratitude must therefore be inadequate.

We would also like to mention our fellow workers at the Department for Psychoanalysis of Ghent University whose ready ears and critical remarks enabled us to channel our efforts.

Furthermore, we are most indebted to Professor Walter Vandereycken of Leuven, who readily provided us with various supplementary resources. He also encouraged us to write this book and gave advice and critical remarks on many topics on the history of psychiatry. In addition to him, Professor Em. François

Duyckaerts provided us with support and guidance when the book was still in its first stages. We would also like to express our special thanks to Jacques Sabbe and to Dany Nobus for their intense collaboration in improving and amending the English manuscript.

Finally, I am most grateful to Professor Irving Louis Horowitz for readily accepting the manuscript for publication. He and his staff at Transaction, particularly Scott B. Bramson, Laurence Mintz and Sheldon Bernbaum gave this book its present form by their guidance and many constructive contributions in preparing the final manuscript.

Notes

1. J.-C. Maleval (1981), *Folies hystériques et psychoses dissociatives*, Paris, Payot.
2. This historiographical aspect has already been broached in K. Librecht (1989), *Hysterische waan: Symptoom of structuur?*, introductory study by J. Quackelbeen, Pegasos series no. 3, Ghent, Idesça.
3. The fact that our historiography entails certain limitations is inherent to any such design, which by necessity carries through a selection of authors and material. This selection, always arbitrary, is the privilege of the author and therefore is his responsibility. A second observation regards the use of the words *hysteria*, *delusion*, *madness* and *psychosis*. The reader will find the respective significance of each of these notions specified each time in the discussion. These concepts incessantly shift in meaning throughout the text.
4. In contradistinction to the self-evidence where a historical sketch or a short historiographical survey of the issue is interpolated in an article or a study, we wish to state the necessity of this, which, in our case, is indisputable.
5. M. Foucault (1972), *Histoire de la folie à l'âge classique*, Paris, Gallimard.
6. S. Freud & J. Breuer (1895d), *Studies on Hysteria*, *S.E.*, 2, pp. 288-290.

Part One

The Turn of the Century

Recognition of Hysterical Madness, Heyday of the Hysterical Fit

Introduction

The period from the second half of the nineteenth century up until the first years of the twentieth century is marked by dialogue and exchange of clinical and nosological concepts between the two great schools that are at the cradle of clinical psychiatry. They are the French and the German Schools, both in their meaning of nationality and tongue.[1] The fact that the German theoretical textbooks are laced with French clinical material is a concrete trace of this exchange.

The originality of the German works lies in the strength of their attempts at synthesis and in dominance of theory in approaching psychopathological problems. The Germans, whose minds focused on systematicity, excelled in exhaustive, dogmatic classification systems and were disposed to a strong conceptual framework.[2]

In spite of a rather meagerly turned out conceptual armature the French revealed an extremely pregnant positivistic mind. They were clearly ahead as far as the clinical method was concerned. Above all, description was their forte. Closely in keeping with clinical practice, they tried to arrive at general features. This clinical development was accompanied by extremely vague and broad doctrinal options. The French eschewed dogmatic and rigid systems. One French criticism of the Germans therefore was that every German-speaking psychiatrist of any importance constructed his own classification system, typified by personal neologisms and newly fleshed-out, already existing categories. There simply was no consensus.[3]

In the year 1860 on French soil we note the birth of the *folie hystérique*, as a specific form of madness, namely mental illness issuing from hysterical neurosis. Characteristic are mental aberrations, without any exception linked with an inherent mental weakness. Clinically it comprises the most diverse phenomena. This form of madness, peculiar to hysteria, is acknowledged during that same period in German-speaking territory. With this, under one signifier or another, hysterical madness near the end of the nineteenth century is a unanimously accepted and studied entity within clinical psychiatry. Although the psychiatrists still argue over the definition of hysteria, the link between hysteria and madness is unmistakable. This denotation of hysterical madness as a distinct clinical entity precedes the neurological emancipation of hysteria, in line with what psychoanalysis will develop.

In France, this neurological emancipation is here and there precedented and the uncoupling of hysteria from madness and also of neurosis from psychosis is initiated: madness as an affiliated disorder of hysteria. German influences are present in the coupling of hysteria to confusion, characterized by dream-like delusions. Finally, there is the French publication in 1910 of a final monograph on *folie hystérique*. Hysterical madness is thus carried to its grave without having theoretically demonstrated its clinical singularity.

However, where the French systematically describe the clinical manifestations of hysterical madness, the German psychiatrists develop classification systems in which hysteria is allocated a position both as a distinct form of madness and as a precursor of it. It is a marked German tendency to let the hysterical character or the hysterical nature (be it acquired or not) prevail over the hysterical symptoms which demonstrate little coherence. In it the disorders revolve around a congenital hysterical nucleus. What is emphasized in German-speaking circles is the evolution of the clinical picture rather than the terminal demential state. This reveals itself in widely ramified classification systems. This classification-character of German textbooks sharply contrasts with the explicit monograph-nature of French works.

Towards the turn of the century hysteria as neurosis will let itself be characterized more and more clearly by physical disorders and psychosis more and more by mental disorders. Hysteria will however continue to comprise, albeit in a limited sense, mental disorders next to the already explicitly studied physical complaints. A second shift concerns the range of the mental disorders which initially referred to disorders of the intelligence. These mental disorders are expanded to include disorders of the intelligence, the will, and the character. The seeds of the present era of personality disorders are already present here.

Notes

1. P. Bercherie (1988), *Géographie du champ psychanalytique*, Bibliothèque des Analytica, Paris, Navarin, p. 137.
2. This is connected with German university psychiatric training, in which scientific and philosophical formation remain strongly associated. P. Bercherie (1980), *Les Fondements de la clinique*, La Bibliothèque d'Ornicar?, Analytica no. 20-21, Paris, pp. 66-67.
3. See for example *Annales médico-psychologiques*, 1881, 6, 5, pp. 335-341. A certain doctor Chatelain discusses Krafft-Ebing's textbook and highly appreciates its frugality, in particular regarding the use of neologisms.

1
The Psychiatric Coordinates

The French Alienists

Let us first and foremost state a few concepts that color the discourse of the French physicians during this period.

Under the heading of *aliénation mentale* (mental derangement), which during those days has the same meaning as *folie* or madness, used in a vulgarizing sense, the entire gamut of mental illnesses is brought together. It is the only classification which is applied at that time and it is essentially characterized by what are called disorders of intellectual functions. When a condition of mental alienation becomes habitual it results in dementia—a general regression of the mental functions. What is notable is the secondary importance assigned to the presence of delusion. The *paralysie générale* (general paralysis) applies as a paradigm.[1] This instantly implies that in the first instance mental disorders of an organic origin find accommodation under that heading. Next to this general paralysis there is the gradual development of a series of symptomatic types of mental derangement which, apart from organically determined entities, also start including functional disorders. Hysteria for example.[2]

Neurosis, the neuropathologist's specific object of study, in its initial, wider sense encompasses all disorders of the nervous system without a known anatomical basis or assignable neurological damage. To this end Charcot introduces the concept of the dynamical (ephemeral) lesion. The School of the Salpêtrière, of which Charcot was the figurehead and founding father, strictly limits the definition of neurosis. The basic model for this is essential epilepsy.

To further elucidate this we would also like to establish the position of the physician-alienist and that of the physician-neuropathologist in their mutual relationship. In nineteenth-century France the physician who devotes himself to the study and treatment of mentally ill patients or *aliénés* in the asylums is given the title of physician-alienist, the specific tag *alienist* clearly conjures up images of mental estrangement. With the rise of psychiatry the title of alienist is more strictly reserved for the medical-judicial sector.[3] On the other hand, there is the fact that neuroses which, strictly speaking, are on one side of the boundary of neuropathology, gradually become the exclusive study and therapy field of the physician-neuro(patho)logist. The entourage of Charcot, during the second half of the nineteenth century, is particularly authoritative both with regard to research into and treatment of neurosis.

Birth of a New Entity

Depending on the source consulted it is either Bénédict-Augustin Morel (1809-1873) or Jacques Moreau de Tours (1804-1884) who get the honor of first reporting and clinically describing the *folie hystérique* (hysterical madness).[4] This means that in 1860 hysterical madness is described for the first time as a separate entity and given credence as an identity. Prior to this it vanished in the amalgam of mental disorders.

In 1860 Morel's *Traité des maladies mentales* was published as the implementation of his innovative vision on pathogenesis.[5] Within madness two groups are distinguished on the basis of etiology. The first of these two groups can be characterized as those forms of madness in which the madness as an original phenomenon fully ties in with the actions of the cause. Among others it comprises madness stemming from the major neuroses (hysteria, hypochondria, epilepsy). Hysterical madness, too, as a transformed hysteria, finds its place there. Transformed means that the somatic disorders typical of neurosis feature less prominently. They make way for mental disorders which mark the transition to mental derangement. As long as the periods of delusion can be distinguished and intelligence and affective life in between those periods remain unaffected there can be no question of true hysterical madness but of hysterical delusion. "Hysterical" in this sense therefore relates to the origins; the madness is the result of hysteria, it is consecutive to hysteria.[6] The second group finds its definition in hereditary degeneration, a concept which, in substitution of moral cause, will have great impact on the further development of theoretical concepts with regard to psychopathology.[7] Morel's observations of *folie hystérique* impel the conclusion that the image, to him, is protean.[8] Specific characteristics are: the linking up of the delusion with neurological disorders that are typical of hysteria, sudden impulsive and potentially dangerous behavior, briefness of occurrence and disappearance of the delusion, and, in conclusion, awareness of the delusion. A terminal demential state is not excluded; hysterical madness is (but) one form of madness.[9]

In 1869, after eight years at the Salpêtrière, Jacques Moreau de Tours, a student of Esquirol's, published his *Traité de la folie névropathique (vulgo hystérique)*.[10] This frequently quoted clinical reference is marked by the confrontation of Moreau as an alienist with the physician-neuropathologists in residence at the Salpêtrière who take the classical neuroses and in particular hysteria as their object of study and therapy.[11] In it Moreau now brings what was still called *folie hystérique* in his first publication, under the heading of *folie névropathique* (neuropathic madness). Hysteria becomes a synonym for neuropathy or neurosis —one for the entirety—whilst Morel still subsumes, next to hysterical madness, epileptical and hypochondriac madness under the same category.[12]

Moreau divides neuropathic madness into three categories, the first of which comprises the phenomena which pertain to hysterical delusion rather than to hysterical madness. With this it is made abundantly clear once more that the hysterical delusion is treated separately from hysterical madness. The second category constitutes actual hysterical madness. The third category covers the cases of hereditary transformation of a hysterical nature (Morel's hysterical madness). The work is, however, essentially devoted to the second category, actual hysterical madness determined by a material neurological disorder. The elaboration is analogous to the previous study. The typification which we include for the sake of completeness, is situated on the same line as Morel's. There is always a certain awareness of the brief, acute state; there are obvious analogies with both the delusion (artificially) induced by narcotics, and the somnambulistic state and stupor where the delusion is intermittent, and finally there is also the presence of various, violently acute ideas and impulses.[13]

With regard to the earlier mentioned analogy with artificial delusion, we would like to add here that Moreau de Tours puts *folie* on a par with the state of dreaming, which implies an alteration with regard to how Morel described *folie*.[14]

Falret and Legrand du Saulle

In Jules Falret (1824-1902), who follows in the path of his father Jean-Pierre Falret, we hear a different and older tale. In 1866 he took part in a discussion before the Société médico-psychologique on *folie raisonnante*, which to his mind is not a separate mental illness but an artificial patchwork of disparate facts belonging to distinct categories. Hysterical madness is also lodged under this heading. He reduces it to two main types, namely the *manie hystérique* and the *folie raisonnante hystérique*. The first category Falret describes as the normal hysterical character which at a given moment gives cause to a general delusory state of a manic kind. The hysterical *folie raisonnante* on the other hand is typified as a pronounced hysterical character which has been intensified in its various components to such an extent that the symptoms have become irreconcilable with reason or just plain common sense.[15] Not hysterical madness as understood by Morel but the hysterical character, more particularly the hysterical disorders of the character, are dominant here. Jules

Falret's criticism of Morel and Moreau, which is directed against the extreme comprehensiveness of hysterical madness, applies just as much to the scope of the contents he gives to the concept. Not the comprehensiveness but the essence of hysterical madness is the actual point of contention. Falret is not dealing with the clinical manifestations of madness as are Morel and Moreau de Tours. He is talking about the aberrations of character in hysteria. His contribution *Folie raisonnante ou folie morale* suggests that true hysteria is one of the most banal types of moral madness. With this he puts the hysterical nature on a par with a type of madness and becomes as moralistic as his friend Morel, albeit in a different manner.[16] Falret takes up the position that is vilified by Moreau. With his point of view he diametrically opposes Moreau's, who does not accept the existence of the *folie morale*. For him every form of mental disorder is organically determined.

Henri Legrand du Saulle (1830-1886), alienist at Bicêtre and later chief-physician at the department for epileptics at the Salpêtrière, focused his interest on the medical-judicial aspect of psychopathology, which later on became the generalized limited meaning that was given to the title alienist. The observations from *L'état mental des hystériques* are therefore lodged in this context. The title confirms his medical-psychological interest from a judicial point of view; the state of mind (madness) is determinative for the reply to the question of accountability. In that sense his work can only be described as a lateral attempt at the clinical study of hysteria.[17]

Permanent intellectual disorders determine the true madness-character which in the medical-judicial sense means that the subject cannot be held accountable and must therefore be placed in an asylum for *aliénés*. The clinical description of hysterical madness mentions the same characteristics as those we find with Morel and Moreau de Tours. Legrand du Saulle picks up a certain idea of Morel's, i.e., the chance for a *folie hystérique* to occur is bigger when neurologically morbid phenomena are present in a less outspoken way (Morel's transformed neurosis).

Hysterical Madness from Three Different Angles

Although Morel, Moreau de Tours and Legrand du Saulle share the same reference in their function as alienists, they seem to define the *folie hystérique* each in their own way, grounding themselves on one and the same clinical picture. To Morel hysteria is undeniably a precursor of madness. The road there is, among other things, strewn with hysterical delusions. In hysteria the madness resounds. Moreau de Tours also couples hysterical madness to neuroses. The shift in the naming voices is keeping in with the scientific neurological model which is then in full incipience; hysteria is neuropathy. Moreau distinguishes three separate categories in which true hysterical madness is restricted to the second form—in between delusion and madness. Legrand specifies Morel's definition (hysteria is predestined for mental derangement) within a strictly medical-judicial frame and within the explicit study of hysteria.[18] And so we find in Legrand a clear emphasis on the mental state of hysteria from a strictly medical-judicial standpoint. Here Legrand voices the social norm. Hysteria belongs to the domain of the neurologists. The alienist only intervenes in the name of the law; the issue of the accountability of the patient brings him to the subject of discussion of the mental derangement in the neuroses. Madness is equivalent to nonresponsibility, to nonguilt.

Generally speaking, these three alienists distinguish a specific form of madness which is coupled with hysteria. Considering the fact that delusion is secondary in the definition of madness, its occurrence is neither decisive nor necessary. The definition of the fourth alienist we discussed, Falret, clearly falls under this second interpretation; the delusion is entirely absent in the description of the clinical picture.

This setting up of hysterical madness as a distinct clinical entity precedes the neurological emancipation of hysteria in which the latter is promoted from being one of the three great neuroses to being *the* neurosis. Its naming, the signifiers couple, implies the creation of a reality which touches upon both hysteria and madness, namely a reality which neither the settled alienists nor the upcoming neuropathologists can pass over. Before it was a matter of hysteria and madness but their potential union was not expressed in language; hysterical madness was no nosological category, no lingual reality.[19] This temporary bridge between hysteria and mental derangement does not make a sharply defined boundary between hysteria and hysterical madness. However, further reflection will reveal that this bridge constitutes the cause or even the prerequisite for the distinction between what is called neurosis in neuropathology and neurology and what is called psychosis in psychiatry. Only an already existing couple can be split up!

Du Saulle ventures furthest into the domain of hysteria. Moreau formulates the intention to include certain types of madness in the frame of neurosis, i.e., hysteria, out of a predominantly therapeutical concern. The displacement that Moreau carries out from hysteria to neurosis or neuropathy is the precursor of the substitution of three great neuroses, being epilepsy, hypochondria and hysteria. One great neurosis, hysteria, will ultimately be constituted as a type by Charcot.

The image hysterical madness evokes is highly protean. The true *folie* is characterized by its chronicity, i.e., dementia. Through its variety, hysterical madness, according to Falret, becomes quasi-synonymous with madness studied in women in general.[20] Although this statement is formulated as a critique of the other alienists, it also captures the essence of Falret's own, dissenting position in the matter. What he does is not so much to try to capture a clinical picture but instead to gather character anomalies, e.g., mythomania, impressionability, and familial tyranny under a pathological denominator.

With Falret hysterical madness becomes a disorder that is typical of the female. This definition will catch on particularly in German psychiatry.

Magnan's Associated Madness

The ideas of Valentin Magnan (1835-1916) are chronicled as a synthesis of the great schools of thought of French psychiatry during the 1880s, the starting point of the period of classical psychiatry. This period is characterized by a certain homogeneity in the various points of view and tenets, more specifically by the role of neurology which assumes the status of model. Psychiatry becomes a mere branch of neurology and gradually integrates into general pathology.[21]

Magnan's vision of hysterical madness is indebted to Charcot's concept of hysteria that is elaborated later in the present volume. Here psychiatry appeals to neurology. Next to a group of miscellaneous states, Magnan distinguishes the group of actual kinds of madness or psychoses. The first category includes those mental disorders that he links to organic brain damage, neuroses, intoxications, and cretinism. In this, hysteria becomes, by definition, a miscellaneous state. Although the introduction of the notion of psychosis is not attributed to Magnan, it is the first time we see the word surface in psychiatric texts. Magnan for that matter essentially owes his renown to those works which he devoted to the category of psychoses. This new concept still emphasizes the mental disorder, in contrast to neurosis which presupposes an organic-neurological lesion. Also the category of the psychoses or actual madness remains coupled to degeneration.

Magnan's contribution, which nonetheless is specific, to the course of hysterical madness consists of a clearing, a purification of the category by means of a dissociation of *folie hystérique*. He endorses a further unlinking of hysteria and madness, a movement which had already been initiated by Moreau and Legrand du Saulle. Hysterical madness is torn apart into hysteria and psychosis. The clinical picture of hysteria comprises a number of typical mental disorders—an amalgam of temporary states of delusion. The persistent psychoses and the behavioral disorders that formerly belonged to the image of hysterical madness, he attributes to morbid associations.[22] To Magnan, therefore, there is no question of an involution from hysteria to psychosis but of a well-defined possibility of cumulation through morbid association.

A new turn in the relationship between hysteria and madness is introduced here. Hysterical madness vacates the domain of psychiatry and madness to join, as a hysterical delusion or a hysterical delusory fit, the field of neurology and the neuroses. The relationship of hysteria-psychosis, through the entrance of mental disorders, becomes that of delusion vs. madness. This in turn fits in with the more rigid demarcation of neurosis and psychosis both of which came to life in the second half of the nineteenth century. They constitute two distinct categories of affliction. The rift between the clinical description of the syndrome or the nosography and the nosological theories that resulted in classification systems, manifested itself in the emphasized differentiation of neurosis-psychosis, and the prevalence of combined clinical pictures. Or put in another way the classification systems prove to be inadequate in seizing the richness of the clinical manifestations.

We find some problems in the volume on afflictions of the brain in *Traité de médecine*, published under the direction of Charcot, Bouchard, and Brissaud in the period 1891-1894.[23] Among other subjects, this volume contains an article on the psychoses by Gilbert Ballet (1853-1916) and an article by Dutil on the neuroses.[24]

The pathology of the mind, according to the psychiatrist Ballet, includes the study of all mental disorders that not only involve disfunctions of intelligence but also those of character and will. He stresses etiology and restricts his discussion to those disorders that find their origin in the mind, i.e., the *vésanies* or psychoses.[25] In his discussion of symptomatic mental afflictions, i.e., those with an other than mental etiology, he refers to those passages in the textbook dealing with the appropriate causes. For madness linked with the neuroses and to which hysterical madness belongs, there is the chapter on the neuroses. For symptomatic afflictions this implies both a different status as well as a different reality from those of the *true* psychoses.

Ballet distinguishes four groups in the *délirants*. The first is determined by organic lesions of the brain, the second includes intoxications, the third the neuroses, and the last constitutes the category of the psychoses. Ballet now attempts to rigorously demarcate the field of the psychoses or the vesanias—his object of study—by transferring the peripheral cases to neurology. Unlike the group of the psychoses, the group of the neuroses cannot be strictly defined according to Ballet, precisely because of the often undetermined nature of symptomatic madness. This implies that it is not always possible to determine whether the mental disorders are part of the neurosis or rather if they are associated with it as complications and therefore belong to the category of the psychoses.[26]

On to Dutil's contribution on the neuroses (hysteria, epilepsy and neurasthenia), which are considered as essential afflictions of the nervous system. This means that the afflictions cannot be reduced to demonstrable lesions of the nerve centers.[27] Hysteria or the great neurosis is a mental illness, typified by functional and dynamical disorders of the nervous system. Regardless of the mobility and the polymorphism that is characteristic of them, they do constitute a separate group within the frame of syndromes and afflictions *sine materia* of the nervous system. Heredity undeniably plays a major part.

In Dutil's definition both elements from Charcot's theory as well as from Janet's theory resound—both theories will be discussed further on. From Charcot he borrows the notion of *dynamical lesion*. From Janet he gets the specification of the genetic predisposition—a cerebral insufficiency that manifests itself in the debilitation of the psychological function of synthesis.[28] His discussion of hysterical madness, the final piece of his clinical description of hysteria, is strangely marked by its conciseness and vagueness. His definition is not limited to certain delusions, but extends to mania, melancholia, and confusion, in other words the main psychotic categories.[29] The nature of the phenomena is not self-obvious.

The Mental Confusion and the Oneiric Delusion

Jules Séglas (1856-1939), the finest clinician the French School produced, is an important representative of the Salpêtrière group during the 1890s. Their position is characterized by a number of subtle differences with regard to Magnan's ideas, which they globally adopted, as well as by a successive importation of German concepts (mental confusion, paranoia, and dementia praecox).[30] Although this group did not explicitly recognize the entity of the *folie hystérique* it is worth mentioning here. For hysteria surfaced in a surprisingly novel and, as will be shown later, an exceptionally interesting place in the writings of this group.

The Salpêtrière group, particularly Chaslin (1857-1923), distinguishes the primitive, symptomatic confusion which encompasses the most divergent disorders, from the secondary confusion which is more definite. Neither of these confusional states are necessarily accompanied by a delusion. The hysterical states of delusion are [wrongly?] classified with symptomatic confusion.[31] Régis (1855-1918) applied himself to the description of the characteristic delusion (the oneiric delusion or the action dream) which may accompany this symptomatic confusion; it is comparable to the dream and is constructed scenically.[32] This typical delusion which Régis had already introduced as far back as 1894, he compares with the secondary states that occur in hysteria, and makes it into the typical example of the mental disorders of toxic origin.[33] In this connection Séglas speaks of toxic and hysterical *oneirisms*.[34]

The Final Monography on Hysterical Madness

La folie hystérique by Mairet and Salager is published in 1910. It was the last French monography on the subject. The authors, entrusted with clinical-psychiatric instruction, see themselves compelled to answer the question "What about hysterical madness?" Considering the fact that the specialist literature did not provide a decisive elucidation on this genre of madness, they appealed to the clinical observation of cases of hysterical madness in order to arrive at some degree of decisiveness. Their interpretation of Charcot's teachings is evident from their definition of hysteria. Hysteria is not to be recognized by the prevalence of convulsive fits, but by stigmata or somatic phenomena, by certain mental manifestations or delusions, and by a certain physiognomy. What they present here, is a Charcotian definition of hysteria, that is elevated to *folie hystérique*. The result of these hysteria observations at the asylum is a differentiation between two groups. On the one hand there is the group of the *folie hystérique*, a form of madness which incontestably—pathogenetically or symptomatically—is supposed to be determined by hysteria. On the other hand there is the *hystéro-vésanie*, a form of madness which is linked with hysteria.[35]

Three out of the seven nosological groups, distinguished by Mairet and Salager—and in our opinion artificially differentiated from each other—are labelled hysterical madness. In our consideration Charcotian hysteria is involved. The determinative diagnostic criterion is hysterical delusion. The hystero-vesania is defined as the simultaneous incidence of a hysterical and a psychotic delusion. Only one out of the seven groups comes under this criterion.[36]

The question of the differentiation between hysteria and psychosis remains undecided. Worse still, after the division of the clinical material into seven groups, a number of these are simply just set aside. The remainder are ranged into two categories. Number one, hysterical madness, is an old category which is taken with a modified content. Number two, hystero-vesania, is a new signifier that implies a miscellaneous delusion. Magnan's attempt to throw some distinction between hysteria and psychosis into relief, albeit with the indispensable preservation of certain miscellaneous states typified by morbid associations, seems to have escaped these authors.[37] Mairet and Salager reserve *folie hystérique*, the very category under discussion, for what in Magnan's opinion were mental disorders typical of hysteria. For the associated psychosis, they introduced a new signifier, *hystéro-vésanie*, which may perfectly indicate the miscellaneous state but which has no classificatorial value to the authors. An important implication connected with the introduction of this signifier passes by the understanding of the authors. For, with this, the real problem cases are returned to their sender, i.e., psychiatry. Hysterical madness which also originated in a psychiatric milieu is referred to neurology, with the retention of the psychiatric label. Later we will show that Mairet and Salager hold an exceptional position in French psychiatry of their day, that lends a special touch to their contribution.[38] Their position is comparable to that of the Belgian psychiatrist Laruelle whose vision will be discussed later.

The German Classification Systems

Griesinger's Vesania Typica

Wilhelm Griesinger (1817-1868) is the founder of the German School. He was active in the first half of the nineteenth century. He paved the way for the construction of a clinical tradition within the German-speaking region.[39] His large-scale psychiatric textbook is recognized as the first one worthy of that name, and lends German psychiatry its international eminence. The basic concept of this work is contained in the statement: "Illnesses of the mind are illnesses of the brain." Mental disorders have an anatomical basis. His theory does however escape the French therapeutic nihilism, an outgrowth of Morel's degeneration theory. Griesinger finds himself at the crossroads of new avenues in psychiatry: the anatomo-pathology of the brain, neuropsychiatry, clinical and dynamical psychiatry. The latter implies that, contrary to the French alienists, he also emphasizes the activity of psychical processes in the human (pathological) mind.[40]

According to Griesinger, hysteria is both a distinct form as well as a cause of mental illness. He defines hysteria as an a-specific affliction of the nervous system with variable manifestations, occurring in various parts of the nervous system. These manifestations are, almost without exception, concomitant with psychical disorders which, in turn, are explained somatically. In this, a privileged position is allocated to afflictions of the female genitals (the uterus theory of hysteria).

Apart from the mild cases with predominantly somatic complaints which, as yet, should not be considered as mental illness, he also distinguishes the heavy hysterical mental afflictions or the acute hysterical madness. The latter manifests itself in spells of manic behavior with delusory fits and is often preceded by discrete convulsive attacks and severe emotional confusion. In typifying these violent, spectacular forms most weight is given to aberrant hysterical character traits.

Griesinger identifies still a third, chronic variant of hysteria—a frequent final state of the previous type which takes the shape of mania or melancholia.[41] Although he devotes only a few pages to hysteria, we can infer from his later writing that the second form, the acute hysterical delusion, is curable and that the third chronic form belongs to the incurable category of madness. A striking detail is the fact that Griesinger makes the remark that, although hysteria is also prevalent in men (boys) he has, as yet, no knowledge of hysterical delusion in male patients.[42]

This vision of hysteria as a non-inherent, devolutive affliction can be traced to his theory on madness in general. Griesinger employs an original conception of madness—the *vesania typica* as the unique and only psychosis. Madness is an involutive process and every stage of this cycle of progressive degradation of the mind represents a specific form of psychosis or madness.[43] This leads to a division into primary and secondary forms. With primary madness the essentially determinative factor of the mental disarray is the emotional confusion. The states of depression and excitation are situated here; we could also place the acute hysterical delusion here as well. The secondary forms of madness are characterized by a fading of the state of disarray, by a mental debilitation, and by the distortion or the dissociation of the ego. The chronic hysterical madness we locate under this stage.[44]

Griesinger's conception of the psychotic cycle leaves permanent traces in the further development of German psychiatry. First, specific attention is kept going for the terminal forms of the acute psychoses. Second, there is the preservation of the contradistinction between the stable, primitive, systematized delusions on the one hand and the psychoses with an acute onset, an evolutive, disintegrating course and a specific demential terminus on the other hand.

Here we must also mention Karl Kahlbaum (1828-1899), whose innovative ideas were strongly influenced by Griesinger and the French alienist J.-P. Falret. His views will only find some degree of acceptance after his death with the works of Kraepelin.[45] He draws up a new classification of mental illnesses and isolates a number of new entities, including hebephrenia and catatonia, to which he devotes a monograph in 1874. Both are either refuted by the psychiatric milieu or acknowledged as clinical forms of already recognized nosological entities, respectively paranoia and idiocy.

The entity of catatonia is of interest in the light of our study because of its clinical definition. The contents of this evolving clinical picture is so capacious that it effortlessly encompasses both the various distinct forms of hysterical madness as well as those of the forthcoming new notion *dementia praecox*.[46]

In this connection we would like to point out that Kahlbaum cautioned us not to rely unthinkingly on one specific clinical sign or on the intensity of a certain phenomenon to make up a diagnosis. He did so in view of the fact that, in the case of catatonia for instance, one comes across the most diverse phenomena that also have the greatest differences in intensity. Kahlbaum therefore gives mental illness a different definition than the one based on a certain sign. The illness is the permanent nucleus of the disruption around which all variants and all variations circle. This conviction is either not heard or not heeded.[47]

The Hysterical Temperament and Paranoia

A third remarkable figure, and the first leading authority in German psychiatry around the turn of the century, is Richard von Krafft-Ebing (1840-1902).[48] He was the first to mention the notion *hysterical psychosis*. Together with Schüle he represented the Illenau School, the dominant trend of that period. The psychiatric textbooks of Schüle and Krafft-Ebing, which were published respectively in 1878 and 1879, were overwhelming successes.

In his *Lehrbuch der Psychiatrie* Krafft-Ebing arranges the *Hysterisches Irresein* (hysterical madness) under a category adopted from Morel's classification, the forms of madness stemming from constitutional neuro(psycho)ses. Contrary to Morel, however, he classifies them under the category of the psychic degenerations, typified by an abnormal constitution. The psychoneuroses, typified by a normal constitution, comprise mania, melancholia, hallucinatory madness, or the amentia of Meynert, stupidity, the secondary systematized delusion, and terminal dementia.[49] So hysterical delusion implies an acquired or congenital constitution—the hysterical degeneracy. Just as with Morel the specification *hysterical* indicates the initial cause of the affliction.[50]

This frequently diagnosed category comprises three orders, analogous to what Krafft-Ebing distinguishes under the heading *epileptisches Irresein* (epileptic madness).

1. *Transitorische Irreseinzustände* (ephemeral hysterical states of delusion):
   - states of anxiety accompanied by obfuscation of consciousness
   - hysterico-epileptical deliriums
   - ecstatic visions
   - hysterical-convulsive fits

- twilight states accompanied by compulsive reproduction of experiences

2. *Protrahirte delirante Zustände* (hysterical hallucinatory madness)
3. *Hysterische Psychosen*:
   - the hysterical psychoneuroses: mania and melancholia
   - the hysterical degenerative forms of madness: paranoia

First there are the ephemeral fits of delusion, which are subsequent to, substitutes of, or unrelated to the hysterical fit. He distinguishes some five types. Second there is the hysterical hallucinatory madness that comprises recurring delusions of the first order. This form is what most French and German authors (besides the hysterical fit) acknowledged as the most typical hysterical delusion. The third and final group, the actual hysterical psychoses, Krafft-Ebing divides into two forms. First there are those that are coupled to psychoneuroses and which consist of acquired hysterical mania and melancholia, both with a favorable prognosis. The distinction with the actual mania and melancholia lies in the absence of the hysterical constitution in the latter. The second subgroup, that of the chronic and therefore permanent hysterical psychoses, constitutes only a stage in the process of progressive functional degeneration.[51] Paranoia on a hysterical basis is the most prevalent type of this hysterical psychosis, which as a rule commences with a hysterical delusion of the first and/or the second order.

Two remarks are necessary here. First the concept of *Irresein* is used here in its broad meaning, namely that of mental disorder as opposed to somatic disorder. Second it turns out that Meynert's amentia especially seems to elicit some differential-diagnostic problems with mania, melancholia, and the acute delirious stages of paranoia. Since hysterical psychosis comprises hysterical mania and melancholia and also paranoia on a hysterical basis, this amplifies the suspicion that amentia is closely related clinically to the German hysterical psychosis.

The association of paranoia and hysteria seems to be a new element with regard to the French, who did not explicitly mention the signifier paranoia within this context. Initially synonymous with mental illness in general, paranoia is in the ascendant, particularly in Germany where through the years it is given the most diverse definitions, ranging from the most restrictive to the most capacious. A constant in this tradition is the fact that this signifier keeps the differentiation terminologically sharp between sheer disorders of intelligence (paranoia) and disorders of affectivity which fall outside paranoia.[52] Therefore, we can conclude that the position paranoia holds is equally as important as the position of madness with the French, but with the emphasis on a systematized delusion.

We shall see that Janet takes Krafft-Ebing's concept as a reference in order to develop his own vision of what he calls the hysterical delusory states. Janet, however, is a clinician-theoretician and not a systematician. He poses the question of the limitation of hysteria while Krafft-Ebing, by virtue of the position he allocates to the hysterical delusion, indicates that to him hysteria is essentially a type of madness which is quite separate from pure clinical pictures, i.e., psychoneuroses such as melancholia and mania.

Krafft-Ebing's view of psychopathology is the product of the synthesis of the ideas of Morel and of the tradition that goes back to Griesinger's *vesania typica*. Two parameters, the etiopathogenesis and the syndromal form, underpin his clinical conception. His view of hysterical psychosis can in no way be considered as an exact copy of Morel's *folie hystérique*.[53] For the word group hysterical psychosis is both reserved for the curable hysterical mania and melancholia, and for the incurable hysterical psychosis, being Morel's notion of hysterical madness.[54]

Schüle's work is richer in clinical material and bears witness to a greater precision than Krafft-Ebing's textbook which is more perspicuous in its composition.[55] Under the heading *das hysterische Irresein* (hysterical madness) Schüle discusses all psychopathological states of the hysterical temperament which he defines as the hysterical-neuropathic character that has transgressed *in sucum et sanguinem*, given content by the reputed malignant female character traits.

The symptomatology of hysterical psychosis is highly protean and may assume and pass through all clinical states. Both acute and chronic, transitory and permanent clinical pictures, with or without demential evolution, find a place under it. The mark which the hysterical temperament makes on each of these pictures constitutes the constant and with that also the etiological framework of the group. The hysterical character binds the group together. Distinct clinical forms include the hystero-epileptical madness, the hysterical *Dämmerzustände* (twilight states) and raptures, hysterical mania and melancholia, and the hysterical *Wahnsinn* (madness), *Verrücktheit* (mental aberration) or paranoia. The latter category gets special notice in view of the fact that it is the only type of hysterical madness that is most intimately entwined with hysterical temperament. Schüle regards it as virtually a part of or still as a natural evolution of the hysterical disposition. This hysterical paranoia is in turn subdivided into seven types of the most divergent nature.[56] We would like to highlight type seven, the chronic, incurable cases of hysteria with symptoms of degeneration. This type is split into the chronic degenerative hysterical *Wahnsinn* and the primary hysterical degenerative dementia, which is coupled with the dementia praecox. Both types of hysterical madness will soon [unjustly?] be lodged under dementia praecox.

We conclude that we find virtually the same capacious clinical definitions as we did with Krafft-Ebing, although it is not as clear-cut and soberly systematized. The fragmentation of categories turns the aggregate into an inextricable tangle of clinical typifications. In this way, our analysis of Schüle's work confirms the critique formulated by Gilles de la Tourette (1857-1904). According to this student of Charcot's, Schüle's concept of hysterical psychosis comprises *all* types of madness.[57]

Just how miscellaneous or arbitrary the contents of the word *paranoia* is in this period, may additionally be illustrated with

Theodore Ziehen (1862-1950). This German psychiatrist, neurologist, and philosopher was a student of Kahlbaum's. Hysterical psychosis, together with the epileptic and the alcoholic psychosis he locates under acute paranoia which in turn is part of the psychoses without intellectual deficiency.[58]

Both Krafft-Ebing and Schüle, who concern themselves only minimally with hysteria, consider hysterical psychosis as a process, which is a legacy of Griesinger. The linking thread, especially elaborated by Schüle, is the hysterical character or the hysterical temperament. In the specification of hysterical madness with regard to the distinct stages of the psychotic process, the course is not fully completed by every subject. They utilize a limited scale of signifiers, including *Wahnsinn*, *Irresein*, and *Paranoia*. The differences concern the position that each of these signifiers are allocated within both their classification systems and also their mutual relations (the context or chain of signifiers which gives rise to meaning). The categories, therefore, are not directly comparable in terms of diagnostic range and theoretical weight. Additionally, one and the same signifier does not just correspond with one and the same clinical typification.

Here the clinical meaning of hysterical madness is extremely vast. All authors with whom we have discussed this subject agree on the amount of space which this phrase, "hysterical madness", has at its disposal. Where Griesinger still emphasized the picture of mania and melancholia, the Illenau School elaborates on this. This expansionary labor, at least with Schüle, leads to a fragmentation of hysterical madness into a countless number of clinical pictures. The fact that such a capacious view of hysterical madness is not shared by the entire medical world is evident from the work of Armin Steyerthal. Among others, this physician refers to Krafft-Ebing, Schüle, and Arndt in order to argue that the diversity of the states described by them, including the assumed ease that hysterical phenomena may go together with numerous other disorders, demonstrates that hysteria is not an autonomous mental illness. Subsequently, it does not exist as such.[59]

As far as the range of the *hysterisches Irresein* is concerned, Griesinger, Krafft-Ebing, and Schüle are close to the French alienist tendency. The criterion for the dementia evolution employed by the French is less prominently present in the rigid German classification systems. These are directed more towards the conditions for the genesis and the actual genesis of the pathology. The hysterical nature, i.e., the hysterical degeneration functions as linking thread. We would still like to emphasize that both Krafft-Ebing and Schüle subscribe to the existence of a transitory, non-involute form of hysterical madness.

The Migration of Hysteria

Another important author within German psychiatry around the turn of the century, the successor and heir to the Illenau School who further extends the clinical tradition and mitigates Morel's influence, is Emil Kraepelin (1856-1926). Outside of Germany his new classification only conquered France with great pains and was subject to alterations. One such obstacle is dementia praecox. The French were familiar with dementia as the terminal state of madness but not as a distinct clinical entity.[60] Nonetheless, his textbook still applies today as an important work of reference. His theory is classically identified with the sixth edition of his textbook, first published in 1883. There were eight editions, the last one was published in 1913.

The first edition closely ties in with Ziehen and keeps its distance with regard to the innovations of the Illenau School. In this classification of syndromes Kraepelin introduces the hysterical and epileptic twilight states under the general heading of *Dämmerzustände*. The epileptic twilight states apply as a reference for the hysterical twilight states.[61]

The 1887 second edition—the second and the third closely tie in with Krafft-Ebing's nosology—distinguishes among the general neuroses. Next to epilepsy and neurasthenia, Kraepelin puts the *hysterisches Irresein* (hysterical madness) which includes the *hysterische Verrücktheit* (hysterical mental aberration) or the hysterical psychoses, adopted from Krafft-Ebing with the emphasis on chronicity.[62]

Editions four (1893) and five (1896) carry the hallmarks of Kahlbaum and with that also the influences of Griesinger and J.-P. Falret. Regarding content, the stress is shifted to clinical-evolutive entities. We find *hysterisches Irresein* or hysterical madness, still a general neurosis, under the congenital mental illnesses. Hysterical constitution is once more emphasized.[63]

The alterations in the sixth edition (1899) contain definitions of dementia praecox, paranoia and the manic-depressive psychosis.[64] The French School has extensively integrated these new orientations.

The seventh edition (1904) lodges hysterical madness under psychogenic neuroses, a subcategory of the general neuroses and typified by a psychogenic development and a hysterical disposition.

In the final eighth edition a monumental and final attempt is made at integration (1909-1913). Psychogenic neuroses have scattered and hysteria is allocated a different position, but a similar definition.[65]

Hysteria migrates through eight successive editions of Kraepelin's textbook. A point of departure is hysterical madness as a general, constitutional disorder. The finishing point is that of hysteria as a reaction disorder, rooted in a hysterical personality. Up to and including the seventh edition, Kraepelin discusses hysteria, as an entity, under the heading of hysterical madness. Only in the final edition does this become hysteria. The last but one registration, psychoneurosis, is new. For under Krafft-Ebing mania and melancholia were still the pre-eminent psychoneuroses.

Contentwise hysteria remains anchored to and determined by the hysterical disposition or personality, which may manifest itself both in physical and psychic afflictions. The twilight states belong to the most reputed and most important of the temporary mental disorders. They include the whole spectrum of classical hysterical delusory states, that were extensively dealt with by Janet, e.g., somnambulism, sleeping fits, delusory fits, and split personality. The twilight state holds a remarkable position in the German region, comparable to that of the hypnotic state in France. The clinical picture is characterized by an alteration of consciousness, i.e., restricted or obfuscated awareness and gaps in one's memory. On top of that it may occur with quite a number of (organic and mental) pathologies. When it occurs with hysteria it is often coupled with hysterical or amnesic *fugues*. The classical tale is that of someone who goes on a trip in a twilight state and suddenly finds himself in a far off place without anyone having noticed something about him.

In 1898 Ganser (1853-1930) described a specific hysterical twilight state, the Ganser syndrome, which could be particularly observed in prison and which allegedly would be specifically characterized by *vorbeireden* (thematic paralogia). Associated characteristics are visual hallucinations, anxiety, and various somatic phenomena. The Ganser syndrome becomes one of the many temporarily recognized clinical syndromes in which hysterical nature and the part of simulation are disputed.[66]

According to Kraepelin, other than typically hysterical psychoses can join the hysterical nature and subsequently carry traces of this. Among others he mentions manic-depressive psychosis and dementia praecox, to be distinguished from *hysterische Psychosen* which are beyond a doubt manifestations of the hysterical nature and which have a short-lived, irregular course that is influenced by coincidences.

So Kraepelin makes the distinction between the hysterical nature or personality and its clinical-pathological manifestations.[67] In this the hysterical personality cannot be identified with a degenerative personality. He also opposes too wide a usage of the adjective hysterical.[68]

The hysterical personality and the typical disruptions like physical accompanying phenomena and twilight states remain decisive for the diagnosis of hysteria or hysterical psychosis. The demarcation with other disorders does however remain vague. With Kraepelin, hysterical psychosis introduced by Krafft-Ebing, does indeed get a psychogenic status but it does not break free from the hysterical personality.

Notes

1. The *paralysie générale* is described for the first time in 1820 by Esquirol as an exclusively motor syndrome and as a complication of the *folie* (particularly dementia). It regards two different, yet related processes; Esquirol used a dualist concept. Bayle's treatise *Recherches sur les maladies mentales* (1822) signifies a radical change; the general paralysis becomes a separate morbid entity. Only twenty years later is he to get recognition for this discovery. Another ten years later his innovation brings about a true revolution within psychiatric circles. The general paralysis becomes the model for all organic mental illnesses and orients the development of psychiatry toward the direction of organo-genesis; the organic substratum becomes the determinative etiological reference for psychopathology. The syndrome of the general paralysis is further developed by quite a few alienists in this period. It is particularly Esquirol's student J. Baillarger who develops a description. Dementia and motor defects remain however typifying. Delusion is not excluded but is secondary. For an elaborate discussion of this clinical picture, which rose to become the basic model for mental alienation, we refer to J. Baillarger (1869), *Des symptômes de la paralysie générale et des rapports de cette maladie avec la folie*, Appendix to «Traité des Maladies mentales» by prof. Griesinger, Paris, Delahaye.
2. A. Porot (1975), *Manuel Alphabétique de Psychiatrie clinique et thérapeutique*, Paris, PUF, p. 40; P. Bercherie (1980), particularly pp. 76-78.
3. A. Porot (1975), p. 40. The journal which represents the view of the alienists and, even now, of the psychiatrists in France, is *Annales médico-psychologiques.*
4. B. Morel (1860), *Traité des maladies mentales*, Paris; J. Moreau de

Tours (1869), *Traité pratique de la folie névropathique (vulgo hystérique)*, Paris.

5. Morel is generally mentioned as the one who replaced symptomatology by a less restricted nosology (systematic classification of diseases). The description of clinical pictures was still to attain great heights in the nosography.
6. According to Morel the neuroses are etiologically determined by a hereditary predisposition; not the degeneration but something close to it, namely the predisposition to an unbalanced nervous system.
7. P. Bercherie (1980), p. 94.
8. Morel described several cases of *folie hystérique* but did not make a synthetic study of it.
9. B. Morel, discussed in A. Mairet & E. Salager (1910), *La folie hystérique*, Paris, Masson & Co, pp. 13-16 and in P. Bercherie (1980), pp. 103-104.
10. The work of 1869 puts hysteria on a par with a form of *folie*, generally considered to be a mental aberration. Previously there was already published: J. Moreau de Tours (1865), *De la folie hystérique et de quelques phénomènes nerveux propres à l'hystérie convulsive, à l'hystéro-épilepsie et à l'épilepsie*, Union médical.
11. Here we find an illustration of both the fertility and the confusion which such a double position brings for a physician or a psychic worker. We quote Moreau (in translation) in his introduction to his work of 1865, "It is in my department of the epileptics at the Salpêtrière that I became convinced of having too frequently mixed up psychological phenomena and similar phenomena presented by ordinary madness." The psychological phenomena refer to hysteria; ordinary madness is a synonym for true madness.
12. The specification "neuropathic" or "neurotic" (the assumption of a material affliction of the nervous system as a diagnostic criterion) indicates a certain attitude. We alienists, are talking about neuropathy, which in the ordinary word (vulgo) is called hysteria. This choice of words implies the distance between alienist and neurologist with regard to the delineation of hysteria—predisposed mental aberration vs. neurologically determined, psychical affliction. It also indicates a wide conception of hysteria. Opposing the moral treatment and also the *folie morale*, Moreau is simultaneously one of the first advocates of the use of medication for research and treatment of mental illnesses. His interest for the artificial delusion also refers to

his interest for the chemical practice.

13. The clinical picture of Moreau's *folie hystérique* is typified by its temporary and ephemeral character. From his (fanatical) conviction that every psychical disorder presupposes an organic, neurological one, he appeals to a law of the pathological physiology in order to explain a characteristic of this clinical picture by means of the organic substratum. He names this law, which lays down the alternating of psychic disorders and nervous afflictions, the law of substitution. J. Moreau de Tours (1865), reported in J.-C. Maleval (1981), *Folies hystériques et psychoses dissociatives*, Paris, Payot, pp. 106-107.
14. P. Bercherie (1980), p. 56. The equalization of the state of madness and that of the dream is also rendered explicit in view of the fact that this analogy, albeit not within the same context, is taken up again further on.
15. I. Veith (1965), *Hysteria*, Chicago and London, The University of Chicago Press, pp. 210-211; P. Bercherie (1980), p. 88. Falret's description of the first form equals the pronounced second phase of the classical major hysterical fit of Charcot. It is probably no coincidence that Falret was active at the Salpêtrière during this period.
16. J. Falret (1890), Folie raisonnante ou folie morale. In *Etudes cliniques sur les maladies mentales et nerveuses*, Paris, Baillière & Fils.
17. H. Legrand du Saulle (1883), *L'état mental des hystériques*, Paris.
18. Not all alienists concerned themselves with the study of hysteria, although the greater part of them, in the course of their formation, called at the Salpêtrière.
19. We proceed on the basis of the assumption that the naming creates a reality. Those not named, those not seized in signifiers, do not exist as such. Every reality is lingually. This implies, within the concrete scope of the relationship category-picture, that we do not proceed on the assumption that a category (a signifier) names and comprises a pre-existing reality, but that the signifying creates a reality.
20. Cited in A. Mairet & E. Salager (1910), p. 19.
21. P. Bercherie (1980), pp. 115-116.
22. *Ibid.*, pp. 129-130.
23. J.-M. Charcot et al. (eds.) (1894), *Traité de médecine*, vol. 6, Paris, Masson.
24. This immediately constitutes an illustration of the lodging of psychiatry within general medicine.
25. *Vésanie* (vesania) is a concept that has fallen into disuse and which

refers to longterm psychoses, generally chronic, that have at their base a strictly mental and no organic disorder. A. Porot (1975), p. 675. Etymology: 1490, Latin *vesania*; synonym to *folie* (madness), which etymologically does not have such a strict affiliation however with being unhealthy: vesanus. *Folie* is the oldest and least explicit name for madness or lunacy; *vésanie* dates back to the Middle Ages. *Psychose* (German) was most recently introduced in 1845 by E. Von Feuchtersleben as counterpart to the *neurosis* (English), introduced by Cullen in the eighteenth century. The dichotomy between mental and neurological (functional neurological state) is central. It is no coincidence that the signifier *psychosis* was introduced by a German, since the Germans, much earlier than the French, used the signifier *psychic*. We would like to take this opportunity to express our gratitude to François Duyckaerts who brought this to our attention.

26. J.-M. Charcot et al. (eds.) (1894), p. 1061.
27. *Ibid.*, pp. 1281-1383.
28. We shall return to this at a later stage.
29. More specifically, Dutil mentions all psychoses which Ballet distinguishes. In this way, he refers to what according to the latter are associated psychic disorders. J.-M. Charcot et al. (eds.) (1894), p. 1382.
30. The mental confusion is characterized by a more or less complete dissolution of consciousness, generally followed by a complete restoration of the personality. Secondary to this confusional state are the oneiric delusion and the polysensorial, predominantly visual hallucinations. Magnan is reticent with regard to this category. According to him it is a pure syndrome and not a nosological entity. Dementia praecox, originally conceived in three (later expanded to nine) distinct forms, was introduced by Kraepelin in the period 1892-1899. The most important criteria are the demential evolution, and the disorders and the loss of affectivity. Paranoia, initially a synonym for mental illness in general, especially caused a furor in Germany where, over the years, it was given the most varied definitions. P. Bercherie (1980), pp. 149-150 and 153-155.
31. *Ibid.*, p. 155. The unclear character of the psychological analysis of hysterical delusion connected too systematically with epilepsy, according to Bercherie, prevented them from being classed with the secondary confusion. This is characterized by a clouded consciousness, i.e., a flight of ideas and hallucinations that are so intense that

the patient can no longer collect his thoughts. More specifically it concerns acute hallucinatory syndromes, including Meynert's amentia.

32. *Ibid.*, p. 156.
33. See Charcot's *état second* and Kraepelin's *hysterische Dämmerzustände* which will be dealt with later. Régis pays attention too to the problem of the differential diagnostics with dementia (not the dementia praecox!). Partly under the influence of his assistant A. Hesnard (1886-1969), he is to give a warm reception to the theories of Freud and is to disseminate them in also France from 1910 onward. J. Postel & C. Quétel (eds.) (1983), *Nouvelle histoire de la psychiatrie*, Toulouse, Privat, p. 701.
34. P. Bercherie (1980), p. 165.
35. An analogy with hystero-epilepsy (the concurring of the hysterical picture and that of epilepsy) comes to the surface here; their possible association would not detract from the established, strictly clinical distinction between hysteria and epilepsy. Here too the authors pull the wool over their own eyes. They are blind to the failure of the clinical, classificatorial method—a failure that is evident from the way in which problematic pictures are classed. The various components of the hybrids are pulled apart, i.e., hysteria and epilepsy, hysteria and psychosis.
36. The distinguished groups are: 1. "délire hystérique lié aux attaques convulsives," 2. "délire équivalentaire," 3. "délire équivalentaire par crises rapprochées constituant des périodes délirantes séparées par des intermissions," 4. "délire hystérique prolongé," 5. "délire hystérique avec amnésie," 6. "délire hystérique et délire vésanique combinés. Hystéro-vésanie," 7. "symptômes hystériques émaillant des aliénations mentales de formes diverses." Group 3, 4 and 5 merit the label *folie hystérique*, 6 is the *hystéro-vésanie*. Three of the seven groups are not taken into account.
37. The above discussed textbook does follow the idea of Magnan.
38. Mairet and Salager's work would have gone unnoticed since it was too unacceptable for contemporary psychiatry which was dominated by the ideas of Babinski, student of Charcot's. J.-C. Maleval (1981), pp. 223-224.
39. The importance of Griesinger in Germany is comparable to that of Pinel (1745-1826) in France—the founder of psychiatry. Griesinger was inspired by the innovative ideas of the Ghent psychiatrist Joseph

Guislain (1797-1860). We made use of the French translation of Griesinger's work, in which it must be mentioned that *mentale* is the translation of *psychisch* (psychic in English) (see the above observation of F. Duyckaerts). W. Griesinger (1865[1845]), *Traité des maladies mentales, pathologie et thérapeutique*, Paris, Delahaye; P. Bercherie (1980), pp. 61-67.

40. H. Ellenberger (1970), *The Discovery of the Unconscious*, New York, Basic Books, pp. 241-242.
41. A recognizable, founding idea is the transformed neurosis of Morel's.
42. W. Griesinger (1865[1845]), pp. 214-217. Discussed in I. Veith (1965), pp. 193-199. It is also remarkable that in Griesinger's textbook two clinical pictures are central which caused a furor with the French alienists in the nineteenth century—mania and melancholia. It is these two pictures that make up the larger part of the curable mental illnesses or the first stage of chronic afflictions.
43. To the French psychiatrists of that period, Morel in particular, madness constituted a unitary genre, which was cut up into different types by mutual comparison of different patients on the basis of observed analogies and contradistinctions among the various clinical manifestations.
44. Here Griesinger places, among others, the *Verrückheit* (mental aberration). The course that is sketched here as the invasion of delirant phenomena with the subsequent distortion of the ego, is to become a basic notion in Freud's early conceptualizations.
45. The method of working which J.-P. Falret advocated was that of a fine analysis which had to permit the description of disease-entities with their specific symptoms and their anticipated course. In P. Bercherie (1980), p. 84.
46. K. Kahlbaum (1874), *Die Katatonie oder das Spannungsirresein*, Berlin. Kahlbaum defines catatonia as a cerebral disease with a cyclical alternating course, in which the psychic symptomatology successively presents the aspects of melancholia, mania, stupor, confusion (*Verwirrtheit*), and dementia (*Blödsinn*). One or more of these symptoms can be absent. In addition to these psychic symptoms, nervous locomotor processes with the general character of convulsions are present as typical symptoms. P. Bercherie (1980), p. 110.
47. J. Quackelbeen (1989), Hysterische psychose? Een probleem!, in K. Libbrecht, *Hysterische waan: Symptoom of structuur?*, Pegasos series

no. 3, Ghent, Idesça, p. 23.

48. Krafft-Ebing sporadically kept in touch with the School of Nancy. His masterpiece *Psychopathia Sexualis* caused a considerable stir in psychiatric circles. Another important figure from this period is Theodor Meynert (1833-1892), the leading figure of Austrian organic psychiatry. Meynert however did not specifically concern himself with hysteria; in his textbook he hardly mentions it. R. von Krafft-Ebing (1886), *Psychopathia Sexualis*, Stuttgart, Ferdinand Enke; T. Meynert (1884), *Psychiatrie*, Vienna, Braumüller.
49. Meynert's amentia (*acute hallucinatorische Verworrenheit*) is a synonym for the mental confusion (*Verwirrtheit*) and is, at that moment (1893), a novelty as a clinical entity. U. Peters (1984), *Wörterbuch der Psychiatrie und medizinischen Psychologie*, München, Vienna, Baltimore, Urban & Schwarzenberg, pp. 23-24 and 603-604; Ch. Lévy-Friesacher (1983), *Meynert-Freud. «L'Amentia»*, Psychiatrie ouverte, Paris, PUF.
50. R. von Krafft-Ebing (1893[1879-1880]), *Lehrbuch der Psychiatrie auf klinischer Grundlage für praktische Ärzte und Studirende*, 5th ed., Stuttgart, Ferdinand Enke, pp. 306-307. The *Psychische Entartungen* (Morel's mental degeneration) together with the *Psychoneurosen* make up the group of the functional psychoses. The psychical degenerations, next to the madness ensuing from constitutional neuro(psycho)ses, comprehend the *folie raisonnante*, the paranoia, and the periodic madness or manic-depressive psychosis.
51. Here Griesinger's view on the unary psychosis shines through.
52. A. Porot (1975), p. 479; U. Peters (1984), p. 395.
53. Morel was the first to give specific attention to the hypochondriac and the hysterical madness, under the heading of transformed neurosis. See P. Bercherie (1980), pp. 103-105.
54. Here too we observe a conceptual gap between the psychiatrists on the one hand and the neuro(patho)logists on the other hand. The former emphasize the clinical picture of mania, melancholia or madness next to possible character anomalies, while the neurologists among others study hysteria as a clinical picture and not as a sheer character anomaly.
55. H. Schüle (1886[1878]), *Klinische Psychiatrie*, 3rd ed., Leipzig, Vogel. Schüle devotes an entire chapter to *das hysterische Irresein*, which comprises all distinct forms of hysteria.
56. Schüle uses a capacious concept of paranoia. In his view the syste-

matized delusion is by no means a predominant or covering feature. The seven subforms are much rather typified by a well-defined hysterical character trait, such as capriciousness, and also by the polymorphism of the clinical picture.

57. G. Gilles de la Tourette (1895), *Traité clinique et thérapeutique de l'hystérie. Seconde partie*, vol. 1, Paris, Plon, Nourrit & Co, pp. 370-371. (v.inf.)
58. Here once again it is obvious that the same concepts get their own definition from every author. We also observe that psychoneuroses here too (cf. Krafft-Ebing) refer to mania and melancholia and not to hysteria. P. Bercherie (1980), pp. 127-128; U. Peters (1984), p. 625.
59. A. Steyerthal (1908), *Was ist Hysterie?*, Sammlung zwangloser Abhandlungen aus dem Gebiete der Nerven- und Geisteskrankheiten, edited by A. Hoche, vol. 8, part 5, Halle a. S., C. Marhold Verlag, pp. 64-69.
60. This does not prevent the fact that virtually all contemporary Anglo-American authors state that Morel was the first to describe dementia praecox. This ascription is however contested by the French historians of psychiatry. J. Garrabé (1992), *Histoire de la schizophrénie*, coll. Médecine et Histoire, Paris, Seghers, p. 17.
61. As will still be apparent from the discussion of Charcot, the differentiation between hysteria and epilepsy in this period was particularly on the agenda in neurology. For a survey, see E. Trillat (1986), *Histoire de l'hystérie*, coll. Médecine et Histoire, Paris, Seghers, pp. 157-162.
62. P. Bercherie (1980), pp. 140-142.
63. The fourth edition also introduces dementia praecox, catatonia (Kahlbaum), and dementia paranoides. The group of psychoneuroses (Krafft-Ebing) has been excised from the fifth edition.
64. The manic-depressive psychosis was already described in France as early as 1851 as *folie circulaire* (J.-P. Falret) and in 1854 as *folie à double forme* (Baillarger). In 1890, one year after the publication of the sixth edition of Kraepelin's textbook, Magnan with his authority consolidates this clinical picture in France. J. Postel & C. Quétel (eds.) (1983), pp. 623-624.
65. Two other categories within the psychogenic neuroses are the traumatic neurosis and the expectation neurosis. P. Bercherie (1980), pp. 220-232.
66. J. Ganser (1898), Über einen eigenartigen hysterischen Dammerzu-

ständ, *Archiv für Psychiatrie und Nervenkrankheiten*, 30, pp. 633-640. The hypothesis of an exclusive hysterical etiology (Ganser and Kraepelin) is still recognized in the 1950s by a number of psychiatrists, but the Ganser syndrome is every bit as much discussed as a psychotic picture over this period. See S. Arieti & J. Meth (1967), Rare, Unclassifiable, Collective, and Exotic Psychotic Syndromes, in S. Arieti (ed.), *American Handbook of Psychiatry*, vol. 1, Basic Books, New York, pp. 547-548; M.-D. Bruno (1979), L'hystérique délirant, doctor's thesis, University of Paris, p. 104.

67. Here we can refer to the thesis of Gilles de la Tourette that hysteria very willingly adheres to a large number of afflictions. The notion of the morbid associations or complications then reigned over psychiatric thinking and will continue to parasitize there. Freud, too, will initially support this view. (v.inf.)

68. We take the sixth edition as a reference. Kraepelin's *Einführung in die psychiatrische Klinik* from 1905 contains a lecture on the *Hysterisches Irresein*. In it he discusses the severe forms of hysteria, known to us from the works of the School of the Salpêtrière (Charcot). E. Kraepelin (1899), *Psychiatrie*, 6th ed., vol. 2, Leipzig, Barth, pp. 492-520; E. Kraepelin (1984[1905]), *Introduction à la psychiatrie clinique*, trans. from the German, Bibliothèque des Analytica, Paris, Navarin, pp. 311-323.

2
The School of the Salpêtrière

Charcot

"While in the nineteenth century, with Duchenne de Boulogne, Vulpian and Charcot a neurology emerges, molded by strongly systematized afflictions that are based on solid anatomical foundations, all that lie outside of this area constitute a sizeable group of the Neuroses, which for many of them will only turn out to be a *waiting group* (chorea, Parkinson's disease, epilepsy). Within this group hysteria takes up a position of precedence that is fortified every day. With its wealth, diversity of manifestations and what is peculiar to it, hysteria knows how to arouse medical interest to its maximum; one sees it everywhere and considers it capable of everything. According to Lasègue, it is the wastebasket in which everything ends up that is non-classifiable."[1]

By the second half of the nineteenth century, hysteria is in its heyday within neurological circles, not least through Charcot's efforts on the subject. This fertile period has its repercussions on hysterical madness. Towards the end of the nineteenth century hysterical madness acquires a specific position within the clinical picture of hysteria that articulates itself in a novel way within the distinct nosological and nosographical systems.

Everything published in the Salpêtrière on hysteria during the 1880s and 1890s, takes Charcot's type-hysteria (the grand hysteria in which the hysterical fit assumes an eminent position as a symptom) as its reference. Charcot's students are singularly attuned to their own divergent ways. Each one takes a different point of view from his teacher. Richer is the best methodological illustration of the master. Gilles de la Tourette finds his message in hysterical suggestibility. Janet develops Charcot's concept of the psychic definition of the hysterical phenomenon. Beyond the nuances their respective clinical contributions testify to madness, as it were, being attracted by the hysterical fit. The dynamics of this operation are comparable to what Freud was to posit some twenty years later on the relationship between conscious and unconscious, particularly on the contribution of the unconscious primally repressed nucleus in the process of repression.[2] The model patients exude a similar attraction as that which Freud connected with the primally repressed nucleus. Blanche Wittmann (Charcot), Madeleine Lebouc (Janet), and others, each knew how to captivate the desire of their respective masters.[3] The fact that this nosographical work demonstrates its bankruptcy in the numerous exceptions, proves that the subject (of the unconscious) does not simply let itself be objectified or neutralized.

Charcot, the Napoleon of the Neuroses

From 1870 until his death in 1893, Jean-Martin Charcot enjoyed world acclaim as a neurologist. Academically, too, he was a highflyer.[4] After his appointment as *chef de clinique* at the Salpêtrière, neurology was gradually deprived of the lion's share of his scientific research activities. After more than ten years of remarkable neuro(patho)logical studies he successively shifted his interest to hysteria (1870), hypnosis (1878), and traumatic hysteria (1885). The results were the *grande hystérie*, the *grande hypnotisme*, and the *hystérie virile*.[5]

Considering Charcot's prestige this turnabout was tolerated in medical and academic circles but hardly accepted with gratitude. This was shown at his death: Charcot's type of hysteria was reduced to cultural (artificial) hysteria, the hypnotic treatment was suddenly rejected as dangerous and immoral (cultural hypnotism) and following on from that, his theory on hysteria was considered worthless.[6]

Because of Charcot's standing, hypnosis was temporarily acknowledged as an official scientific object of research. In 1882 hypnosis made its official entry into the *Académie des sciences*. For the first time hypnotic suggestion was found to be respectable. This golden age however lasted for just ten years—from 1882 until 1892.[7]

The permanent scientific recognition of his neurological studies does not extend to Charcot's contributions on hysteria. Nonetheless the name of Charcot is primarily linked with hysteria. This anatomo-pathologist has gone down in history not as an eminent neurologist, but as the creator of the great hysterical fit and of hysterical hypnotism. The attribution of creator is not a token of scientific recognition for two new clinical entities, but rather it stresses the artificial nature of both entities. Just about every study which refers to Charcot attaches more importance to the mythic dimension of his person than to the analysis of his theory on hysteria, which, as we shall demonstrate, reaches further than the (mere) creation of a new category.[8] We do not dispute the fact that Charcot cultivated the show-element within the Salpêtrière and created a stage on which the mostly female patients could perform *his* hysteria (the grand hysteria and the grand hypnotism).[9] It does, however, become suspicious when this spectacular element is abused by Charcot's critics in order to integrally reduce the scientific value of his work to nil.[10] We shall clarify our position.

The initiative for Charcot's turnaround—his encounter with hysteria—is a reorganization within the Salpêtrière. This resulted in the formation of a new department, constituting the merger of the female non-alienated epileptics and the hysterics who came under his responsibility. The hysterics of this *quartier des épileptiques simples* very soon founded their attacks on the convulsive list of the *authentic* epileptics.[11] Considering the circumstances under which Charcot's encounter with hysteria took place, it is no coincidence that the epileptic fit is allocated a central position in his type-hysteria, the hystero-epilepsy. One should also take into account that epilepsy then constituted the referent and the challenge for whomever took up the study of the neuroses—essential afflictions of the nervous system, i.e., (as yet) without demonstrable lesions.[12]

Another element that lodges itself in Charcot's grand hysteria is a fascination with the possession of medieval days. In the demonic and ecstatic states that reigned there Charcot acknowledges a manifestation of hysteria, a form of expression of hysteria which by the end of the nineteenth century had virtually disappeared from everyday clinical practice.[13] The fact that this fascination of Charcot essentially regards the visual aspect of "hysterical possession" is shown in the studied material of plastic arts.

The Hystero-Epilepsy or Major Hysteria

In the year 1870 Charcot succeeded—with the collaboration of his hysterical patients—in introducing a then supposedly outdated manifestation of hysteria into the Salpêtrière. Patients identified with the image of the ideal (female) patient that was manifest in the way the masters, Charcot and his assistants, spoke about hysteria. In this way they consciously or not enacted Charcot's theory on hysteria and "constituted" his type-hysteria. Concerning the various phases determining the process of inducing a hypnotic state, one and the same process is active. Charcot's research into hysteria, however, has more to offer than his visual packaging.

The master is seeking to define a clinical type, a ground form to which every individual case can be traced back and upon which a diagnosis can be based—a nosography of hysteria. This means that Charcot attempts to introduce a scientific approach to hysteria.[14] His method is that of observation, description and systematization of what presents itself to the eye: Charcot spoke of himself in terms of a *visuel*. These clinical observations from 1878 onward are replaced by hypnotic experiments.

In subjecting hysteria to his anatomo-clinical method it becomes an illness just like any other and it enters into the scientific realm, into the realm of neurological knowledge. Implementing hypnotic suggestion Charcot moves on from passive observation into the active creation of hysterical phenomena. In doing so his neurological knowledge advances and becomes independent of the incidental occurrence of hysterical phenomena. It is this transition which signed the public death-warrant for Charcot.

First Charcot believed he had found the type in the entity of hystero-epilepsy, in which he defined four phases. This hystero-epilepsy is the result of a systematization of clinical pictures he had witnessed in his ward for essential epileptics. Subsequently, the *hystérie major* or the grand hysteria makes its entrance. The major hysterical paroxysms continue to hold a central part.[15] Opposite the major form Charcot places the everyday, veiled forms of hysteria or the *hystérie minor*. Hysteria becomes the neurosis which manifests itself through periodic fits, the accidents and permanent symptoms, and the stigmata.[16] The major form is the ground form, the reference for every particular case. In order to explain hysterical phenomena Charcot introduces the dynamical lesion, i.e., an essentially temporary functional disorder at the level of the cortex.[17] The division into accidental or periodical and permanent is adopted by Charcot's students and propagated by interested foreign visitors including Sigmund Freud.[18]

A second merit of Charcot's is that he wanted to liberate hysteria from the prefix *simulation*.[19] This fits in with his revaluation of the hysterical state of mind which up until then had been considered by the alienists as perverse and deceitful.[20] This unlinking of simulation is rejected outside of the Salpêtrière for Charcot's type-hysteria is considered to be a cultural hysteria. Within the confines of the Salpêtrière, simulation will make way for a new attribution, i.e., hysterical suggestibility. Both reactions appeal to one and the same argument, which strangely enough is the instrument with which Charcot conducted his experimental research into the nature of hysterical phenomena of hypnotic suggestion.[21]

The relation between simulation and suggestion allows for clarification by means of the concept of hysterical mimicry, founded on the observation that the hysterical picture conforms to the image presented by the master. Simulation and suggestion constitute two interpretations of this fact. It is said that the patient simulates, in which the emphasis falls on a certain malicious gain through sickness on the part of the patient, or that the patient is impressionable, which focuses attention on the suggestibility by the physician or the environment. Charcot observed the imitation and refused to identify it with simulation, but he did not know how to theoretically grasp the mechanism. More specifically he did not see that the hysterical patients were aware of his fascination with hypnotic suggestion and possession of medieval days, and that they mirrored this fascination by means of their symptoms.[22]

Charcot also noticed a certain dynamics in the mutual relationships between patients when they imitated each other. Freud will call this the psychic infection on the basis of hysterical identification.[23] This second phenomenon is hysterical identification by means of one single trait. Both hysterical mimicry and hysterical contamination, two typical hysterical phenomena which extend far beyond the confines of the Salpêtrière, are identifications. The mechanism of mimicry is a mirroring that results in the taking on of a picture in reference to a master figure. The so-called perfect example of the (female) model patient is the product of such an identification. Hysterical contamination, on the other hand, grounds itself on a communality and results in the taking on of a trait which indicates the point of desire on which the identification is based. This identification with an indifferent similar other, apart from the trait, does not result in a model copy because it is not grounded on an overall picture or a Gestalt. Therefore, by no means, is it a true copy. Why? First, there is no master figure (ideal) involved in the mechanism. The female patient does not mirror herself in the speech of this *ideal*, but creates a bond with a similar other, a fellow patient. The master's fascination with the clinical picture is, when present, only secondary in the sense that this fascination is not the substratum upon which the mechanism of the identification is grounded. Second, the identical element, the point of similarity between the similar others, is no picture but a trait, namely a hysterical phenomenon. Hysterical identification by means of the trait introduces a social bond between subjects. The distinct subjects only have the hysterical phenomenon in common. Clinically this means that the nosographical image, apart from the communal trait, carries the hallmark of the particular subject. This explains why the seclusion of the so-called contaminated subjects does not always produce the expected disappearance of the contamination; it concerns more than a mere imitation.[24]

Charcot unlinks hysteria from its univocal association with the genital organs. In doing so he reacts against the uterus theory, which reduces hysteria to an affliction of the womb and also generalizes it to women. This implies that Charcot no longer reserves hysteria exclusively to the female gender (as had Briquet). This does not imply though that Charcot denies the role of the sexual element within hysteria. Along with other factors, such as emotions, he allocates the sexual element a part in the outbreak of hysteria.[25] This brings us to Charcot's theory of trauma, psychical or physical by nature, which is designated a specific position in the case of hysteria. Charcot develops the notion that the impression left by a trauma on the psyche, causes a hysterical phenomenon.[26] This new idea, which is rarely mentioned and which Charcot only elaborated later in his career, is subsequently taken up by Janet and Freud and elaborated on in an entirely different way.

The *folie hystérique* does not receive specific status in Charcot's teachings. Rather than investigating the relationship between hysteria and madness, the fringe area of hysteria, he directs his efforts to the construction of a basic type and to the pathogenesis of the hysterical symptom. A number of mental disorders, namely delusory states which correspond to distinct phases of the complete major fit have their established position within this type-hysteria. These states may present themselves in extremely various ways, e.g., as dream states with obfuscation of consciousness, as ecmnestic delusions, and as secondary or as twilight states. Each of them encompasses an element typical of the hypnotic state.[27]

Charcot's clinical and nosographical work aims at establishing hysteria as a definite clinical identity. In doing so he positions himself directly opposite the current view considering hysteria as a phenomenon which may encompass the entire scale of pathologies—and with that including *madness*. To Charcot the polymorphism of the hysterical picture is the impetus to introduce order and to look for systematicity in the clinical picture, and not to go and emphasize the aspecificity of the hysterical phenomenon, an attitude which ultimately results in the issue of simulation. Charcot was gripped by the scientific ideology of his day in such a way that he interprets the positive results of his research, the type-hysteria, as pure confirmation of his basic thesis and of the scientific ideal he cherishes. He did not realize, for example, that the additional observation of his new experimental method, hypnotic suggestion, which both successfully makes hysterical phenomena disappear as it creates them, precisely knocks the very ground from under the feet of his basic thesis that hysteria is a clinical-neurological entity. This is a conclusion that his student Babinski draws. Charcot was convinced that the experimentally induced hysterical symptoms would ultimately allow him to learn the laws that govern the production of the normal symptom or the pathogenesis. In this connection his theory on male hysteria is very fertile.

The Orthodox Duo

Paul Richer (1849-1933) and Georges Gilles de la Tourette rank as Charcot's most orthodox pupils. Richer turns out to be the stricter of the two whereas Gilles de la Tourette is the more militant.

The cooperation between Richer and Charcot was extremely intense. Richer's work constitutes a streamlined, systematized reproduction of Charcot's ideas on the major hysterical fit and on the hypnotisms, i.e., the hypnotic states that may occur in hysteria.[28] The major hysteria and the major hypnotism constitute a twofold paradigm for hysteria. The paradigm is twofold considering the fact that the various hypnotic phenomena do not simply allow themselves to be fitted into the scheme of the great hysterical fit.

Richer's *Etudes cliniques sur l'hystéro-épilepsie ou grande hystérie* was published in 1881 and, as usual, was introduced by Charcot. A passage from the preface:

> However it may be, your studies on the hysterical fit have put you in a position capable of demonstrating that there is at least nothing left to coincidence. On the contrary, everything takes its course along certain, well-defined rules, common to hospital practice and to that of this city, valid for all times, for all countries, in all races. Variations of the rules do not affect their universality in view of the fact that these variations, no matter how numerous they may seem, are always logically connected with the basic type.[29]

Just how much Richer is convinced of this regularity, may appear from the naiveté that he believes to disprove the criticisms regarding the role of the imitation. According to Richer, imitation irrefutably plays a part but only as far as the shape is concerned. Patients will imitate the shouts, the bizarre gestures. In short, that which is spectacular; but the foundations, the secret pattern that links the various phases of the fit and that is similar in all patients cannot be ascribed to imitation.

The basic type, the grand hysteria, is mentioned in one and the same breath here as the hystero-epilepsy. The differential diagnosis of hysteria and epilepsy, much rather than the combination of hysteria with mental derangement, was therefore the order of the day during that period.

Richer's condensed description is as follows. After an epileptoid period and a clonic phase (that of the great movements) passionate attitudes occur. The patient becomes a victim of hallucinations which bring him into a dream state; he experiences his delusion. The fourth and final period is a delusion of reminiscence and deals with events that have marked the patient's life; the patient recounts his delusion. The delusory fit, the isolated prevalence of the third or fourth phase, is only one of many possible variants and may occur isolated without preceding convulsive fits in anamnesis. Somnambulism and related dream states (the hypnotic phenomena) are linked with the third phase of the fit.

According to Richer, the presence of hallucinations and delusory states as part of the phenomena of the hysterical fit does not necessarily constitute the prefiguration of mental derangement, although this can be a possible complication. No more than what Charcot believes, however, does he make any clear statements on the legitimacy of the *folie hystérique*. Villechenoux links this to the scant attention given to the mental state, out of a fixation on the positive, or the scientific aspect of the neurological discourse.[30] And indeed, the emphasis comes to fall on the quantification (objectification and positivation by means of graphs and figures) of the periodical fits and the permanent symptoms.[31] The conclusion therefore seems evident: the more scientific the discourse, the less madness crops up in it. If hysteria can still be grasped by means of tables, madness cannot. Yet this explanation is not to the point in our opinion. For in the first instance objectification means that all subjectivity is excluded, regardless of the studied pathology, albeit hysteria or madness. In our opinion, the exclusion of the word madness from the lexicon of the neuropathologists is rather connected with neurological knowledge as such than with the quantification project or the process of objectivation. Madness forfeits its right to existence within neuropathology because it does not fit in with the knowledge of this (new) discipline. Put otherwise: since neuro(patho)logy cannot explain the occurrence of madness, madness falls outside of the neurological corpus. Contrary to hysteria, madness is not considered to be a neurological disorder.

The anything but smooth relationship of Charcot's adepts to the alienists may be situated along the same lines as a consequence of the above reasoning. The School of the Salpêtrière reacts against the levelling out within the asylum—stronghold of the alienists—of hysteria with all kinds of madness. For this levelling out in the first instance affects their scientific status. Consequently, the *folie* as a signifier by definition falls outside the boundaries of hysteria.

Among the characteristics of the delusory state connected with the hysterical fit, Richer stresses the analogy with toxic delusions. More particularly, the delusory fit that is part of the third phase of the hysterical fit can artificially be reproduced by the inhalation of ether. Apart from this analogy, Richer also mentions the presence of a certain consciousness of the delusion, a nimbleness of the ideas, the presence of a fixed idea, and the discernible influence of old emotions and present preoccupations.[32] These last elements are worthy of attention in view of the fact that they indicate the link between the phenomenon, the delusory state, and the reality of the hysterical subject. This link may have been known up until then, but it received little attention. In this sense the hysterical fit, in its variants and often incomplete appearances, more than once turns out to be the acting out of an earlier psychical trauma. Generally, they go back to an event of a sexual nature. A third possibility is that the fit expresses certain secret desires of the patient.[33]

Gilles de la Tourette remained faithful to the master, even after Charcot's death. Of his *Traité clinique et thérapeutique de l'hystérie* the final two volumes were published in 1895; Charcot died in 1893.[34] Unlike the work of Richer it is not the result of years of quantifying research, but a classical nosographical product in which the glorification of Charcot's work and an uncompromising hatred for his opponents are predominant.

In this way, he delineates the ideas of the master more rigidly and brings them to a number of caricatural heights. The hysterical fit and hypnotism are the most important, visual-diagnostic references. The clinical picture of hysteria is—classically—reduced to that of the hysterical fit and hysterical becomes a synonym for suggestible; the moralizing tone is not quite so classical. A symptom is considered as pertaining to hysteria when it can either be brought back to the hysterical fit or when it accompanies hysterical fits, or when it can be manipulated by means of suggestion.[35] This implies that the fit in its most minimal presence becomes the criterion to determine whether phenomena such as catalepsy, the severe manic fit and the toxic delusion, which can be present in both hysteria and madness, are hysterical or not.[36] This process is possibly responsible for the reproof, from the psychiatric corner, that the School of the Salpêtrière makes hysteria into a *fourre-tout*, an all-embracing category, the same reproach that Gilles de la Tourette hurls at the psychiatrists.[37]

Whereas Richer, as a clinician, does not automatically equate delusion with madness, Gilles de la Tourette dogmatically states that hysteria docs not lead to dementia. This does not mean though that there can be no question of protracted states of illness.[38] The study of the hysterical fit according to Gilles dc la Tourette sheds light on the tangle of psychic manifestations of hysteria and constitutes the condition for its demarcation with regard to the most various forms of madness. Although hysteria very tractably bonds with quite a number of nervous afflictions, it does not blend with it. In his opinion it is these very morbid associations that are responsible for the belief in a chronic hysterical delusion, a so-called hysterical madness. He reproaches the alienists for having described the clinical picture of mental degeneration linked with hysteria, as the hysterical state of mind, neglecting the fact that the hysterics of the asylums were not interned for their hysteria but for acts arising from their associated mental degeneration.[39]

In our opinion, the above development does not so much show a clinical concern for the hysterical subject but rather a concern to keep the clinical picture pure, in order to have it take precedence. In this, Richer makes use of tables and numerical data. Gilles de la Tourette becomes moralistic.

Gilles de la Tourette also believes it is necessary to purify hysteria of all that concerns the domain of the sexual, which is directly given a perverse connotation. In this he loses sight of the fact that hysteria as such is little served by such fanaticism. Illustrative of his zealotry is the fervor with which he attacks Colin's dissertation. This dissertation voices the same positive disposition with regard to hysteria but does not make any mention of Gilles de la Tourette. Therefore, he believes he is classed with those regarding hysteria with disfavor. Yet he adopts the following passage from that same Colin:

> Hysteria is a *caput mortuum*, in which all that seems strange, in which all that our mind—devotee of the theory of the goal causes—cannot explain, is compressed. This propensity is particularly evident in the case of *mentally ill* patients. Whether it is an unknown patient who presents himself, one or another unbalanced person, one rather coquettish, or rather frivolous mentally defective. She's a hysteric, it is propounded, and with that just about all is said.[40]

In case the reader should still suspect that Gilles de la Tourette means to confirm the view of Charcot, namely that certain mental illnesses may be counted within the clinical picture of hysteria, he is way off the mark. The point of contention is rather the (moral) appreciation of hysteria.

Where, in the first instance, it would seem that our author renounces the malign female characteristics that are attributed to hysteria by the alienists (mythomania, perversion, and simulation) in favor of the benign characteristics, the truth lies elsewhere. Gilles de la Tourette equates hysteria with suggestibility, which becomes equivalent to weakness and impressionability. With this hysterics become highly gullible, absent minded, and averse from physical sexuality. In this way he succeeds in letting the diversification and nuance which Charcot and Richer advocated, based on their scientific attitude, degenerate into a caricature. The fact that this fanatical-militant attitude is also fed and refreshed at the source of a revindication of the master, is demonstrated by the comparison with an earlier work; the analysis of a case of possession (the seventeenth-century Sœur Jeanne des Anges) first published in 1886, before Charcot's death.[41] This solid illustration of the master doctrine contrasts in one crucial point with the work discussed earlier. The appreciation of hysteria is kept in the background by means of the quantitative research. Neither of the two studies, however, is pervaded with much concern for the hysterical subject.

The above digression is necessary as background for Gilles de la Tourette's explicit stand in the *Traité* concerning the *folie hystérique*. In it he first denies this entity, which is defined on the basis of the fit, the right to exist; madness has nothing whatsoever to do with neurosis. Second the only reality of the so-called hysterical madness is that of the chronic hysterical delusion and this does not appear in the clinical picture of hysteria. Subsequently, as in a recoiling movement, he still allocates the *folie hystérique* as a signifier, a possible position within hysteria as an equivalent to or an extension of the fit. In that he makes the distinction between the true hysterical delusion, being the hallucinatory and the manic delusions on the one hand, and all phenomena infected by hypnosis (the somnambulistic delusions, and the ambulant automatism, which causes fugues or the running away from home) on the other hand.[42] Old news, if it were not for the fact that Gilles de la Tourette here pilots the signifier into the field of neuropathology by giving it the definition of the just mentioned paroxysmic or hypnotic states. An operation which retranslates, and in doing so creates quite a bit of confusion, i.e., the distinction between hysterical madness and hysterical delusion into the distinction between the hysterical madness of the alienists and the hysterical madness of Gilles de la Tourette. His definition of hysterical madness by the way is, paradoxically, restrictive and capacious—restrictive because it only includes the delusory fit and the hypnotic states, capacious because every hysterical paroxysm, even the most minimal of references, suffices to arrive at a diagnosis of hysteria. The hysterical fit and the hypnotism have the same impact for him as madness has for the alienists. Gilles de la Tourette puts himself in the same position as Mairet and Salager, with the difference that these alienists found their question on a pedagogic problem.

Apart from attesting to a militant and moralistic stance, the work of Gilles de la Tourette hardly proffers any new relevant clinical material concerning hysterical delusory states, a feather which does adorn Richer's cap. Gilles de la Tourette's great merit is having broached the problem of the *folie hystérique* within the Salpêtrière. His inconsistent solution, however, nurtures the already existing confusion more than it provides clarity.

The Psychologist Pierre Janet

Original and constructive theoretical contributions can be found with Pierre Janet (1859-1947).[43] Philosopher by training, he became physician via the roundabout path of hypnosis. He called himself psychologist and stood rather aloof from the world of medicine. In 1890 Charcot introduced Janet into the Salpêtrière and set up a laboratory for experimental psychology for him.[44] Possibly Charcot expected Janet—to no avail as it will turn out—to paint the psychological tableau of hysteria on completion of his own rounded out neurological tableau.

In the controversy between Charcot and Bernheim he opened a third avenue, building on the doctrine of the eminent physiologist and Nobel Prize winner Charles Richet (1850-1935), pioneer in the scientific study of hypnosis.[45] This avenue is the study and understanding of suggestion and hypnotism in their own right and the exposure of their psychological laws.[46]

The notion of a total or a partial *psychological automatism* is central to his early development of a psychological theory (on hysteria). The automatism which he defines as a psychological phenomenon, always accompanied by a rudimentary consciousness, functions as a basis of explanation for specific amnesiac phenomena that occur with the splitting of personality, an essentially hysterical symptom. Janet distinguishes two groups: total automatism and partial automatism. Under the total automatism that regards the subject in its totality he puts catalepsy, the hypnotic state or the artificial somnambulism as well as the so-called succession of existences or alternating personalities. Partial automatism comprises the partial catalepsy and certain types of confusion.[47] His preference for somnambulistic states and dual personalities can easily be understood from his position of departure, namely research into hypnosis by means of the clinical observation of hysterical patients. And so Janet arrives, via hypnosis, at hysteria—the inverse way Charcot followed.

Contrary to Gilles de la Tourette and Richer he does not proclaim a definite or established knowledge; he is not a disciple but a researcher.[48] He seeks to gather direct knowledge on the secret of hysteria. In this he is scared to death of superficiality and descriptiveness. Above all, he wants to avoid "drilling" his hysterical patients—compare with Bernheim's criticism on Charcot's type-hysteria.[49] Penetrating to the essence, into the very heart of the hysterical organization means only one thing, namely the psychological analysis of the hysterics' mental state.[50]

Therefore Janet makes a distinction between permanent and incidental mental disorders, i.e., mental stigmata vs. additional mental symptoms.[51] Mental stigmata are explained by a narrowed field of consciousness, which in itself is determined by a hereditarily transmitted debility. He stresses that what is at hand there is a frailty of the function of synthesis and not a dissolution of this function, for this characterizes madness. The subconsciously fixed ideas, developed from events that were experienced as traumatic, are ultimately explained identically and are responsible for the incidental symptoms, which manifest themselves pre-eminently in the form of a fit. The hysterical delusion lodges itself here.

Janet here acknowledges, like the majority of his "hypnotic" contemporaries, the existence of two states of consciousness (the dual personality). The second state is accessible under hypnosis.[52] The digging up, under hypnosis, of the fixed idea implies the drawing up of a biography, of a history. With this Janet introduces, at least in France, the historical dimension of the (hysterical) subject; the relevance of the past for present suffering.

Under the heading "L'état mental hystérique," which to him is a neuropathological state, in *Les Névroses*, he describes what in his opinion is an original delusion, *les idées fixes à forme somnambulique*. It regards a period of delusion entirely dominated and determined by an underlying, subconsciously fixed idea. After the ebbing away it is veiled by a complete amnesia, that is lifted by hypnosis.[53] This specific delusion is to Janet what the major fit was to Charcot and constituted already seventeen years earlier the informal fixed nucleus of his elaboration on hysterical delusion.[54] The central issue here is the nature of the delusions which may present themselves in hysteria.[55] Janet implicitly distinguishes between delusions emanating from a subsequently added mental illness on the one hand and those belonging to the development of hysteria on the other hand.[56] This thesis shines through like a recurrent motif throughout his dissertation. Without somatic stigmata there is no question of hysteria, which is characterized by its high impressionability. The definition of the second category, of particular concern to us, clearly deviates from the restrictions imposed by Gilles de la Tourette and from the even stricter definition of Colin, which reduces hysteria to somatic symptoms and the classical hysterical fit.[57] The basic model of the hysterical fit is discarded.

Janet appeals to the clinical definition of the three forms of hysterical madness, distinguished by Krafft-Ebing. He respectively typifies them as the ephemeral delusory fits, the delusions that persevere during the intervals between fits, and the definitive chronic psychoses.[58] Each of these forms, according to Janet, beyond any doubt is still prevalent with hysterics. Whether one still counts the respective patients as part of the population of hysterics is dependent on the significance allocated to hysteria. The mental illnesses, according to Janet, are not characterized clearly enough for their respective demarcations to be fixed. Installing order in the field of neuroses was one of Janet's ambitions. He himself came onto a system of two basic neuroses, hysteria and psychasthenia, which he consecutively studied thoroughly and defined theoretically.

Which delusions can be attributed to the clinical picture of hysteria? Is the presence of a hysterical stigma sufficient? Janet's reasoning is that this way the concept of hysteria becomes pretty capacious. Without any explicit argumentation he makes the following choice. The delusion must meet two conditions: it must be the development, i.e., the consequence or an intensification of a hysterical phenomenon and the hysterical state of mind must be discernible in the delusion. With this second condition Janet specifies an important differential-diagnostic criterion. Krafft-Ebing too emphasized the hysterical constitution, but Janet defines it differently as the splitting of the mind, variable states of consciousness, and the formation of truly subconscious phenomena such as subconsciously-fixed ideas, for example. Another distinction with regard to Krafft-Ebing is that this constitution or mental state is, according to Janet, a criterion to classify certain delusory states with hysteria as a pathological entity. To Krafft-Ebing it was an argument to stick the supplementary predicate *hysterical* onto certain types of madness. In this way Janet does not report or bring into account the taxonomy, the German context, in which Krafft-Ebing's categories obtain their specific definition and value. Rather than study madness he applies himself to hysteria.

Within the just indicated boundaries longer lasting delusions may appear according to Janet. We notice here that the development of a new theory does not just simply rearrange or put into order a pre-existing clinical field: it makes another clinical field possible.

To these conditions Janet immediately adds that the second (which in our opinion is essentially innovative) is generally very hard to ascertain in view of the fact that the delusory state veils the hysteria.[59] The subsequent clinical observation provides an additional diagnostic criterion; if one succeeds in discovering the psychogenesis, being the meaning and the origin of the disorders, by means of hypnosis, it can be posited with certainty that there is question of a case of hysterical delusion.

Here hypnosis is given a different status. Charcot used hypnosis as an experimental means to arrive at the development of a theory on hysteria. Because of his attention to the mental state of hysteria, Janet deviates from this cleared path. Hypnosis is no longer primarily at the service of the development of a theory, but has become an instrument of therapy. With that Janet falls outside of the Charcot net, in which hysterics played their role of teaching "aids." Not the reproducibility of the pathological phenomenon but the discovery of its psychical anchoring directs Janet's research into hypnosis. This alternative line of approach is also obvious from the position both researchers take up with regard to their patients. Janet on the one hand takes up a position that is characterized by discretion and respect for the patient. His demand that after his death all records of his patients should be destroyed, typifies his attitude. Charcot on the other hand did not take this dimension of respect into account. This is obvious from his teachings. Not only were symptoms suggested away, the recovery of the patients was also made undone in the name of science and therefore without Charcot finding it necessary to justify himself to the patient in question.[60]

Janet does not succeed either in unequivocally delineating hysterical delusion. It seems that the departure from the certain, though artificial boundaries of the hysterical fit, again submerges the clinician in the scorching quagmire of symptoms and complexes of symptoms or syndromes, which is beyond his theoretical postulate of a narrowed field of consciousness. Neurosis and madness, by the way, remain deficiency states which sharply contrasts to Janet's understanding attitude in his clinical work.

Azam and Felida

Before continuing the historiography, we pause at the influence of the then generalized interest in the use of hypnosis in the field of psychopathology. All kinds of pathological incarnations of the hypnotic state (e.g., somnambulistic states and dual personalities) captivated the attention of the physician who, out of his desire to hypnotize, very often cultivated these states.

A harrowing example is Felida X., a patient of *maître de pro-*

vince Charles Azam (1822-1899). It is often cited as a type example of vigilambulism or the perfect, total somnambulism.[61] Felida shows two alternating states of consciousness the second of which, the psychically more healthy one, in time gradually takes the upper hand. During the first state periods Felida has no recollections of what happened during the second state periods. This implies that the ever more sporadic and shorter first state periods become ever more painful to Felida, who is left in a state of uncertainty by Azam about the nature of her condition.

We cannot escape the impression that neither the subject nor the treatment take precedence over the unexpected scientific glory and recognition which this unique case may bring Azam. This may be confirmed by the fact that Azam's "scientific" publications keep taking this singular case as a reference. His outspoken preference for the second, healthier, state gives rise to the suspicion that he, possibly unconsciously, cultivated this state and in doing so permanently installed the ever more frequently and lengthier occurring second state.[62] Oddly enough Azam concludes his synthesis labor on Felida with a diatribe against the charlatanism and the malpractice of hypnosis, faith, and suggestion.

The Anglo-American Countries

From Smith-Rosenberg's analysis of the hysterical woman it is obvious that the hysterical fit also reigned in the Anglo-American countries.[63] There, during the first half of the nineteenth century, hysteria is phenomenologically compressed and identified with the hysterical or epileptoid fits; the hysterical fit is the most characteristic and dramatic symptom of hysteria. This true to type imitation of the epileptic fit is classically preceded by an acute or deeply felt emotion (e.g., fear or shock) or by a psychic trauma. The role ascribed to emotion and to the psychic trauma is comparable with the views of Krafft-Ebing and of Freud for German-speaking Europe, and with those of Morel and of Charcot for French-speaking Europe.

From the 1870s onward the star of the hysterical personality is rising to the detriment of the pathognomonic symptom of the fit. The hysterical symptomatology meanwhile covers just about all possible disorders, including all kinds of hysterical delusory states. Some of the women diagnosed as hysterical, therefore, because of bizarre behavior like automutilation and hallucinations, would doubtlessly be labelled as ambulant schizophrenic these days. Typical characteristics include high impressionability, suggestibility and also a marked narcissism—the pejorative typification we found with the French and German psychiatrists.

Also with regard to gender differentiation one and the same line is present; male hysteria is an accepted clinical entity towards the end of the nineteenth century, but that the frequency especially hits fertile women, between ages fifteen and forty.

A recognizable problem is the question whether or not hysteria is an illness and what it is that may be counted as pertaining to its domain. In other words, does it come under the area of neurology, which at that moment was still in its infancy in Anglo-American countries and would it command respect within the adult world of science, or not?

According to our observations, several elements point out that there, too, hysteria is excluded from scientific circles. First, there is the conclusion that hysterical neurological afflictions do not comply with known neurological laws. Second, the simulation of disorders—which is hard to see through—is generally acknowledged as a problem with which to reckon. Finally, there is the confusion between hysteria and complex clinical pictures and the often occurring sudden changes in the hysterical symptomatology. All this leads to the suspicion that Babinski will find overseas connections for his *pithiatism*.[64]

S. Weir Mitchell (1829-1914), one of America's leading neurologists at the end of the nineteenth century and an ardent opponent of psychoanalysis, is one of the few who, out of a therapeutical concern for his hysterical patients, does not attempt to squeeze hysteria into the dichotomy ideational-simulation vs. neurological-disease. In 1855 he writes:

Looking at the pain evoked by ideas and beliefs, we are hardly wise to stamp these pains as non-existent.[65]

Notes

1. A. Porot (ed.) (1975), *Manuel Alphabétique de Psychiatrie clinique et thérapeutique*, Paris, PUF, p. 328. Author's translation.
2. S. Freud (1915d), Repression, *S.E.*, 14, pp. 148-149.
3. H. Ellenberger (1970), *The Discovery of the Unconscious*, New York, Basic Books, pp. 98-99 and 342. Blanche was given the epithet *Queen of Hysterics*, Madeleine was Janet's patient for twenty-two years. P. Janet (1926-1928), *De l'angoisse à l'extase I & II*, Paris, Félix Alcan.
4. Charcot was active for over thirty years at the Salpêtrière, where his career as a neurologist had its permanent base after six years of working in Lourcine. Charcot's academic career is more often than not placed in the shadow of his work at the Salpêtrière. Unjustly so, in view of the fact that Charcot also scored academically high. Already *chef de clinique* of the Faculty of Medicine in Paris in 1853, he held the chair of pathological anatomy in 1872, until he was awarded the then newly established chair of afflictions of the nervous system in 1882 which, incidentally, was the first chair in neurology in the world.
5. The third and final segment of Charcot's work concerns the study of traumatic hysteria (1885-1888) as well as the study of hysteria in the male or virile hysteria. Both become virtually synonymous. Sigmund Freud, who during this period resides at the Salpêtrière for several months, is to propagate and further develop this part of Charcot's teachings. E. Trillat (1986), *Histoire de l'hystérie*, coll. Médecine et Histoire, Paris, Seghers, pp. 147-148.
6. The fact that this criticism not only existed outside the walls of the Salpêtrière, is confirmed by such figures as Babinski and Janet who were both rather late arrivals at the Salpêtrière (respectively in 1886 and 1890) but who were the first to square the demise of the master by rejecting his teachings.
7. Just like hysteria, hypnosis is subject to specific laws, according to Charcot. The basic type is the grand hypnotism. The critical study by

Chertok and Stengers sketches in a refreshingly sharp manner the relation between hypnosis on the one hand, and science and suggestion, on the other hand. J.-M. Charcot (1882), Sur les divers états nerveux déterminés par l'hypnotisation chez les hystériques, *Comptes Rendues hebdomadaires Académie des sciences*, 44, pp. 403-405; L. Chertok & I. Stengers (1989), *Le cœur et la raison*, Paris, Payot, pp. 227-229.

8. In France, meanwhile, we have to wait for any kind of ritual tribute until the 100th anniversary of Charcot's date of birth. There Charcot's neurological studies get all the attention and space they merit while his study on hysteria is covered with the cloak of veniality and diffidence. We find that same extenuating attitude back in some of the existing biographies: P. Marie (1925), Discours à l'occasion du centenaire de Charcot, *Revue neurologique*, 1, 6, pp. 731-745; A. Souques & H. Peige (1939), J.-M. Charcot (1825-1893), *Les biographies médicales*, Paris, Baillière, pp. 329-352; G. Guillain (1955), *J.-M. Charcot (1825-1893)*, Paris, Masson.
9. See, for instance, Didi-Huberman's critical comment on this element of "spectacle": G. Didi-Huberman (1982), *Invention de l'hystérie*, Scènes, Paris, Macula. Just what kind of miserable situations this gave cause to can be read in a series of anecdotes, gathered by Axel Munthe (1857-1949) who frequented Charcot's ward for a period of time. His account is exceptionally hard on the master. For the French translation of the tale of Geneviève who caused the rift between Munthe and Charcot, which supposedly took place in 1883, we refer to Leroux-Hugon. A. Munthe (1930), *The Story of San Michele*, New York, Dutton; V. Leroux-Hugon (1987), L'évasion manquée de Geneviève, ou des aléas de la traduction, *Frénésie*, 4, pp. 103-112.
10. Such a crusade can be found in the writings of Ellenberger, for example. The following article is exemplary in this sense: H. Ellenberger (1965), Charcot and the Salpêtrière School, *American Journal of Psychotherapy*, 19, pp. 253-267.
11. Before epileptics, hysterics and the insane were still hospitalized together. The newly established ward borrows its name, i.e., essential epileptics, from the most important common symptom of its occupants: the convulsive fits. J. Postel & C. Quétel (eds.) (1983), *Nouvelle histoire de la psychiatrie*, Toulouse, Privat, pp. 603-605; I. Veith (1965), *Hysteria*, Chicago and London, The University of Chicago Press, pp. 230-231.

12. Trillat compares epilepsy and hysteria to two siblings of the same family. Both have family traits but each still has a different physiognomy which allows for and makes individualization possible. E. Trillat (1986), p. 133.
13. See among others J.-M. Charcot & P. Richer (1887), *Les démoniaques dans l'art*, Paris.
14. Charcot's ideas go back to those of Briquet, who heralded the beginning of a scientifically fertile period in the history of hysteria. Briquet's work passes as the first systematic and objective study on hysteria. In his opinion this neurosis is an affliction of the encephalon, more specifically of that part, destined to receive the sensations and the affective impressions. Briquet refutes the role of sexual frustration, refuses to accept the coupling of hysteria to the genital organs and links the illness, which presents itself in predestined subjects, with persistent emotions or severe distress. In reference to Briquet, Charcot emphasizes the part of emotions. The emotional content of the hysterical fit to him is self-evident. P. Briquet (1859), *Traité clinique et thérapeutique de l'hystérie*, Paris, Ballière.
15. The analogy with the *grand mal* will not have escaped the attention of the reader. The basic work on this, the great hysterical fit, is the fruit of an intensive collaboration between Charcot and Richer. P. Richer (1881), *Etudes cliniques sur l'hystéro-épilepsie ou grande hystérie*, Paris, Delahaye & Lecrosnier.
16. The permanent stigmata include, in particular, anaesthesias and hyperaesthesias, visual disorders, contractures, and paralyses. The paroxysmic accidents, apart from the major hysterical fit and the phenomena of the grand hypnotism (lethargy, somnambulism, catalepsy) also comprehend vegetative disorders. A description of the hysterical fit can be found later in the present volume.
17. See C. Villechenoux (1968), Le cadre de la folie hystérique de 1870 à 1918, doctor's thesis, University of Paris, p. 34.
18. With Freud this becomes the acute vs. the chronic hysteria. (v.inf.)
19. Which does not mean that Charcot considered hysteria to be clear of any attempt at simulation. It is obvious from his clinical presentations that he incessantly demanded an answer to the question of differentiation between the *neuromimésie* (the imitation of clinical pictures which is typical of hysteria), and (conscious) simulation. See for example J.-M. Charcot (1887), *Leçons sur les maladies du système nerveux faites à la Salpêtrière*, Paris, Delahaye & Lecrosnier,

pp. 16-17 and 48-49.

20. An example of this is the following contribution by Ernest Lasègue (1816-1883): E. Lasègue (1881), Les hystériques, leur perversité, leurs mensonges, *Annales médico-psychologiques*, 6, 6, pp. 111-118.
21. A striking detail which surfaces here and there in publications on Charcot is that he supposedly left the induction of the hypnotic state to his assistants. It was these disciples, according to the various interpretations, who told the patients how to live up to the master's expectations. Quite apart from the reality value of such an interpretation, we note that it rather invalidates Charcot than it indemnifies him against possible blame, which is presumably the intention of a similar "nuance." I. Veith (1965), pp. 238-239.
22. See K. Libbrecht (1989), L'usage imitatif du symptôme: le mimétisme hystérique, *Quarto*, 37-38, pp. 75-79.
23. See S. Freud (1921c), *Group Psychology and the Analysis of the Ego*, *S.E.*, 18, pp. 105-110.
24. This is pre-eminently apparent in the numerous described examples of mass hysteria and epidemics of possession. We may refer here to Richer (1881). A more recent (psychoanalytic) work which is devoted to the relationship between hysteria and epidemics of possession is that of Wajeman's. Both mechanisms can also be demonstrated within Jacques Lacan's schema with the two mirrors (a further elaboration of his 'mirror phase'). G. Wajeman (1982), *Le Maître et l'Hystérique*, Paris, Navarin/Seuil; J. Lacan (1966[1958]), Remarque sur le rapport de Daniel Lagache «Psychanalyse et structure de la personnalité», *Ecrits*, Paris, Seuil, especially pp. 674-678.
25. We briefly refer here to Charcot's view on hysteria in the male. Charcot is both of the opinion that male hysteria not only appears with a certain regularity in the lower social classes, and that the clinical picture comprises the same phenomena as its female counterpart. Both theses at that time are novel. Hysteria in the male—one was agreed on that—occurred sporadically, was class bound and evidently less outspoken than its female pendant. An additional element in this is that Charcot couples male hysteria to *traumatic hysteria*. In this matter too he takes up a distinct position. E. Roudinesco (1986), *L'histoire de la psychanalyse en France*, vol. 1, Paris, Seuil, pp. 50 et seq.; J.-M. Charcot (1887).
26. Charcot discovers this during his research (1884-1885) into the hysterical and traumatic paralyses. H. Ellenberger (1970), pp. 90-91.

27. Charcot's experiments with hypnosis (from 1878) produced a threefold sequence: the lethargic, the cataleptic, and the somnambulistic phase. Each of these states is a hand down from magnetism, the obscure precursor of hypnosis. The injection of it into hysteria avails the definition of the hysterical delusion (see Janet). Through these findings (grand hypnotism) Charcot propels hypnosis onto the scientific stage, which in no time is converted into a scaffold. During the 1880s Charcot's harshest opponent is Bernheim. H. Ellenberger (1970); E. Trillat (1986), pp. 167-179.
28. Charcot's clinical contributions (*leçons cliniques*) are therefore much more subtle and variegated than Richer's work would have us believe.
29. P. Richer (1881), p. viii. Author's translation. The iconography of the patients at the Salpêtrière, the visual aspect of the nosography, must—for the larger part—be attributed to Richer's archives. Charcot saw and Richer recorded the image. J. Postel & C. Quétel (eds.) (1983), pp. 703-704.
30. C. Villechenoux (1968), p. 27.
31. The fact that this determination on quantification (which is not restricted to Richer) may produce grotesque results is for example illustrated by Legrand du Saulle who reports a case in which there is a question of tens of thousands of fits. In such cases one speaks of a state of illness and not of a phenomenon. H. Legrand du Saulle (1885), Cas insolite de névrose convulsive, *Annales médico-psychologiques*, 7, 1, pp. 499-500.
32. This fixed idea becomes the salient point of Janet's psychological doctrine.
33. These clinical references with regard to the presence of sexual or psychical traumata on the one hand and the sometimes obvious wishful character of the hallucinations on the other hand is to be taken up again and theorized by Freud. (v.inf.)
34. G. Gilles de la Tourette (1891), *Traité clinique et thérapeutique de l'hystérie. Première Partie*, Paris, Plon, Nourrit & Co; G. Gilles de la Tourette (1895), *Traité clinique et thérapeutique de l'hystérie. Seconde partie*, 2 vol., Paris, Plon, Nourrit & Co.
35. Hysteria is explicitly subdivided into paroxysmic and inter-paroxysmic hysteria; the fit is the only reference.
36. G. Gilles de la Tourette (1891), p. 490. His reproach regards the statements of, among others, Morel, Legrand du Saulle, Moreau de

Tours, Lasègue, and Tardieu.

37. Just as Charcot and Richer, Gilles de la Tourette considers hysteria as a psychic affliction which must also be treated psychically, i.e., with hypnosis, but which finds its cause in a functional lesion in the nervous system.
38. This statement he takes from Charcot.
39. G. Gilles de la Tourette (1895), pp. 371 et seq. and 533-534.
40. H. Colin (1890), Essai sur l'état mental des hystériques, doctor's thesis, univ. of Paris, p. 69. Author's translation.
41. G. Legué & G. Gilles de la Tourette (eds.) (1985[1886]), *Sœur Jeanne des Anges*, Montbonnot-St. Martin, Jerôme Millon. Extensively discussed in K. Libbrecht (1992), La possession de Loudun: les deux scénarios religieux de Sœur Jeanne des Anges, *Quarto*, 48-49, pp. 53-58.
42. G. Gilles de la Tourette (1891), in particular the chapter on the mental state of hysteria and pp. 368-369.
43. Janet completed the first part of one of his most prominent writings on hysteria (*L'état mental des hystériques*), just prior to Charcot's death in 1892. Certain sources report that Charcot, shortly before his death (in the same period that is) started doubting his theories on hysteria, in the sense that he, after all, was receptive for innovation and was prepared to review his doctrine. The first sign of this was an article on the healing power of faith. J.-M. Charcot (1892), La foi qui guérit, *Revue Hebdomadaire*, Dec., pp. 112-132,; I. Veith (1965), pp. 245-247.
44. J. Postel & C. Quétel (eds.) (1983), pp. 650-652.
45. In France the School of the Salpêtrière was not the only authority in the domain of the study and the therapeutical use of hypnosis. There was also the School of Nancy, headed by the physician Hippolyte Bernheim (1840-1919). The polemic between both schools, which is to result in a direct dispute over the right to exist of hysteria, is determined by three signifiers: hysteria, hypnosis, and suggestion. At every single point Bernheim opposes Charcot's views. He posits that there is neither a specific nor a privileged relationship between hysteria and hypnosis. The hypnotic state is no privilege for hysterics, whose symptoms have come into being by means of suggestion. The consequence is that Charcot's hysteria does not exist for it is artificial. Suggestion, which is omnipresent and omniactive, he detaches from hypnosis. It becomes Bernheim's all explaining gimmick; only

that which cannot be influenced by suggestion is pathological. What is certain is that both schools, under a different guise, abused suggestion on willing (hysterical) "guinea pigs."

46. According to Janet, Charcot's error lies in the application of the neurological method in both the study of hysteria and hypnosis. Both demand psychological analysis. His critique of Bernheim regards the latter's lack of theory as well as the fact that he deserted the sinking ship of hypnosis. P. Janet (1919), *Les Médications psychologiques*, Paris, Félix Alcan, vol. 2, pp. 182, 186 and 187.
47. P. Janet (1889), *Automatisme psychologique*, Paris, Félix Alcan. With this study Janet obtained the *doctorat-ès-lettres* in philosophy. In the same year he started his studies in medicine which he crowned with a dissertation on hysteria: P. Janet (1893), Contribution à l'étude des accidents mentaux chez les hystériques, doctor's thesis, University of Paris.
48. Janet and Gilles de la Tourette, who worked together at the Salpêtrière, were not quite the best of friends because of their diverging recognition of the master.
49. Janet too considered Charcot's grand hysteria and his grand hypnotism as the product of a drill. E. Trillat (1986), pp. 181-185.
50. The psychological analysis of the mental state of the hysteric allows the isolation of the fundamental mechanisms, more precisely of the source of the production of hysterical symptoms.
51. P. Janet (1911[1892-1894]), *L'état mental des hystériques*, 2nd ed., Paris, Félix Alcan. The book falls into two parts, respectively "Les stigmates mentaux" (1892) and "Les accidents mentaux" (1894).
52. Subconsciously means that the ideas emerge under hypnosis or in a natural somnambulistic state. Janet reacts against Möbius who also emphasizes the importance of ideas in the formation of symptoms but who claims that these ideas are conscious. (v.inf.)
53. P. Janet (1910), *Les névroses*, Paris, Flammarion, p. 310-311.
54. P. Janet (1911[1992-1994), pp. 387-410.
55. We would like to point out that Janet speaks of *délire* and not of *folie*: the signifier shifts and the hysterical delusion acquires the status of hysterical symptom.
56. Compare with the difference between morbid associations (Magnan) and hysterical delusions (Gilles de la Tourette).
57. H. Colin (1890), passim. As far as the hysterical fit is concerned we can say that Richer's rigid pattern is adopted with the explicit restric-

tion that the separately occurring delusory fit presents itself only seldom and highly restrained in duration.

58. Although it is no question that the French get their basic insights from the Germans, with this it is beyond dispute that Janet was a well-read scientist and that he kept himself abreast of the latest developments in clinical psychiatry. Janet's typification drops one of the subcategories introduced by Krafft-Ebing—that of the acquired hysterical mania and melancholia. He does not take up the reference to paranoia either.
59. This brings Morel's transformed neurosis to mind. The criterion of the development could already be read with, among others, Jules Falret.
60. See, for example, J.-M. Charcot (1887), p. 297.
61. Ch. Azam (1893), *Hypnotisme et double conscience*, Paris, Félix Alcan.
62. This installation technique at present applies to the multiple personalities who "inhabit" America from the 1950s. (v.inf.)
63. C. Smith-Rosenberg (1972), The Hysterical Woman: Sex Roles and Role Conflict in 19th Century America, *Social Research*, 39, pp. 652-678.
64. See, for example, T. Williams (1910), The Simulation of Hysteria, *American Journal of Insanity*, 67, 2, pp. 287-297.
65. S. Mitchell (1885), *Lectures on the Diseases of the Nervous System, especially in Women*, Philadelphia, Lea Brothers & Co, p. 66.

3
German Neurological Studies
Freud

Hysteria and Hypnosis

Charcot's authority and with it also his influence reach far beyond France's borders. First of all his fame as a neuropathologist combined with his interest in hysteria lends the latter a certain aura and places it under scientific scrutiny. It would however be a misconception to say that Charcot's ideas with regard to hysteria, more specifically the unlinking which he carries through between hysteria and simulation on the one hand and between hysteria and afflictions of the genital organs on the other hand, were unanimously accepted.

German authorities such as Paul Möbius, Sigmund Freud, Emil Kraepelin and later on also Otto Binswanger and Ernst Kretschmer indulge in an elaborate study of hysteria, which results in specific and often voluminous monographs.[1] In this way Binswanger (1852-1929), professor at the University of Jena, devotes some one thousand pages to scrutinizing the numerous varieties of hysterical phenomena. Next to the known (neurological) gamut of illusions and hallucinations, fits and twilight states including the Ganser syndrome, he also devotes a few pages to the hysterical psychoses. In his opinion though, this label is not legitimate since hysteria—the problem child of neuropathology—in essence is a psychic disorder, and therefore not a mental illness. Hysteria and mental illness may occur in one and the same individual, but have nothing to do with each other. This sharp division between hysteria or psychically determined disorder on the one hand, and psychosis or degenerative affliction on the other, is only disrupted by the rare degenerative cases in which a mental illness obviously stems from earlier hysterical suffering. Only in those cases is the use of the notion *hysterical psychosis* legitimized. Binswanger's study above all makes clear that the neurological or psychological study of hysterical phenomena in light of the constitution of a clinical unity or an explanatory theory automatically gives rise to the question of the delineation of neurosis and psychosis.

Apart from Charcot's influence on the study of hysteria, there is also his influence on the interest in hypnosis. The general temporary rehabilitation of hypnosis which was effected in France during the 1880s through the agency of Charcot and Bernheim, albeit with a different drive and from an antagonistic view of the phenomenon, is hesitatingly and mistrustingly followed in contemporary Vienna.[2] There, too, a renewed interest in hypnosis is burgeoning, but primarily directed at theoretical physiology and less, as is the case in France, on the clinical treatment.[3] Hysteria and hypnosis become intertwined, although never as exclusively as with Charcot.[4]

The unifying faith in hypnotic suggestion as the dominant element in the etiology and treatment of hysteria at the end of the nineteenth century, also gets off the ground in Vienna.[5] The most important figure of this period is Sigmund Freud (1856-1939), the founding father of psychoanalysis. His theory of hysteria and his propositions regarding the relationship between hysteria and madness are worthy of extensive consideration here.

Charcot's name attracts quite a number of foreign students and researchers to Paris. Freud, therefore, is not Charcot's first German-speaking caller when he visits him in 1885. A Viennese doctor, worth mentioning because of his original contributions on hysteria, is Moritz Benedikt (1835-1920) who already met Charcot in 1866 and who struck up a tightly knit friendship with him. Notwithstanding his interesting and early contributions in the domain of hypnosis and hysteria he disappears into the vaults of history, in contrast to Freud, whose theory he very much anticipates in certain aspects. The *Wieners* of 1860 were not ripe for it yet.[6]

Benedikt couples hysteria, to which women, considering their specific organs are more sensitive, to early functional disorders of the sexual life or to maltreatment during childhood. These elements constitute a specific vulnerability of the nervous system, i.e., a predisposition to hysteria. With this he expands the assumption, unilaterally posited by Charcot, of a congenital, organic-neurological predestination with an acquired predisposition. This implies a less nihilistic therapeutical conception of hysteria.

Separatly from Charcot, Benedikt experiments with the induction of the hypnotic state (which in his opinion is an artificial state of catalepsy) in cases of severe hysteria. In contrast to Charcot he keeps pointing ever more emphatically to the dangers of this use of hypnosis with hysterics; the ghost of simulations or mock healings, the classical argument by which the study of hypnosis is condemned. The psychic influencing on the level of consciousness becomes the beatific therapeutic procedure. The prerequisite to recovery is the conscious acknowledgement of the pathogenic *secret*, which often is sexual in nature. This means that the emphasis falls on the conscious revelation or the public enunciation of something which is carefully kept hidden.[7] Benedikt later expands the notion of the concealed or fantasy life to that of the more general *second life*.[8]

The crucial elements of sexuality and fantasy will resound in Freud's theory on hysteria.

In order of importance, *hysterical delirium* and *hysterical psychosis* get a few sporadic mentions when, around the turn of the century, Freud develops a first theory of hysteria. The former mentioned entity refers to the fourth phase of Charcot's grand hysteria and therefore is derived from the field of neurology. The second concerns a psychiatric reference insofar as the hysterical psychosis in name, though not in meaning, remains a reference to Krafft-Ebing's *hysterical psychosis*. Freud's disparate mentions of hysterical delirium and hysterical psychosis, however, are not intended to constitute a separate class or category of clinical pictures. They pop up almost incidentally and do so under the heading of psychiatric typifications of clinical observations. Nonetheless, these do make up the point of departure of Freud's development of theories, in which he mainly attempts to seize the psychic mechanisms that are active in hysteria. For the sake of completeness we would still like to mention that the paranoia and the (acute) hallucinatory confusion or Meynert's amentia interlard this early Freudian discourse on hysteria.

We reread Freud's first theory proceeding from what ideas or theories were active in the then French and German neurological and psychiatric circles, on the look-out for specific (theoretical) articulations of hysteria and madness. To this end we resume his initial steps in the field of psychopathology.[9]

At the origin of psychoanalysis in general and the initial psychoanalytic theorizations on hysteria in particular, Freud puts two major figures. These fertile "transference" figures are Jean-Martin Charcot and Josef Breuer (1842-1925).

The Hysterical Delirium—1886-1896

In 1885 Freud left for Paris. Although at that moment he had been appointed Docent in neuropathology in Vienna, he wanted to continue his studies in this field at the Salpêtrière.

Freud's master in neuropathology up until then had been Theodor Meynert, standard bearer of the Austrian organic psychiatry which had sought its salvation in the anatomy of the brain.[10] Meynert was in 1870 the first to be given the chair in psychiatry. This academic psychiatry seeks to find explanations only in anatomy and physiology and therefore presents a therapeutical nihilism. Kraepelin and Krafft-Ebing (the latter succeeded Meynert at the University of Vienna but could not really halt the dominance of organic psychiatry) belong to the clinical school and react against a purely organic psychiatry. To a considerable greater extent they specialize in clinical description. With them hysteria is also given more space.

The encounter with Charcot permanently sends Freud's scientific career into a different direction, that of psychopathology. His love for Charcot makes a transfer of the latter's theory possible. Enthusiastic about what the short stay at the Salpêtrière has done for him, Freud conceives the plan to go and translate a few of Charcot's clinical works into German.[11]

Freud sinks his teeth into the study of hysteria with the attitude of a researcher and not that of an enthusiastic expert. His emancipation of Charcot's view will occur soon after the first acquaintance. We already find the first clues in his contribution on hysteria in the Villaret encyclopedia in the edition of 1888, in which he argues that hysteria perverts the laws of anatomy.[12] Physical hysterical disorders are in no way a copy of the anatomical conditions of the central nervous system.

This observation is theoretically framed in a comparative study on hysterical and organic paralyses which was already in the making then but which was not published until five years later. Proceeding from Charcot's clinical-anatomical method Freud demonstrates its impossibility when applied to hysteria. For he comes to the conclusion that hysterical paralysis does not obey the general laws of neurology. This means the kiss of death for the theory and method of Charcot, who rounds out his neurological knowledge with what the hysterical symptoms teach him. After having demonstrated the hiatus in Charcot's conception, Freud can in the second instance unfold his own theory. Now it is no longer purely novel or revolutionary though, but rather a necessary conceptualization because no other theory takes into consideration the specificity of the hysterical symptom. Oddly enough to this end Freud proceeds from Charcot's theory regarding the dynamical lesion anyway. He comes to the conclusion that the lesion must be entirely independent from the anatomy of the nervous system since the hysteria behaves as if this anatomy does not exist or as if it has no knowledge of it whatsoever. The hysterical paralysis functions according to its own specific laws.

It is coupled to a knowledge about the anatomy, about the body as something which speaks itself. Hysteria takes the parts of the body in their everyday, vulgar meaning and not in their anatomical sense, which proves that there is a question there of a body, other than the anatomical one—an image, constituted by parts, bits, cut up along the lines of ordinary language.[13]

The article from 1888 also gives an almost integral Charcotian reading of hysteria.[14] In his discussion of psychic disorders Freud posits that a psychosis, in the psychiatric sense of the word, is not part of the hysteria, although it may develop on the foundation of the hereditarily determined hysterical status. In this case the psychosis must be considered as a complication. Here we recognize the official view of the Salpêtrière on the relationship between hysteria and madness. The Charcotian legacy is also very apparent in the assumption of a congenital hysterical disposition.[15]

Freud's emancipation becomes clearer in his necrology on Charcot in which he, without detracting from Charcot's clinical qualities as a *visuel*, ventilates fundamental criticism on his inadequate explanation of hysterical phenomena and the etiology of hysteria in general.[16] This critique is extensively resumed in 1896 and elaborated further.[17] With this, Freud breaks with the contemporary trend in the view of hysteria, which allocates the innate or acquired hysterical predisposition a part that explains all and which subsequently focuses on the function of the *agent provocateurs* (Charcot), the illness eliciting elements. Freud's movement proceeds from an accurate analysis of this generally supposed neuropathological constitution; it is neither specific for hysteria, nor therapeutically usable. This does not mean that Freud does not allow any role for heredity. As long as it is not known or purified however, he prefers to concentrate on the therapeutically usable factors. Freud does not, therefore, leave the congenital determination aside but focuses on the workable part, namely the psychic determination. This therapeutical orientation shines through in, among others, a series of three lectures which he gave in 1895 before the Viennese *Doktorenkollegium*.[18]

Two other texts from the period 1893-1896 develop what is to become a constant: the psychic definition of hysteria as an alternative for the neuropathological constitution. In *On the Psychical Mechanism of Hysterical Phenomena*, a lecture from 1893, Freud expands Charcot's theory on the etiology of traumatic paralysis. For in his study of this traumatic hysterical paralysis Charcot acknowledges the eliciting role of a physical lesion (*agent provocateur*), which in the first instance starts off a physiological process of temporary, partial paralysis (a topical shock), subsequently gives rise in the seized subject to the idea of a motor incompetence, in order to finally result, through autosuggestion, in the hysterical paralysis. Freud's contribution will consist of expanding this etiological role of the trauma to every case of hysteria and of emphasizing its psychic nature.[19] Hysterics suffer from traumata that have not been sufficiently abreacted.[20] Later on he is to specify the trauma as the memory of a premature sexual experience.[21]

Let us return, however, to the above mentioned text from 1893. In it Freud mentions hysterical *Delirien* (deliria). The contents of these deliria is often a series of ideas which the patient under normal conditions has rejected, inhibited, or suppressed.[22] Freud in this period repeatedly speaks of the hysterical delirium, whether or not explicitly in reference to the fourth phase of the hysterical fit.[23]

Other authors too stress the importance of ideas or memories in the genesis of hysterical phenomena. In France there is Janet with the *fixed idea*, preceded in Germany by Möbius (1853-1907).[24] As early as 1888 the latter enunciates that under specific conditions defined as a congenital hysterical disposition and a state comparable to that of hypnosis, ideas may restrain or excite physical and neurological processes. It is these particularities which explain the suggestibility of hysterics, their tendency to autosuggestion and the ease with which they actualize neurological or mental syndromes.[25] Janet and Möbius employ a psychological view of hysteria, although with an outspoken degenerative basic postulate, which is akin to Möbius' view of women in general.[26] Möbius holds the Salpêtrière view on hysterical madness. Apart from the delusions connected with fits, it is impossible in his opinion to speak of a truly hysterical madness (*hysterisches Irresein*).[27]

The Charcotian Delirium as an Illustration of Freud's Trauma Theory

In a ten year time span—from 1886 to 1896—Freud purifies Charcot's theory on hysteria of popular but scientifically arguable elements; among others, the general neuropathological constitution is replaced by the sexual constitution. Next to this, he further elaborates the clinically verifiable and usable elements and generalizes these on the basis of his own clinical experiences to arrive at the trauma theory.[28] This rigorous and subtle analysis of Charcot's theory shows Freud his own direction.[29] His scientific commitment is reflected in his study of the etiology of hysteria and the pathogenesis of the hysterical symptoms. Rather than compounding a catalog of possible symptoms Freud, proceeding from clinical material, attempts to seize and theoretically find the psychic mechanisms. This results in his theory of the psychic defense against traumata.[30] This theory on the pathological defense against psychic traumata Freud particularly develops in two articles on the *Neuropsychoses of Defense*, and also in his co-publications with Breuer. In these it is apparent that, apart from the rejection of a congenital predisposition, a second crucial element installs a rift between Freud and his contemporaries, i.e., the role of the "affect," the quantum of energy connected with an idea or a memory, as a crucial factor in the genesis of hysterical symptoms.[31]

Which position does hysterical madness hold within this seemingly Charcotian démarche? Freud adopts the policy view of the Salpêtrière (the hysterical delusory fits) but passes Charcot as far as the explanation is concerned.[32] In reference to the fourth phase of the hysterical fit Freud speaks of the hysterical *deliria*, which repeat the traumatic moment (the idea and the accompanying affect) in a specific way. The contents of the delirium represents the held off, traumatic memory. The affect initially accompanying the ideational content, is flown off into the paths of the sensory innervation—the hallucination. The hysterical delirium, or—put more broadly—the hysterical fit, is the type example of the hysterical symptom.[33]

A second observation applies to the signifier *delirium* which does not have the same meaning as *delusion.* A delirium in the first place refers to a state of decreased consciousness in which hallucinations occur. A delusion emphasizes illusions more and a delusory construction—what is commonly called intellectual disorders—without implying a specific state of consciousness.[34] Charcot, but above all Janet speak of the *délire hystérique* which we translated as the hysterical delusion. Their use of *délire* indeed in the first instance refers to an intellectual defect which in Janet even ties in with his explanation of hysteria. This does not mean to say, however, that quite a number of Janet's clinical descriptions of hysterical delusory states cannot be typified as a delirium. In particular we refer to the delusory states that are linked to hypnosis and to the hysterical fit.[35]

Freud refers to the fourth phase of the hysterical fit in terms of a terminal delirium and not in terms of a terminal delusion. This option may be framed in two ways. First and foremost this implies that Freud here chooses for a different signifier with a different reality, i.e., the psychic state, which still referring to a state of consciousness, is directly contained in the name. Just as it holds for Janet that his choice for the *délire* registers itself in his theory on hysteria, we can say for Freud that his choice for the psychic state reveals his theoretical démarche—the discovery of the unconscious. Also, Freud attests to the German tradition which was always well disposed towards the study of the disorders of consciousness. The reference to the acute hallucinatory confusion which—with observance of the inherent decrease of consciousness—places itself between the delusion and the delirium, may be read in the same fashion.

In our opinion *delirium* is a fertile signifier to seize hysterical madness. Our definition, strictly speaking, does not correspond with the psychiatric definition. To our mind, it takes into account three clinical typifications: hysterical *Dämmerzustand* which is to outlive, by far, hysterical psychosis with the Germans; hypnotism with the inclusion of the *état second*; and the *double conscience*, and the dream state and following on from that oneiric delusion (Régis). Central to delirium is the alteration of consciousness or the presence of another psychic state. The structural affinity between the hysterical symptom and the dream as formations of the unconscious, evident in Freud's later elaborations of the hysterical fantasies and in his magisterial work on the dream, leads to a second important element for the theoretical foundation of hysterical madness as a hysterical phenomenon, namely wish-fulfilment.

The Breuer Epoch
Hypnoid Hysteria and Hysterical Psychosis

In 1895 Freud and Breuer jointly published their now classic *Studies on Hysteria*, preceded in 1893 by the article *On the Psychical Mechanism of Hysterical Phenomena: Preliminary Communication.* The publication of these studies on hysteria, in which the *Preliminary Communication* figures anew as the first chapter, also marks the end of a collaboration which dates back to 1882, the moment when Breuer tells Freud of his new treatment of a case of severe hysteria. It concerns the patient who is to go down in history under the pseudonym of Anna O. and who later, under her real name of Bertha Pappenheim, will make important contributions in both the literary as well as in the social domain.[36]

Her case study was included as the first of six in the *Studies.* The others are Emmy von N., Frau Cäcilie, Elisabeth von R., Lucy R. and Katharina, the last three treated exclusively by Freud. The case of Cäcilie, mentioned sporadically in footnotes but whose history is not extensively treated for reasons of discretion, led directly to the publication of the *Preliminary Com-*

munication. Just like the case study of Căcilie, that of Emmy von N. is an example of the intense collaboration between Breuer and Freud. Emmy's treatment was Freud's first application of the hypno-cathartic method.

Although Breuer spoke positively of the therapeutical result of the Anna O. case in the *Studies*, her treatment can hardly be called a success. Her recovery was not complete, nor was it permanent. There remained some considerable residual phenomena and later several admissions followed into specialized sanatoria. Hirschmüller's analysis of the diverging versions of the hapless outcome of the treatment leads to two central themes which are not even mentioned during the therapy or in the written case study, but which can explain the eventual failure—"transference-love" and sexuality. Jones' version—a myth according to Hirschmüller—says that his strange experience not only kept Breuer from publishing the case study for years but also brought about his break with psychoanalysis. Freud himself puts Breuer's explicit rejection of the role of sexuality in the etiology of hysteria as a determinative element in their eventual split. We can still mention that Freud had the case study in his pocket when he left for Charcot, though the latter did not show any particular interest in it.[37]

Breuer's new technique, which is given the name hypno-cathartic method, is the systematic elaboration of a chance discovery; Anna's symptoms disappear when in a quasi-hypnotic state. The events under which the symptom made its entry and which were subject to amnesia, are revived, described, and reacted to. The essential components upon which the method is founded may therefore be described as making forgotten traumatic events newly conscious and procuring an adequate abreaction of their accompanying affects or energy quanta.

This hypno-cathartic method, which was metaphorically described by Anna as *chimney sweeping* and which was framed in a subsequent movement within the theory on the *abreaction*, constitutes for Freud the fertile moment of the collaboration. Where Freud purifies Charcot's theory on hysteria, with regard to Breuer, he develops the latter's therapeutical method into the classical psychoanalytic cure.[38]

To Breuer, who only temporarily perpetrates the study of hysteria, Anna O. functions as a once-only therapeutic model and theoretical paradigm, that Freud initially supports by and large.[39] Central to Breuer's theory on hysteria, enunciated in his theoretical chapter in the *Studies*, are the hypnoid states.[40] These states of consciousness, comparable to hypnosis and affiliated with the dream, which occur spontaneously with Anna O., constitute the basis and the conditio sine qua non of hysteria.[41] Considering the dreamlike nature of their contents they often merit the name *delirium hystericum*. The ideas (accompanied by energy quanta) that emerge in such circumstances, are cut off from any associative connection. The contents are inaccessible to the normal state of consciousness and the affect- or energy quantum that accompanies the idea cannot be associatively abreacted. During this traumatic moment a splitting of the mind into two states of consciousness is produced and the somatic symptoms are formed by the "conversion" of the affect.[42] Once the *Spaltung* or split is completed, the explicit delineation between both states of consciousness expires and the second, hypnoid state can penetrate the normal state—hysterical psychosis.[43]

This splitting of consciousness (the *double conscience* which Freud will take up again as distinct psychic states) is pathognomonical to hysteria to Freud, Breuer, and Janet. Their explanations of this clinically observable phenomenon determine the singularity of their respective theories. To Freud it becomes one of the many victories of his hysterical tour. Breuer will give up after a single stage victory, contested by Janet.[44]

In 1893, Freud, unanimously with Breuer, posits that every case of hysteria finds its origins in a hypnoid state—a shared physiological explanation.[45] In 1894 Freud already places two other forms of hysteria next to this "hypnoid hysteria"—the "retention hysteria" and the "defense hysteria."[46] The splitting of consciousness at the occasion of which separate psychic groups or complexes are formed, loses its pathognomonical character in favor of the new explanation, being the specific defense mechanism of conversion.[47] The *unerträgliche* (unbearable or incompatible) idea, generally sexual by nature, is rendered innocuous by separating it from the accompanying affect. The consequences are that the traumatic idea is isolated in the consciousness and forms the nucleus of a second psychic group, and the affect is flown off. The way in which the latter occurs, defines the specificity of the neurosis. With hysteria this energy is transformed, converted into a somatic innervation of sensory (hallucination) or motor nature. The hysterical fit functions as major reference.

Here, the idea which Freud is to adduce as criticism of Bleuler's notion of schizophrenia some fifteen years later, lies already dormant; the splitting of consciousness is neither pathognomonical to the neuroses nor to the psychoses. This *Spaltung* or split Freud will again generalize to perversion in his study on fetishism, some fifteen years later.[48]

According to Breuer, the hypnoid element is most evident in the hysterical fit and in acute hysteria, a syndrome which generally introduces the severe forms of hysteria and which exhibits distinct psychotic features. It comprises manic and aggressive states, quickly altering hysterical phenomena, hallucinations, etc. These psychotic states often last for months on end and do not restrict themselves, in their appearance, to the aura, namely to the initial stage of the severe hysteria. Although not essentially different from the hysterical delusory fits or the hysterical deliria, they often must be described, according to Breuer, as hallucinatory confusion and categorized as *hysterisches Irresein* or hysterical psychosis. They do not only look like a psychosis, they are a psychosis. This type of madness exclusively emanates from hysteria; it is a typically hysterical psychosis.[49] Arguments for the diagnosis include the duration of the state, the clinical picture that is comparable to the hallucinatory confusion, and the emphatic mental disorders.[50]

Breuer defends the thesis that hysteria is a neurosis that may degenerate into psychosis, implying the recognition of a hysterical psychosis. Here, too, Anna O. applies as a type example. This view clearly differs from what Freud advocates in 1888. Still, what opinion does he hold in 1890?

On Neurosis and Psychosis

Freud is particularly oriented towards neurology, and Breuer is, in the first instance, a physiologist. When their study on hysteria is published, they have only little practical experience in clinical psychiatry.[51] Still they are not entirely ignorant of psychiatry, which precludes the ascription of their so-called loose psychiatric use of words to ignorance or lack of skill. Additionally, their points of view are based on more than just the few, extensively reported case studies.[52]

Breuer is skeptical of Meynert's approach and directs himself towards the latter's clinical counterpart, Krafft-Ebing, whose degeneration concept of hysteria he throws overboard, saying a certain physiological-organic predisposition is reintroduced via the hypnoid state. He would also have avoided fashionable psychiatric diagnoses that carry an element of prognosis (dementia paranoides, dementia praecox, and circular psychosis).[53]

Freud directs himself more broadly towards a number of viewpoints of Griesinger's and towards the nomenclatures of Krafft-Ebing, Kraepelin and, to a lesser extent, Meynert.[54] Freud was also familiar with the theories of Esquirol and Morel.

As indicated, the psychiatric labels under which hysterical madness may hide within Freud's first theory on hysteria, are first and foremost descriptive, namely not constructive in the sense of category founding. Let us list them again: hysterical psychosis (Krafft-Ebing), (acute) hysterical confusion or amentia (Meynert) and *Überwältigungspsychose* (Griesinger).

Which possible explanations can we invoke for these loose references? First of all there is the goal of the research. Freud is looking for the psychic mechanisms that are active in hysteria and is therefore not disposed towards a psychiatric classification system or a new nosology. Secondly, Freud sets his first steps in the domain of psychopathology, a relatively unknown terrain to him. Therefore, he appeals to all his skill and information, and that means also on his psychiatric background. Thirdly there is the ambiguous use of the diagnostic categories *Hysterie* and *hysterisches Irresein*; hysteria in those days was every bit as often called a neurosis as it was called a psychosis. By 1895-1900 neurosis and psychosis have already been part of the nosological vocabulary for a long time but as yet do not constitute a couple of polarities. Both develop within two conceptually different fields: neurology and psychiatry. Far from excluding each other mutually, they may occur jointly. One and the same clinical entity is often circumscribed as being both a psychosis and a neurosis. *Psychosis* is a clinical notion and indicates a psychiatric affliction; *neurosis* is an etiological and nosological concept. Neuroses are functional neurological afflictions. Breuer's view of hysteria as neurosis and psychosis is therefore rather the rule than the exception. The conceptual opposition neurosis-psychosis is strictly Freudian, according to Bercherie.[55]

An illustration of the double definition of hysteria is the *Handwörterbuch der gesamten Medizin*, edition 1898-1900. *Hysterisches Irresein* (hysterical madness) is discussed there under the heading *Psychoses* but the use of words slips from hysterical madness to hysteria. The specific typification of this psychosis includes, next to characteristic psychic anomalies such as absurdities and a tendency to exaggeration, disorders of the consciousness with hallucinations and delusions, dreamlike states, and transitory manic excitement. The contents of the deliria are often erotic and occasionally serve as grounds for accusing the environment and also the physician. Additionally, mania, melancholia, and paranoia can be encountered with hysterics. Under the transitory madness it is also mentioned that this may occur as a hysterical mental disorder.[56] The article on hysteria by Dr. Gossner commences with the thesis that hysteria over the last decade is ever more emphatically labelled as psychosis in the broad sense; the author specifies this implicitly as the weakness of the will, the basis of all mental disfunctions. The specific psychic symptoms comprise the typification of the hysterical psychosis of Kron with emphasis on anxiety states (alarming visions and hallucinatory deliria, and hysterical twilight states). In Gossner's view hysteria and psychosis evidently go together, but to him there is no such thing as a specific hysterical psychosis. It is remarkable that not the psychic disorders but the physical afflictions often hamper the diagnosis, especially when the characteristic fit is absent.[57] We conclude that on the basis of this clinical dictionary no difference can be made between hysterical madness and hysteria.

Freud's view on hysteria and with that also on hysterical madness evolves away from Breuer. This diverging evolution is contained in the development of Freud's theory on the defense neuroses.[58] In 1893 both still unanimously posit that the hypnoid states cast some light on the difference between the dictum *hysteria is a psychosis* (compare with the Villaret encyclopedia) and the observation that among hysterics one encounters the most lucid of spirit, the strongest of will, the most distinctive of character, and the most discerning of people. The latter characteristics namely apply to their alert thinking, while the hysterics in hypnoid states are *alieniert*, such as all of us are in our dreams. Where these *dream psychoses* do not influence the waking life, the hypnoid states do infringe upon it. They do so in the shape of hysterical phenomena.

On the one hand the ascription *psychotic* is reduced here to the hypnoid states, which does not constitute a violation of Freud's view on the hysterical deliria. On the other hand the title *dream psychoses* encompasses both Breuer's and Freud's further démarches. The hypnoid states of which Breuer stresses the frequently psychotic nature, to him become the terminal station. Freud pursues the path of hysteria along the lines of the dream- and the symptom formation, both characterized by the wish-fulfilment and the (psychic) compromise.[59]

In the *Studies*, too, Freud neither explicitly nor rigorously determines the relationship between hysteria and madness, but within his definition of hysteria (its acute and its chronic form) leaves enough space for hysterical delusory states. Acute hysteria, with the hysterical fit as its type example, is typified by a flourishing and permanent production of hysterical symptoms; the ego is overwhelmed by it (compare with the intrusion of the hypnoid states into the normal state of consciousness). Hypno-cathartic labor here is often a Danaic task. Chronic hysteria is signified by a mild and constant production of hysterical symptoms. The hypno-cathartic method is highly suitable here. The more detailed elaboration with Freud of this opposition between acute and chronic, confirms our conjecture, with his contribution on hysteria in the Villaret encyclopedia from 1888, to the effect that the introduction of the distinction was brought about by him and not by Breuer. Psychiatric notions such as the acute psychosis or madness (Krafft-Ebing) and the hallucinatory confusion (Meynert) are tentative clinical indications. Freud uses them to typify the clinical picture of the acute (defense) hysteria but does not credit them with an immediate diagnostic value. His commentary on the deliria of Emmy demonstrates this exploratory attitude. He posits that the picture can be seen as an acute psychosis (typifying description), that it would probably be classed as a condition of hallucinatory confusion (diagnosis) but in fact is analogous to or even the equivalent of a hysterical fit (mechanism).[60]

Freud's application of the notion *hysterical psychosis* can also be framed in another way. This one does not however preclude its first use, i.e., to clinically typify the picture. In the *Studies* he only mentions this psychiatric notion in those case studies that are the result of an intense collaboration with Breuer, namely Cäcilie and Emmy von N. And apart from a single, in time concurring mention in his correspondence with Fliess, Freud no longer comes back to it.[61] The explicit application of the notion of hysterical psychosis would therefore partially be the result of Freud's collaboration with Breuer and exchangeable for the hallucinatory confusion, amentia and acute psychosis.

The Overwhelming of the Ego and the Success of the Unconscious Wish-Fantasy

The defense hysteria is the first in a series of neuropsychoses of defense. In his first article on that subject (1894) Freud distinguishes three neuropsychoses of defense on the basis of the specific defense mode: hysteria, characterized by the somatic conversion (of psychical excitation); obsessive-compulsive neurosis and phobia, characterized by the transposition (of affect); and the hallucinatory confusion characterized by the rejection (of both the idea and its affect).[62] Here he speaks of hysteria and hallucinatory confusion in terms of two distinct neuropsychoses of defense. He does not connect them with one another, in spite of the fact that in the case fragment, inserted as an illustration of hallucinatory confusion, he makes mention of hysterical conversion before the outbreak of the confusion.[63]

In the manuscript H from 1895 he adds a fourth neuropsychosis of defense, i.e., paranoia characterized by projection.[64] Oddly enough hysterical psychosis—which reveals itself in the hysterical fit and in the *état secondaire*—is mentioned here as a [sixth?] distinct neuropsychosis of defense.[65] Even more astonishing seem the results of the comparison of the typifications of hysteria, hallucinatory confusion, and hysterical psychosis. With hysteria there is question of an unstable defense with a satisfactory gain; the hallucinatory confusion results in a permanent defense with a brilliant gain and hysterical psychosis is evidently a failure of the defense. Additionally, the hallucinations are respectively absent, ego- and defense friendly, ego- and defense hostile. Hallucinatory confusion and hysterical psychosis seem like two extremes—complete success vs. utter failure. This opposition will turn out to be only ostensible when we resume Freud's theory on the dream as a wish-fulfilment (1900), more specifically in its application to the anxiety dream.[66]

We, first of all, would like to complete our episode on the neuropsychoses of defense.

After first having studied hallucinatory confusion, via the entrance of hysteria, Freud subsequently changes over to the study of paranoia. Next to that, after first having directed his attention to the specific defense modes, Freud will subsequently focus on the analogies between unconscious hysterical fantasies and paranoic delusions.

In 1896 another manuscript follows on the four neuroses of defense [sic], shortly thereafter followed by a second article on the neuropsychoses of defense [sic] in which the hallucinatory confusion is missing.[67] In it Freud brings a general sketch of the course of the illness, which is clearly based on the study of the obsessive-compulsive neurosis and which may be typified as *repression (successful defense)* and *return of the repressed material (failure of the defense)*. The process supposedly starts off with a premature traumatic sexual experience or series of experiences. The later reminiscence of this trauma (*Nachträglichkeit*) is followed by the repression with the formation of a primary symptom. Subsequently, there follows a period which can be typified as a successful defense, which keeps ending in the return of the repressed ideas and the formation of new symptoms. The end result takes on the shape of an adaptation, an overwhelming or a recovery.

Freud here employs the notions *neuroses of defense* and *neuropsychoses of defense* interchangeably. Paranoia and hallucinatory confusion he sometimes refers to as *psychoses of defense*. At any rate it is obvious that the study of the specific defense mechanism is given more weight than the differentiation between neurosis and psychosis. As his enthusiasm over the treatment of psychoses decreases, he translates this distinctive criterion into the splitting up of the psychoneuroses (neuroses of defense) into the transference and the narcissistic neuroses (1914).[68]

From the years 1896-1897 onwards Freud only speaks of three *sexual psychoneuroses*: hysteria, obsessional neurosis, and paranoia.[69] The fact that old love does not rust (literal translation of a Flemish proverb), is confirmed here; sporadically Freud comes back to the amentia or hallucinatory confusion.[70] The nature of the reference, namely the dream, is an indication of which mechanism in this psychiatric picture has lastingly affected him, i.e., the wish-fulfilment.[71]

On the Wish-fulfilment and Psychic Reality
Dream Psychosis

In the light of Freud's later work his initial references to hallucinatory confusion turn out to be fertile for the study of hysterical madness.

His views on hysteria and hysterical madness around 1900 converge on two focusing points:
1. The mechanism of the hysterical conversion covers the occurrence of hallucinations and deliria; the hysterical fit and the *état second* are explained by means of the conversion.
2. Hysteria does not turn into psychosis but may be interrupted temporarily by a psychosis of defense or be definitely replaced by it, i.e., the temporary or definite overwhelming of the ego.[72]

At the level of the progress of the illness the second situation constitutes the failure of the defense. The how, the why and which psychoses of defense are eligible for this (paranoia or amentia?) Freud does not specify, but the cited examples demonstrate that this honor especially befalls amentia or hallucinatory confusion. Another indication for the coupling of hysteria and amentia is that Freud, in his search for the initial traumatic experience, places that of amentia or the psychosis of overwhelming earlier in childhood than that of hysteria.[73]

The second point further implies Freud's rejection of the notion of a continuum, nurtured by the concept of degeneration or involution; this is clearly a logical consequence of his view, considering that both hysteria and amentia are neuropsychoses of defense and therefore are determined by a specific defense mechanism. This regards a different view from what postulates psychosis as a complication of hysteria. The difference also runs parallel with Freud's altered view of the curability of hysteria. At the time of the *Studies* Freud thought hysteria only symptomatically and not causally treatable. The moderate pessimism quickly tilts into a therapeutical optimism that hysteria is curable. This implies that it can be replaced by another pathology. Around 1900, the year of the publication of *The Interpretation of Dreams*, Freud is already firmly convinced of the role of fantasies in the genesis of (hysterical) symptoms.[74] The hysterical symptom follows the laws of the dream and is a wish-fulfilment. The structural affiliation with the dream applies most particularly to the hysterical delusion. That much is evident from, among other things, the discussion of Jensen's *Gradiva*, in which Freud labels the long-drawn-out delusion of the protagonist Hanold as a hysterical delusion. The same applies to his case study of the painter Christoph Haizmann in which he recognizes an example of hysteria from days gone by.[75]

This development permits the resumption of the above sketched, apparent contradiction between the hysterical psychosis as a failure of the defense and the hallucinatory confusion as a successful defense, in terms of the wish-fulfilment. Both are wish-fulfilments, although for another entity, respectively the unconscious and the preconscious. Both are the result of a conflict between two entities—the unsuccessful vs. the successful compromise between two opposed drive impulses.[76] Freud further elaborates this in *Hysterical Fantasies and their Relation to Bisexuality*, and in *General Remarks on Hysterical Attacks*, and additionally brings an application of this in his study on Dostoevski.[77] Both amentia and the hysterical (delusory) fit may be framed by means of the theory on the wish-fulfilment. The question is now whether Freud does not claim every single symptom to be the wish-fulfilment of an unconscious fantasy. When Freud's initial therapeutical optimism on the treatment of paranoia ultimately changes into pessimism, because of his excavation work on unconscious fantasies any effect fails to appear, we observe that he never adheres to the same opinion on amentia. On the contrary, when in 1917, for the last time, he extensively brings up the subject of amentia, he does so in order to elaborate on the relationship of the dream, amentia, and the hallucinatory phase of schizophrenia. It is remarkable that there he particularly finds amentia and not schizophrenia as a grateful analogy object for the dream.[78]

Epilogue

The clinical features of Freud's cases of hysteria and hysterical madness are analogous to the clinical manifestations of hysteria and hysterical madness which serve as references in French and German psychiatric circles. All clinical-psychiatric notions, reported by Freud, can be traced back to either France or Germany. The link Freud makes between hysteria and the hallucinatory confusion is not original, by the way, and goes almost without saying to all those familiar with the psychiatry of those days. As we have already indicated, the confusion is one of the clinical pictures which closely resembles what is described and categorized under hysterical madness.

What innovation does Freud introduce here with regard to psychiatry as then constituted? His contribution is neither situated in the field of the description of the clinical picture nor in that of the rigorous synthesis of the existing opinions but in that of the explanation of hysteria, more specifically, the psychic definition of its symptoms.

In his first theory, in which the defense of the incompatible idea and the accompanying affect is central, the expansive tableau of the defense hysteria constitutes the basis and the model for his view on neurosis and on psychosis; conversion hysteria vs. amentia or (hallucinatory) wishful psychosis. With that hysteria is the first source of Freud's conception of psychosis, i.e., amentia. We now posit that where amentia (still) surfaces in Freud's work, we can frame this reference on the basis of hysteria, that is allocate it to a position within hysteria.

Freud's mentions of amentia or wishful psychosis time and again include references to an unbearable reality, a loss, which is rejected in a remarkable fashion. This means that in amentia the relationship with an unbearable reality is patently obvious and that the link between the eliciting moment and the delusory reality is irrefutably present, almost logically evident. Put into dream terminology, reality ties in with unconscious fantasies and ideas. Freud cannot distinguish this link as clearly with paranoia or with schizophrenia. His standard example of amentia is that of the woman who rocks her dead child in her arms. This specific relationship between the clinical picture of the pathology and the event which precedes it, he then names as the fulfilment of a wish. Unbearable reality is discarded, the (unconscious) wishful fantasy makes up the new world view.

Freud continues however to maintain the distinction between psychoses that tie in closely with the dream and psychoses which do not show this link with the dream, i.e., amentia vs. paranoia. The study of paranoia will ultimately become the second basis for Freud's theory on the psychoses and, in contrast to amentia which constituted a sublime illustration of his first theory, will necessitate a new development, i.e., the libido theory.[79] Although this theory in the first instance attempts to bring an explanation of the mechanisms that are active in the psychoses or the narcissistic neuroses, it also proffers him a new basis for the explanation of the transference neuroses.

The development of the libido theory evolves analogously with Freud's (informal) run in with psychiatry, more specifically with the Burghölzli-Klinik in Zürich where Eugen Bleuler and Carl Gustav Jung are the most important figures at that time. In this way Freud's correspondence with Jung (from 1907 to 1913) is to leave deep marks. Dementia praecox, schizophrenia, and paraphrenia will make their entry into psychoanalytic theory.

Notes

1. P. Möbius (1888), Über den Begriff der Hysterie, *Zentralblatt für Nervenheilkunde*, 11, pp. 66-71; O. Binswanger (1904), *Die Hysterie*, Specielle Pathologie und Therapie, edited by H. Nothnagel, vol. 12, part I.2., Vienna, Alfred Hölder; E. Kretschmer (1923), *Über Hysterie*, Leipzig, Georg Thieme. With regard to Freud we refer to his earliest published works on hysteria which all exude a Salpêtrière-

spirit; they will be discussed later.

2. See P. Janet (1980[1923]), *La médecine psychologique*, Paris, La société Pierre Janet & le laboratoire de psychologie pathologique de la Sorbonne, pp. 14-19. The Viennese reticence and the physicians' view of hysteria in a generalized sense goes against Charcot. It is evident, for example, from the discussion ensuing from Freud's first contribution on (male) hysteria in 1886, before the Viennese Imperial and Royal Society of Physicians. See S. Freud (1886), Über männliche Hysterie, *Wiener medizinische Wochenschrift*, 23 Okt., pp. 1444-1446; S. Freud (1886d), Observation of a Severe Case of Hemi-Anaesthesia in a Hysterical Male, *S.E.*, 1, pp. 25-31; J. Quackelbeen & K. Libbrecht (1991), Over mannelijke hysterie, *Rondzendbrief uit het Freudiaanse Veld*, 49, pp. 29-41.
3. A. Hirschmüller (1989[1978]), *The Life and Work of Josef Breuer*, trans. from the German, New York, London, New York University Press, pp. 91-94.
4. Sigmund Freud visited both masters (Charcot in 1885, Bernheim in 1889) and in the debate between Charcot and Bernheim he sticks to a compromise. He does not explicitly choose this or the other side but neither does he spare either of them in his critiques. See—among others—Freud's letter of 29 August 1888 to Fliess in J. Masson (ed.) (1985), *The Complete Letters of Sigmund Freud to Wilhelm Fliess, 1887-1904*, Cambridge, Mass. and London, Belknap Press, pp. 24-26 and n. 1; J. Strachey (1966), Editor's Introduction to Freud's Papers on Hypnotism and Suggestion, *S.E.*, 1, pp. 67-88.
5. I. Veith (1965), *Hysteria*, Chicago and London, The University of Chicago Press, p. 257; H. Ellenberger (1970), *The Discovery of the Unconscious*, New York, Basic Books, pp. 171-174.
6. We mention Benedikt because of his theory on hysteria and not because of any specific contributions on the relationship between madness and hysteria which conforms to the accepted one and includes the typical physical disorders and fits (Charcot's type-hysteria). His contributions include, among others, the development of electro-therapy as a treatment of hysteria and the therapeutical application of hypnosis. According to Ellenberger, he belongs to the group of scientists who, in spite of their brilliance, do not make it into science's history book because they are part of the vanquished. Freud and Benedikt were no strangers to each other. Benedikt pro-

vides Freud with an introductory letter for his visit to Charcot. H. Ellenberger (1970), pp. 269 and 436.

7. Benedikt's method is based on the "moral treatment" (re-educational methods) which was customarily used then for the treatment of hysterical patients. Essentially new is the fact that Benedikt places the patient's story on central stage and not that of the physician. The role of the pathogenic secret is analogous to the role of psychical trauma—which invariably has a sexual content—in the theory of Freud. P. Janet (1980[1923]), pp. 29-33.

8. H. Ellenberger (1970), pp. 301 and 764; J. Postel & C. Quétel (eds.) (1983), *Nouvelle histoire de la psychiatrie*, Toulouse, Privat, p. 581. In 1893 both Freud and Breuer refer to Benedikt as an author who enunciates comparable ideas concerning the psychical determination. In 1900 Freud refers a second time to Benedikt with regard to the importance of fantasy, stressed by the latter, in the psychical life of every subject. S. Freud & J. Breuer (1893a), On the Psychical Mechanism of Hysterical Phenomena: Preliminary Communication, *S.E.*, 2, pp. 7-8 n. 3; S. Freud (1900a), *The Interpretation of Dreams*, *S.E.*, 5, p. 491.

9. With this we give only one reading of this theory, namely a reading aimed at the relationship between hysteria and madness. Verhaeghe gives a different, Lacanian reading which centers on a certain historical dimension in Freud's work. See P. Verhaeghe (1987), *Tussen hysterie en vrouw—een weg door honderd jaar psychoanalyse*, Medusa series no. 2, Leuven, Amersfoort, Acco, in particular pp. 9-64.

10. During the period from 1877 to 1893 Freud published some 120 physiological and neuropathological articles.

11. Freud translated several of Charcot's texts and provided them with an introduction and (critical) comments. With this he unmistakably bore testimony to his fascination with both the figure and the work of Charcot. Both introductions by Freud can be found in the *Standard Edition*: S. Freud (1886f), Preface to the Translation of Charcot's 'Lectures on the diseases of the nervous system' (1860), *S.E.*, 1, pp. 21-22; S. Freud (1892-1894), Preface and Footnotes to Charcot's 'Tuesday Lectures' (1887-1888), *S.E.*, 1, pp. 133-136. Certain footnotes are critical of Charcot's theses, which the latter supposedly took ill of. See E. Jones (1980[1954-1957]), *Sigmund Freud*, 4th ed., vol. 1, London, Hogarth Press, p. 251.

12. S. Freud (1888b), Hysteria, *S.E.*, 1, pp. 41-57. Towards the end of the article Freud mentions the hypno-cathartic method as developed by Breuer as the most appropriate one for hysteria, because it imitates the mechanism of the development and the disappearance of the hysterical disorders. He rather links it however with an efficient use of suggestion than with the "abreaction." A more elaborate discussion of the figure and the merits of Josef Breuer can be found later in this study.
13. S. Freud (1893c[1888-1893]), Some Points for a Comparative Study of Organic and Hysterical Motor Paralyses, *S.E.*, 1, pp. 160-172.
14. Among other things Freud gives an elaborate description of Charcot's grand hysteria with the inclusion of the convulsive fits but he does not breathe a word on the fourth phase, that of the terminal delusion. Charcot himself generally specified four phases in the great hysterical fit. Contrary to his student Richer though, he was not always quite as punctilious about this; occasionally the fourth phase is omitted.
15. Here Freud still emphasizes the hereditary disposition of the nervous system, one of the elements which is to be challenged first and the hardest in Freud's own theory in which he replaces the neuropathic constitution by the role of sexuality. Here he already credits the latter with a larger part than Charcot had done. He does so by stating that conditions, functionally related to the sexual life, have an important share in the etiology of hysteria, all the more so considering the important psychical meaning of sexuality to the female gender. Although Freud, in imitation of Charcot, acknowledges hysteria in the male, it remains reserved first and foremost for the female.
16. S. Freud (1893f), Charcot, *S.E.*, 3, pp. 11-23. See also the critical analysis of Charcot's theory on the neuroses by Ferenczi, pupil of Freud's. S. Ferenczi (1925), Charcot, *Internationale Zeitschrift für Psychoanalyse*, 11, 3, pp. 257-260.
17. S. Freud (1896a), Heredity and the Aetiology of the Neuroses, *S.E.*, 3, pp. 143-156. Ellenberger reproaches Freud for not having expressed any criticism on the artificial (show) element and the effect of psychical infection at the Salpêtrière. Indeed Freud was not as much fascinated with the hysterical performances as he was by the figure and the theory of Charcot. Anyway, Freud departs from the path of the therapeutical hypnotic suggestion (see also Benedikt).

H. Ellenberger (1968), La conférence de Freud sur l'hystérie masculine (15 octobre 1886), *Information Psychiatrique*, 44, 10, p. 926.

18. S. Freud (1895g), Über Hysterie, *G.W.*, Nachtragsband, pp. 328-351.
19. Freud's familiarity with Charcot's considerations regarding the etiology of traumatic hysteria goes back to the period when he attended the latter's lectures at the Salpêtrière (Oct. 1885-Feb. 1886). It is worth mentioning that Janet is to further elaborate on the notion of the motor incapacity and that Babinski is to adopt the role of autosuggestion. See P. Bruno et al. (1986), 1886-1986: L'Hystérie masculine, in *Hystérie et obsession*, Proceedings of the Fourth International Meeting of the Freudian Field, 14-17 February 1986, Paris, Fondation du Champ freudien, p. 184.
20. *Abreagieren* refers to *Abreaktion*, a crucial concept which for the first time is extensively developed in the *Studies on Hysteria* (1895d), and must be ascribed to Breuer.
21. S. Freud (1896c), The Aetiology of Hysteria, *S.E.*, 3, pp. 191-219.
22. S. Freud (1893h), On the Psychical Mechanism of Hysterical Phenomena, *S.E.*, 3, pp. 27-39. Virtually the identical passage we find back in the *Preliminary Communication* (1893a). The conditions under which the memories of a psychical trauma become pathogenic, Freud splits up into two categories: 1. the content has a traumatic effect (e.g., the hysterical deliria), 2. the patient was under a special condition (the hypnoid or auto-hypnotic state) at the time of the trauma. From 1894-1895 the former group becomes the Freudian "defense hysteria;" the second group, the hypnoid hysteria, Freud from 1900 on explicitly ascribes to Breuer. In *The Neuro-Psychoses of Defense* (1894a) Freud, for the first time, speaks of a third form, the retention hysteria. In it a reaction to the trauma is, because of external conditions, impossible. In the *Studies* (1895d) Freud classifies this third form (which is ascribed to Breuer) with the defense hysteria.
23. See, for example, S. Freud (1892-1893), A Case of Successful Treatment by Hypnotism, *S.E.*, 1, pp. 117-128. From what follows it will be evident that Freud labels a longer lasting delirium as hallucinatory confusion.
24. Contrary to Benedikt's views (the importance of functional sexual disorders and the fantasy life), those of Möbius do find acceptance. Particularly Breuer refers elaborately to Möbius' *ideas*-theory on

hysteria. However he does put into perspective the latter's definition of the hysterical phenomenon as being *ideogenic* by definition, i.e., engendered by ideas. Breuer proceeds from the view that only certain hysterical phenomena have a psychical source. Möbius supposedly would not take the splitting of the psyche, a specific psychical condition, into account. Another idea adopted by Breuer is that of a hypnosis related state (Breuer's hypnoid state) as a condition for the pathogenic effect of an idea. Freud for his part is more sceptical with regard to the explanation of hysteria by means of auto-hypnotic states. S. Freud & J. Breuer (1895d), pp. 186-188.

25. P. Möbius (1888); P. Möbius (1890), Über Astasie-Abasie (1890), *Neurologische Beiträge*, vol. 1, Leipzig, Ambrosius Abel, pp. 8-19. The hypnosis related state also anticipates Babinski's definition of hysteria (1901) in which the capability for auto-suggestion is the determinative element.
26. P. Möbius (1908[1901]), *Über den physiologischen Schwachsinn des Weibes*, 8th ed., revised and enlarged, Halle a. S., Marhold. Möbius considers the woman as an inferior being—intellectually minimally developed and prey to essentially instinctive manifestations. Regarding physical and mental capacities he situates her halfway between the child and the adult male.
27. P. Möbius (1895), Über die gegenwärtige Auffassung der Hysterie, *Monatschrift Geburtsheilkundige Gynäkologie*, 1, p. 12. Möbius praises both Charcot's as well as Janet's work and mentions the joint publication by Breuer and Freud; no mention, however, of the role of sexuality—an element which Janet too refuted, by the way.
28. Just like Charcot, Freud too repudiates the psychiatric view of hysteria, focalized on its perversities and lies.
29. Freud is one of the few who placed Charcot's scientific value permanently to the fore. The label *Napoleon of Neuroses* conveys the popular reading of Charcot.
30. S. Freud (1906a[1905]), My Views on the Part Played by Sexuality in the Aetiology of the Neuroses, *S.E.*, 7, pp. 272-274.
31. S. Freud (1894a), The Neuro-Psychoses of Defense, *S.E.*, 3, pp. 45-61; S. Freud (1896b), Further Remarks on the Neuro-Psychoses of Defense, *S.E.*, 3, pp. 162-185.
32. S. Freud & J. Breuer (1940d[1892]), Zur Theorie des hysterischen Anfalls, *G.W.*, 17, pp. 9-13. It regards a sketch of the fourth part of

the *Preliminary Communication.*

33. This upgrading of the hysterical fit as a paradigm of the hysterical symptom applies both to acute and chronic hysteria.
34. A. Porot (ed.) (1975), *Manuel Alphabétique de Psychiatrie clinique et thérapeutique*, Paris, PUF, pp. 177-179; U. Peters (1984), *Wörterbuch der Psychiatrie und medizinischen Psychologie*, München, Vienna, Baltimore, Urban & Schwarzenberg, p. 110.
35. At the same time it is certain that the hysterical madness of the alienists far exceeds the *delirium.*
36. P. Verhaeghe (1987), pp. 141-143.
37. E. Jones (1980[1954-1957]), vol. 1, p. 275; A. Hirschmüller (1989 [1978]), pp. 126-132; S. Freud (1914d), On the History of the Psycho-Analytic Movement, *S.E.*, 14, pp. 11-15.
38. Freud's treatment of hysteria evolves from suggestion under hypnosis (Charcot and Bernheim) along the hypno-cathartic method (Breuer-Anna O.) to free association (Freud-Emmy von N.). And so Freud too is instructed by his hysterical patients; Emmy von N. is the source of "free association," the basic rule of the psychoanalytic cure. For a critical comparison between Breuer's hypno-cathartic method and the procedure Janet employed, more particularly the role of suggestion in it, we refer to Hirschmüller. Janet's claim on the patent for this method was the beginning of a bitter controversy between Freud and Janet which certainly did not heat up the rather cool reception of psychoanalysis in France. S. Freud & J. Breuer (1895d), p. 56; A. Hirschmüller (1989[1978]), pp. 177-183.
39. Since the joint publications even out the differences, we also appeal to other sources in order to juxtapose their respective views on the relationship between hysteria and madness. S. Freud (1894a); S. Freud (1896b); J. Strachey (1955), Editor's Introduction to Freud's Studies on Hysteria, *S.E.*, 2, pp. xxv-xxviii; A. Hirschmüller (1989 [1978]); E. Jones (1954-1957), vol. 1, pp. 301-304; S. Freud (1914d), mainly pp. 7-11.
40. Freud subscribes to this thesis without any reserve in the preliminary communication (1893a). As early as 1896 he puts the universal validity of it into perspective, but only in 1900 is he to entirely repudiate it. S. Freud (1896c), pp. 194-195; S. Freud (1905e[1901]), Fragment of an Analysis of a Case of Hysteria, *S.E.*, 7, pp. 27 n. 1 and 41.

41. Anna has two states of consciousness, the normal and the pathological one. The second is alternately typified by Breuer as *absence*, evening-hypnosis, somnolent-hypnotic state, shadow-hypnosis, autohypnosis, hypnoid state. Just as in France (Charcot's hypnotism, Janet's spontaneous somnambulism, dual personalities) there is an interest in German-speaking Europe for the study of consciousness and of sleep. It is to Breuer's credit that he discovered that a *spontaneous* hypnotic state of consciousness can be used in a clinical treatment; the typical hysterical amnesia is suspended during this state, just as with an induced hypnotic state. Hence the guideline that in the absence of hypnotic moments the hypnotic state should be induced.
42. Not the idea but the specific state of consciousness makes up the pathognomonical element. It explains why apparently normal ideas may become traumatic anyway for a certain subject.
43. For this is the way it goes with Anna O.'s *private theater*. The intrusion of the second state into the normal one makes up the difference with the dream state.
44. Contrary to Freud, Janet postulates this splitting of consciousness as a primary theme. He speaks of the constriction of the field of consciousness and the creation of an *état second* and links this to an inherently debilitated synthesis function. In his early writings Freud repeatedly refers to these ideas of Janet's though the mentions gradually get more critical. Apart from the epistemological and theoretical breach, the harshness of the critique is especially infused by the already mentioned grim polemic over the discovery of the hypnocathartic method, which is to result in a downright Janetian crusade against the heretical psychoanalysis. P. Janet (1980[1923]), pp. 22-26; J. Postel & C. Quétel (eds.) (1983), pp. 650-651. For a thorough comparative analysis of the scientific work of Janet and Freud, see E. Trillat (1986), *Histoire de l'hystérie*, coll. Médecine et histoire, Paris, Seghers, pp. 181-195 and 213.
45. This reveals Breuer's background, i.e., his career as a physiologist. C. Oberndorf (1953), Autobiography of Josef Breuer (1824-1925), *International Journal of Psycho-Analysis*, 34, pp. 64-67.
46. S. Freud (1894a), p. 47. In retention hysteria the reaction to the traumatic stimuli is externally impossible, in defense hysteria the idea that is incompatible with the ego is repressed. The idea is gener-

ally of a sexual origin.

47. Two remarks: 1. Breuer adopts the conversion concept, but in an explicit reference to Freud; 2. Both the hypnoid states and the psychical defense attempt to fit in salient clinical facts such as the gaps in the memory, the *états seconds* and the disappearance of the amnesia under hypnosis. Breuer stresses the link of the second state of consciousness with hypnosis, Freud rather stresses the dynamically emerged and maintained break between both states.
48. S. Freud (1894a), pp. 49-50; S. Freud (1911c[1910]), Psycho-Analytic Notes Upon an Autobiographical Account of a Case of Paranoia (Dementia Paranoides), *S.E.*, 12, p. 75; S. Freud (1927e), Fetishism, *S.E.*, 21, p. 156.
49. Here it is obvious that Breuer, in contrast to Möbius, explicitly acknowledges the existence of a hysterical psychosis. The bearing of this clinical notion differs however from that of Krafft-Ebing, insofar as Breuer refutes the hysterical degeneration and its, by definition, chronic nature. The evolution from a hysterical delusion to a hysterical psychosis, as contained in Breuer's view, may on the other hand be encountered in Krafft-Ebing's typification of hysterical psychosis. Breuer's reference to the (hallucinatory) confusion in addition confirms our earlier formulated conjecture that amentia bears a clinically close resemblance to the German hysterical psychosis.
50. The French definition of *folie* (madness), too, places the mental disorders central stage (in neurosis the somatic phenomena are unmistakable). From Hirschmüller's sources concerning other case studies of Breuer (time span 1881-1912) it is apparent that he already reported a temporary hysterical psychosis in a hysterical patient as early as 1888. A. Hirschmüller (1989[1978]), p. 140.
51. In 1880, Freud attended some lectures of Meynert on psychiatry. In 1883 he did a five month housemanship in the latter's clinic and got a lasting impression of the hallucinatory confusion. Subsequently, up until his study tour to Paris, he worked at Meynert's laboratory for eighteen months. Freud shares the widespread view that Meynert is the greatest brain anatomist of his day, but he holds a rather more modest opinion on his qualities as a psychiatrist. Meynert gradually reveals himself as one of the tough opponents of Freud's theory. This polemic is fed by the source of rivalry and envy and expresses

itself in themes such as male hysteria and hypnosis. S. Freud (1900a), *The Interpretation of Dreams, S.E.*, 5, pp. 437-438; S. Freud, (1925d [1924], *An Autobiographical Study, S.E.*, 20, pp. 15-16; E. Jones (1954-1957), vol. 1, pp. 62, 72-82 and 252-265.

52. Neither of their clinical activities focus on *pure* hysteria but cover the wide field of hysteria, neurasthenia, and the severe psychoses. As a beginning physician Freud is (automatically) allocated the severe (hopeless) cases. A. Hirschmüller (1989[1978]), p. 144; S. Freud (1905e[1901]), pp. 20-21 n. 1.
53. A. Hirschmüller (1989[1978]), pp. 147-148.
54. From Krafft-Ebing Freud takes up the notion of hysterical psychosis and from Meynert that of amentia without their subscription to respectively a degenerative view on hysteria and an organically oriented psychiatry. Therefore, his references to Meynert's amentia are only by way of indicating the clinical picture. From Griesinger on the other hand Freud adopts, among other things, the idea of the *Überwältigungspsychose* (psychosis as an overwhelming of the ego).
55. This was already apparent from the discussion of the psychiatric coordinates. P. Bercherie (1988), *Géographie du champ psychanalytique*, Bibliothèque des Analytica, Paris, Navarin, pp. 158-161.
56. Both mentioned contributions are by Dr. Kron. We observe clear analogies with the capacious view of Krafft-Ebing as well as the emphasis on the delirium; noteworthy is the specification of the sexual subject matter. Under the heading "Psychosen" we find the *hysterisches Irresein* classed with the group of functional psychoses. A. Villaret (ed.) (1898-1900), *Handwörterbuch der gesamten Medizin*, 2nd ed., vol. 2, Stuttgart, Ferdinand Enke, pp. 50, 52 and 637-638.
57. This contribution illustrates the already indicated expansion of the mental or psychical disorders (additional introduction of the will and the character) and confirms the emphasis on the delirium and the twilight states. A. Villaret (ed.) (1898-1900), vol. 1, pp. 1074-1083.
58. The fact that they each go their own way may also be linked with the employed therapeutical methods. Breuer uses the hypno-cathartic method which implies the induction of a hypnotic state. Freud, on the other hand, drops this hypnotic condition early on and from 1892 changes over to free association. This confronts him with a certain resistance from the patients which manifests itself mainly in the field

of the reminiscence of the traumatic scenes. This resistance is circumvented by the induction of the hypnotic state. S. Freud (1914d), p. 16.

59. This view constitutes the starting point for the publication of the case fragment of Dora (1905e[1901]). Freud's correspondence with Wilhelm Fliess gives a detailed account of the evolution of his theory over the period from 1887 to 1904. On 2 February 1899 (the year before the publication of *The Interpretation of Dreams*) Freud announces to Fliess that the psychical processes active in the dream are the key to those that are active in hysteria. Already in 1895 (the year in which the *Studies* are published) Freud develops a first attempt at a coherent dream theory in the posthumously published *Project for a Scientific Psychology*. A few important elements from it are: the wish-fulfilling and hallucinatory nature of the dream, the regressive way of functioning of the psyche in the hallucination and the dream, the analogy between the mechanisms of the dream and those of the hysterical symptoms. S. Freud (1950[1895]), *Project for a Scientific Psychology*, *S.E.*, 1, pp. 295-391. For an thorough discussion of the status of this *Project* (neurological or psychological), we refer to: F. Geerardyn (1993), *Freuds psychologie van het oordeel*, Pegasos series no. 10, Ghent, Idesça.

60. The transitions between the delirium and the normal state of consciousness are generally so smooth that Freud can only distinguish between them *nachträglich* on the basis of Emmy's tale, more specifically on the basis of the gaps it holds (hysterical amnesia). For in a normal state of consciousness the patient has no recollection of the delirium. This brings Freud to the conclusion that both states are separated in memory. Freud's report on Emmy's deliria brings also to mind the description of Felida's state by Azam, a history known to Freud. The fact that Freud, in contrast to Azam, did succeed in liberating his patient from her delirium fits, conveys something about the desire of the therapist which takes hysteria as its object. S. Freud & J. Breuer (1895d), pp. 40-85.

61. S. Freud (1985[1895]), Draft H, Paranoia, in J. Masson (ed.), pp. 107-112.

62. S. Freud (1894a), pp. 58-59. In fact, Freud employs the verb *verwirfen*. Considering the fact that the *Verwerfung* or the *foreclosure* of a crucial signifier in Lacan's theory on the psychoses gets the status of

a fundamental mechanism and the fact that Lacan takes the signifier from Freud, we would like to opt for the signifier *rejection* here in order to exclude any confusion.

63. S. Freud (1894a), pp. 58-59.
64. A detailed and clear account of Freud's early theorizations on paranoia can be found in: L. Billiet (1988), Libido en Oedipuscomplex versus symbolisering en Naam-van-de-Vader, Ph.D. diss., University of Ghent, pp. 28-35.
65. S. Freud (1985[1895]), pp. 107-112. This mention is neither commented nor elsewhere confirmed. We would like to point out that this manuscript was written prior to the publication of the *Studies*, so that Breuer's influence still makes itself felt. This does not detract however from Freud's typifications. Additionally, we would like to remind the reader that paranoia and mental confusion, in particular the hallucinatory confusion, make up two classical poles in the German psychiatric classifications.
66. We may add here that where Freud uses the hysterical psychosis and the hallucinatory confusion within the context of one and the same case study the sequence of events is always identical—starting off with acute hysteria which takes the shape of a hysterical psychosis and which ossifies or ends, i.e., becomes chronic, in a hallucinatory confusion (see for example the letter to Fliess dated 11 January 1897). Confusion as a terminal state of a mental disorder in Germany has a comparable value as dementia has as a terminal state of the *folie* in France.
67. S. Freud (1985[1896]), Draft K, The Neuroses of Defense, in J. Masson (ed.), pp. 162-169; S. Freud (1896b); S. Freud (1916-1917 [1915-1917]), *Introductory Lectures on Psycho-Analysis*, Lecture 27: Transference, *S.E.*, 16, pp. 439-447.
68. We shall return to this later.
69. See the correspondence between Freud and Fliess.
70. It should be said that Freud no longer mentions amentia and (acute) hysteria in one and the same breath.
71. S. Freud (1917d[1915]), Metapsychological Supplement to the Theory of Dreams, *S.E.*, 14, pp. 229-230.
72. The latter is not quite far off from his earliest statement on hysterical madness, i.e., psychosis as a possible complication of hysteria.
73. J. Masson (ed.) (1985), letters from 30 May 1896 and 11 January

1897. Since Freud's hysterical patients provide him with traumatic memories going back further and further, he situates the moment of the initial trauma (the sexual scene) earlier and earlier in earliest childhood (until the age of four). The main characteristic of this first psychical period is that the memory remnants have not been put into words. The sexual scene in cases of hysterical psychosis (confusion) and of hysterical epilepsy (hysterical fit) goes back furthest (before one and a half years of age). The sexual scene in paranoia takes place in puberty, i.e., the third psychical period (separated from the two foregoing ones by a period of suppression).

74. S. Freud (1900a). In his letter to Fliess from 6 April 1897 Freud for the first time mentions the hysterical fantasies as a new source for the answer to hysteria. These fantasies are protective structures based on what was heard on the trauma afterwards. Still Freud continues to link the hysterical symptoms with memories and as yet not with fantasies. In May 1897 he comes to the conclusion that symptoms are wish-fulfilments. The book of dreams is in the making. On 21 September 1897 he renounces his trauma theory in which the infantile seduction by the father was the pivoting point. He has discovered the "psychical reality." The real trauma has served its turn; from now on, the subjective experience of the trauma is the material in use. J. Masson (ed.) (1985), pp. 234-235, 251 and 264-266.

75. S. Freud (1907a[1906]), Delusions and Dreams in Jensen's 'Gradiva', *S.E.*, 9, p. 45 n. 1; S. Freud (1923d[1922]), A Seventeenth-Century Demonological Neurosis, *S.E.*, 19, p. 72.

76. In *The Interpretation of dreams* we read, "There is no longer anything contradictory to us in the notion that a psychical process which develops anxiety can nevertheless be the fulfilment of a wish. We know that it can be explained by the fact that the wish belongs to one system, the *Ucs.*, while it has been repudiated and suppressed by the other system, the *Pcs.*" S. Freud (1900a), p. 581, italics by Freud.

77. S. Freud (1908a), Hysterical Fantasies and their Relation to Bisexuality, *S.E.*, 9, pp. 159-166; S. Freud (1909a[1908]), General Remarks on Hysterical Attacks, *S.E.*, 9, pp. 229-234; S. Freud (1928b[1927]), Dostoevski and Parricide, *S.E.*, 21, pp. 181-182. In the first article Freud states that hysterical symptoms are unconscious fantasies brought to expression by conversion. Insofar as somatic symptoms are concerned, these are often adopted from the domain of the sexual

sensations and motor innervations which initially accompanied the then still conscious fantasies. This is elaborated in the second article for the hysterical fit and confirms our hypothesis that Freud long took the hysterical fit to be a paradigmatic symptom for hysteria. In the second article Freud also emphasizes the analogy with the dream-work and the dream-interpretation, as well as the hysterical fit as a substitute for an earlier autoerotic satisfaction. This is to be elaborated by Freud's disciple Karl Abraham. (v.inf.)

78. S. Freud (1917d[1915]).
79. When Freud discusses the relation between hysteria and psychosis, it is remarkable how hallucinatory confusion and later on how dementia praecox and schizophrenia emerge. This does not mean, however, that Freud does not look for or indicate any analogies between hysteria and paranoia. He especially juxtaposes the unconscious hysterical fantasies against the conscious delusory development in paranoia. An essential difference which Freud gradually stresses and which exhorts him to his new theory, is the inert nature of the symptoms in paranoia.

4
Congresses on Hysteria

The ideas of the alienists and the neuro(patho)logists on hysteria and hysterical madness can be learned by their respective contributions to congresses and the subjects treated there. We would like to discuss three of those congresses here held by French neurologists and alienists and one by Belgian neurologists and psychiatrists. They took place respectively in 1894, 1907, 1921, and 1908:

- 1894: "Sur la folie hystérique" (Clermont-Ferrand)
- 1907: "Définition et nature de l'Hystérie" (Lausanne)
- 1908: "Les Psychoses hystériques" (Ghent)
- 1921: "L'Hystérie et les fonctions psychomotrices" (Brussels)

The evolutions in the lines of force which manifested themselves at these congresses, confirmed the developments which we have already touched upon in the previous pages, and which introduced the new trend figures.

The Still Unanimous Endorsement

The contributions and subsequent discussions of the 1894 congress confirm and illustrate the already mentioned antagonism between neurologists and alienists. In a manner of speaking, hysterical madness is torn between neurology and psychiatry.

The psychiatric contribution of Ballet on hysteria and madness expresses the view of the Salpêtrière and refers to Breuer and

Freud. Hysterical madness according to him comprises a number of diverging states which include the *folie hystérique* of the alienists as well as the hysterical delusory states of the neurologists for example, confusional states, mania, melancholia, delusions, and secondary states. In spite of the fact that no unanimous declaration is reached, the existence of specific delusory states with hysterics, different from ordinary madness, is endorsed.

The discussion is, however, streaked with morally tinted views on the essence of hysteria and with references to simulation. The psychological theory of Janet, the first Francophone who explicitly emphasizes the psychic determination and who highlights the theorization on the subject, is unanimously rejected by the alienists. For the rest Breuer and Freud are ignored.[1]

Not theorization but clinical observation and chemical research in support of the diagnosis, may provide a way out according to the alienists. Babinski (1857-1932), who is to become Charcot's official successor, has already got his future made.

Babinski's Pithiatism

After Charcot's death in 1893 Babinski turns from well-liked successor into the most important protagonist in the crucifixion of Charcot's hysteria.[2] He explicitly takes the side of the (scientific) neurology against the psychological trend of Janet and focuses his research on signs that allow the differentiation between hysterical and neurological (lesional) disorders. In 1901 this brings him to a definition of hysteria in which the capacity of autosuggestion is the determinative element. His definition is purely pragmatical; hysteria is a collection of symptoms that can be produced by suggestion and which may disappear by means of counter-suggestion or persuasion. Charcot's experimental method of research is used here as a diagnostic means.

Babinski concludes that certain Charcotian symptoms, including hysterical delusory states, must necessarily disappear from the collection of hysterical phenomena. Hysteria is stripped of every trace of madness.

The fragmentation of Charcot's concept of hysteria carried through in this way by Babinski is generally adopted. It is, however, not only unanimously accepted, but additionally and erroneously interpreted that hysteria is simulation and therefore does not exist. This was by no means Babinski's initial intention since he crowns his definition of hysteria with a new signifier which seems more appropriate to him. He introduces the neologism *pithiatism*, i.e., curable by persuasion or conviction. His purification of Charcot's major hysteria this way unintentionally becomes the coup de grâce of hysteria as such, since the misinterpretation of his view quickly finds general acceptance.[3]

The Belgian Compromise

At the 1907 congress the tendency with regard to the moral nature of hysteria, which was already on hand at the preceding congress, is markedly present. The congress in Ghent, which took place a year later, signals the adapted version for hysterical psychosis. The psychiatric contribution at this Belgian congress for neurology and psychiatry comprehends the clinical study of Laruelle on the hysterical psychoses.[4]

First of all, we observe a discrepancy in the use of concepts there. The Belgian psychiatrist speaks of hysterical psychosis, while the French alienists stick to *folie hystérique* (hysterical madness). From the discussion, in which Laruelle abjures the existence of the *folie hystérique* as a specific form of madness, we deduce that he still undertakes a fierce attempt to save mad hysteria from a certain death, against the ever more forceful tendency to get rid of every form of hysterical madness. He does so by means of the re-introduction of an already existing German category for the coordination of all kinds of mental afflictions that either are or not autonomous to the hysterical fit. The inference, therefore, is especially compromised in the use of the signifier *psychosis*. As already indicated, the notion of hysterical psychosis was introduced long before by Krafft-Ebing. His description, however, especially included chronic states.

The new clinical definition of the group of the hysterical psychoses restores Charcot's hysteria concept, although Laruelle puts the exclusive return to the hysterical fit into perspective. The polymorphous hysterical psychoses apart from the hysterical fit also include the hysterical fugue, stupor, mania, melancholia, lethargy and also various somnambulistic and twilight states, including the Ganser syndrome. In this way he brings a summary of the meanwhile already waning French and German entities.

Laruelle rejects the existence of a chronic hysterical psychosis, namely the demential evolution of hysteria, but he formulates the proposal to reserve the *folie hystérique* for the cyclic and therefore periodically recurrent hysterical psychosis.[5] Just as Janet had done, he acknowledges psychic mechanisms. In this way the hysterical delusion, which he finds in other authors' work under the names of sensorial delusion, hallucinatory dream delusion and oneiric delusion, has an essentially psychogenic character.[6] From Freud he borrows the view that the hysterical fugue complies with a certain desire or an unconscious deception. Each of the hysterical psychoses is either related to the dream or to the hypnotic state.

From his survey of accepted views we may conclude, however, that what is characteristic of hysterical psychosis, to Laruelle too, is not primarily determined by the prevalence of delusions or hallucinations, but by an omnipresent psychopathy, i.e., something which goes against reason. He specifies the fundamental features as a pathological suggestibility—Babinski's influence—and anomalies of the instincts. This last conclusion confirms what the previous congresses already suspected. The hysterical state of mind or the hysterical character has become, with the neurologists too, the determinant element.

Still Laruelle's own view, in his explicit affirmation and definition of hysterical psychosis, dissents from what could be heard at the previous congresses. His contribution is also of interest for other reasons. Apart from the observation that he, as a psychiatrist, endorses the view of the neuropathologists of the Salpêtrière, it appears from the discussion that the *folie hystérique* not only loses value in favor of the mental confusion but also makes room for dementia praecox and for the manic-depressive psychosis, which before had been the hysterical mania and melancholia. Particularly the differential diagnosis with dementia praecox, which is mentioned for the first time, creates serious problems.

> Hysteria and dementia praecox show such a close resemblance, that we may wonder if dementia praecox does not commence with hysteriform symptoms or shows essentially hysterical symptoms in its initial stages. In this case we would possibly be justified in making our conclusions as to the identity of both afflictions.[7]

Is this a clear return to the hysteria concept of the early alienists such as Esquirol because they saw hysteria as a first phase of madness?

The already imminent trading in of dementia praecox for schizophrenia will not make this differential diagnosis any simpler, since the stumbling block of the demential evolution which is primary in presenile dementia but which is referred to the background in schizophrenia, disappears.

In this period and over the years to come, simulation and suggestion color the discourse on diagnosis and treatment of hysteria. Laruelle seizes at this to explain the plasticity of hysteria and the hysterical psychoses, while Babinski, by means of the same criterion, excludes every trace of madness from hysteria (pithiatism), since it is foreign to suggestion. This contrast can be framed from their respective fields of interest. Laruelle, as a psychiatrist, is still interested in the syndrome character of severe hysteria which he means to separate from true madness, while Babinski strictly reserves the developing science of neurology to organic disorders, where the pithiatism falls outside. Hysteria is typified by its female, i.e., infantile character. This was in evidence at the congress in Lausanne, which was entirely dominated by Babinski's and Bernheim's contributions.[8] The *folie hystérique* (also in the sense of Laruelle) is rejected there and is transferred to dementia praecox.

Hysterical psychosis is wiped off the map. Reviled by the neurologists and the alienists, it is divided between the (incurable) dementia praecox and the (curable) manic-depressive psychosis.[9]

Why this turnabout? The development of neurology as a scientific discipline is certainly not alien to this defaming of hysterical madness. For does not hysteria take the slightest notice of all neurological laws?[10] The increasing interest in dementia praecox falls under the wider scope of the polemic surrounding the textbook of Kraepelin.

The End of a Glorious Period

It is obvious from these congress reports that the attention to hysteria, both from the neurological as from the psychiatric corner, is waning. The heyday of hysteria, still to be glorified by the surrealists, draws to a close.[11] The gradual disappearance of the *folie hystérique* is but one sign of this. Laruelle's monograph, together with that of Mairet and Salager, is the last of its kind. The classical hysteria or the cultural hysteria of Charcot is excluded from the neurological centers and ends up in the asylums as cultural psychosis.[12] Parallel with this and clearly marked by the First World War, clinical interest is shifted to the traumatic neuroses and the medical-judicial aspect of pathology. Simulation becomes the main concern of the alienists.[13]

At the 1921 congress in Brussels it is evident to what extent Babinski's impact has surged. In his inaugural report, the psychiatrist Baruk draws up a balance where the pithiatism turns out to have become an almost negligible nosographical group and the most spectacular manifestations of the old hysteria are now part of the psychoses in the asylums. Janet's swipe at the alienists in his *Névroses et idées fixes*, in which he reproaches them of all too easily renaming the patients, having come over from centers for neurotics, into *aliénés*, neglecting the fact that they showed hysterical symptoms in these centers, is one of the few, albeit unheard, signs of protest.[14] Hearing this outburst from Janet is no coincidence. Janet's clinical-scientific activities are distinctly directed towards the study of the neuroses, i.e., hysteria and psychasthenia. From his commentary on a lecture by Minkowski on schizophrenia in 1927, it seems that he does not just simply take up new entities like that either. He rather verifies the new with his own clinical experience and his theory on the neuroses.[15] Janet's orientation towards neuroses possibly suggests his ardent protest against all those who mean to harm, erase, or absorb this group, but he remains one of the few who, from the field of the neuroses, dares to put his finger on the diseased spot in the differential diagnostics.

Conclusion

The French and the German psychiatric schools are also authoritative outside of Europe. Only during the second half of the twentieth century a certain anglophile tendency becomes detectable in Europe.

Can we speak of a classical French and a classical German line of development? French and German psychiatry are at any rate going through an evolution of their own, which automatically demonstrates itself in diverging nosological systems and accents. Regarding hysterical madness we see, in France halfway through the nineteenth century, a unanimous recognition of the existence of a *folie hystérique*, a characterized form of madness. In the parallel neurological circuit which we joined around the 1880s, various hypnotic pathologies appear, including the *délire hystérique* as part of the neuropathological view of hysteria.

In Germany the clinic of hysterical madness (*das hysterische Irresein*) is much more typified by the degenerative, hysterical character. There we find all kinds of hysterical madness under the *Dämmerzustände* and the *halluzinatorische Verworrenheit* or *Verwirtheit*. Until after the First World War, the hysterical twilight states, together with the traumatic neuroses, are given a certain position in German psychiatry. Kretschmer (1888-1964), strongly influenced by his impressions of war hysteria, researches the hysterical reaction type as a biologically-physiologically determined predisposition. His theoretically uninteresting work on hysteria denies the existence of the unconscious and excessively highlights the biological reference to the hysterical predisposition. We mention it here anyway since the clinical phenomena, referred to as typical, still include the twilight states. Kretschmer's elaboration of it ties in especially well with Breuer's hypnoid explanation in the splitting of consciousness.[16]

In France we find this temporary pathological state, characterized by an alteration of consciousness, back as an import under the heading *état crépusculaire*.[17] The *état second*, causing a furor within neurological circles, is of French origin. This label does not find the same dissemination in Germany.

Both entities, the twilight- and the secondary states, stress the alteration of consciousness, which also applies to the delirium. It is remarkable that, where they are still in use today or made mention of, they function as synonyms. This illustrates the thesis that, once unlinked from the original context and framework, it becomes an impossible task to keep clinical entities still separated from each other.[18] The presently still encountered division of psychotic states into those with and those without disorders of consciousness, in which the latter category still includes the neurotic delusory states, must therefore be interpreted as the carrying on of the classical German line, which also gained entry in France.

The coupling hysteria-psychosis, a trend which first presses ahead in France but which also spreads elsewhere, is the coup de grâce for hysteria. The word is discarded as if it were infected. Janet is the last to undertake a scientific study of hysteria and, in doing so, still takes hysteria seriously. Those who still keep occupied with hysteria after the turn of the century, ring the therapeutical bell. Not the study or the fundamental research, but the treatment has taken precedence. The contrast between the gradual increase of studies on hysteria and its sudden strong decrease is remarkable. This is proven by the often noted thesis that hysteria had disappeared by the turn of the century. The one exception to this thesis is Sigmund Freud. The analysis of his early works teaches us that he avoids the nosological puddle and in his study of hysteria propounds the mechanism of the conversion as a characteristic factor for hysteria next to the wish-fulfilment and the psychic reality. This mechanism grounds both the typical physical disorders as the hysterical (delirious) fits. With the dropping of hypnosis so too disappears the hysterical delirium from the specter of symptoms.

Hysteria is on the rebound. Does the disappearance of the diagnosis hysteria prove that it is a product of its time? Its history which dates back to Hippocrates provides an indication in the other direction, namely that it has been absorbed, or has allowed itself to be taken in by other nosological entities. The problematic differential diagnoses show us the way. After the mania, melancholia, and the mental confusion there follow dementia praecox and schizophrenia.

Notes

1. It is essential to remind the reader that Janet does acknowledge psychic mechanisms but situates the ultimate etiology of hysteria in a hereditary predisposition which manifests itself in a psychic impairment: the constriction of the field of consciousness.
2. Therefore Babinski assumes a hostile demeanor against the theory of Janet, whom he reproaches for repeating and thus perpetuating the same mistakes as the master (the use of hypnosis). H. Ellenberger (1970), *The Discovery of the Unconscious*, New York, Basic Books, p. 343.
3. P. Bercherie (1980), *Les Fondements de la Clinique*, La Bibliothèque d'Ornicar?, Analytica no. 20-21, pp. 183-185; H. Ellenberger (1970), pp. 785-786.
4. Laruelle's study is averse from any ambition to present new theory,

but means to bring clinical material. Apart from that, this study also presents a successful synthesis of the then, anno 1908, common ideas regarding hysteria and hysterical psychosis. He makes up the balance of all possible positions concerning hysterical madness. L. Laruelle (1908a), Les psychoses hystériques (étude clinique), *Bulletin de la Société de Médecine Mentale de Belgique*, 140, pp. 245-307 and 141, pp. 346-401; L. Laruelle (1908b), Les psychoses hystériques, Psychiatric Report of the Belgian Conference of Neurology and Psychiatry, 26-27 September 1908, *Encéphale*, 2, 3, pp. 606-612.

5. At the same time Laruelle makes it known that he is not averse to the (German) definition of the chronic hysterical psychosis which takes the pathological hysterical character to be the chronic element. L. Laruelle (1908b), pp. 306-307.
6. Again this conjures up the analogy between hysterical delusion and toxic or artificial delusory states.
7. L. Laruelle (1908b), pp. 610-611. Author's translation.
8. Bernheim did stand alone with his refusal to acknowledge hysteria as a morbid entity.
9. The isolation of dementia praecox (incurable, deterioration) and the manic-depressive psychosis (curable, no deterioration) from the chaos of endogenous psychoses is considered as one of Kraepelin's most important merits. A. Porot (ed.) (1975), *Manuel Alphabétique de Psychiatrie clinique et thérapeutique*, Paris, PUF, p. 190 et seq. and p. 401 et seq.; H. Ellenberger (1970), p. 285.
10. Mairet's work on simulation shows that the typification of hysteria is analogous to that of malingering. The malingerer is characterized by his imperfect simulation, his behavior deviates from the average *aliéné* or mental patient. The physician's job consists of making the malingerer having to own up. For hysteria the criterion becomes that the symptoms should, by means of suggestion, both be able to be made to disappear as well as be newly installed. A. Mairet (1908), *La simulation de la folie*, Montpellier, Coulet & fils.
11. L. Aragon & A. Breton (1928), Le cinquantenaire de l'hystérie (1878-1928), *La Révolution surréaliste*, 11, pp. 20-22. The article is an accolade to hysteria, more particularly to Charcot's hysterics. It mocks the amorous implications of the physicians of the Salpêtrière who first courted their patients in order to subsequently brand their passionate carriages as pathological.
12. C. Villechenoux (1968), Le cadre de la folie hystérique de 1870 à

1918, doctor's thesis, University of Paris, pp. 57-59.

13. See, for example, the work of A. Mairet in which the simulation is studied within the medical-judicial frame, namely within the jurisdiction.
14. P. Janet (1914), *Névroses et idées fixes*, 3rd ed., vol. 2, Paris, Félix Alcan, p. 221.
15. P. Janet (1927), A propos de la schizophrénie, *Journal de Psychologie*, 24, pp. 477-492. In this contribution Janet introduces two female patients who supposedly answer to the clinical picture of schizophrenia as sketched by Bleuler and Minkowski. Subsequently he asks the following question: "Is what the just named authors understand by schizophrenia not the chronic, perpetuated psychasthenia?" This (again) demonstrates that Janet is not capable of applying a section within the field of psychopathology between neurosis and psychosis.
16. E. Kretschmer (1923), *Über Hysterie*, Leipzig, Georg Thieme, mainly pp. 98-115.
17. This state is related to the mental confusion; it is an involutive variant of it, characterized by its transience.
18. In this respect, Porot's psychiatric manual is a very illustrative example.

Part Two

The Interbellum

Hysteria in the Margin, Schizophrenia as a Refuge of Hysterical Madness

Introduction

The *fin de siècle* is a prime period for the study of hysteria. Both neurologists and psychiatrists, representatives of two disciplines in the making, concentrate on hysteria and hysterical madness in order to subsequently dispose of it, after the failure of their knowledge on the matter.

As neurology and psychiatry register themselves explicitly as subdisciplines of medicine, their respective spheres of activity are passed through the objective-scientific grid and purified of their superfluities. Hysteria and hysterical madness are the first and most important victims. Hysteria is essentially psychic, namely not an illness; therefore there can be no question whatsoever of something like a specifically hysterical madness, namely a mental illness exclusively originating from hysteria. First eliminated as a possible diagnosis and as a signifier by the French neurologists under the influence of Babinski, hysterical madness and hysteria become outdated and old-fashioned entities; the diagnoses remain forthcoming. The fact that this deletion from the register after more than 2,000 years of historiography on hysteria caused little controversy may seem surprising to us but for the medical world another awkward patient is again shown the door. "In 1914 one no longer dares to mention hysteria. For over thirty years it has already deceived too many people and its name is linked with too many bitter memories."[1] The war cools down, even freezes the relationship between German and French neurologists and psychiatrists, but on the subject of hysteria there is a marked unanimity for it has disappeared, vanished into thin air.

Janet in Paris and Freud in Vienna are two exceptions who fasten their teeth into the study of hysteria at a time when its obituary is already at the printer's. Both their theoretical elaborations on hysteria are known but are kept in the dark in medical circles, which are directed towards therapy and not theory. Additionally, the role of sexuality in the genesis of hysterical symptoms, as discovered by Freud, is rejected by Janet as well.

By 1914 hysteria has just about disappeared altogether from the hospitals. With the outbreak of war, however, it temporarily reappears on the international scene together with its mad or psychotic variant as traumatic neurosis, i.e., a neurosis caused or elicited by an accident.[2]

Another parallel development within psychiatry is the study of the psychoses, more precisely dementia praecox and schizophrenia. This evolution exerts a more lasting attraction to hysteria which is classified under it together with its psychotic variant. Oddly enough it is Freud's students and the Anglo-American Postfreudians who internationally propagate schizophrenia.

Notes

1. E. Trillat (1986), *Histoire de l'hystérie*, coll. Médecine et Histoire, Paris, Seghers, p. 241. Own translation.
2. The occurrence of this traumatic neurosis takes the shape of an epidemic during the period 1860-1920 that can be subdivided into two episodes. The first episode (until the First World War) is typified by the prevalence of the railway spine (railway accidents), while the second one (during the War) is dominated by the shell shock (war accidents). See E. Fischer-Homberger (1975), *Die traumatische Neurose*, Bern, Stuttgart, Vienna, Hans Huber Verlag, p. 7.

5
The War Neuroses
Twilight States
Confusion

During the First World War and up until the 1920s the neurological focus is shifted to the feverish search for emergency treatments for the gamut of disorders engendered by the experiences at the front.

In spite of Freud's efforts, Charcot's theory on traumatic hysteria, i.e., hysteria caused by a physical trauma, did not find acceptance in a first episode of the traumatic neurosis on the continent (1880s) where it was generally classified as a neurological-lesional affliction.[1] Some thirty years later there is a growing body of opinion which acknowledges hysterical manifestations in the war pathologies, but neither Charcot's major hysteria nor his traumatic hysteria are brought up again.[2]

The connection between war pathology and hysteria does not present itself fortuitously in the German-speaking field; the burial of hysteria has clearly not been forgotten at the French front.

The Germans and the French are agreed on the clinical description of the disorders but not on the appropriate diagnostic categories.[3] In French literature emotional and pithiatistic syndromes predominate, i.e., the mental confusion with oneirisms from the Régis-doctrine, and the pithiatism of Babinski. The *état confuso-onirique* is attributed to a biological intoxication and therefore gets an organic explanation. Pithiatism essentially emerges as an euphemism for simulation. The disorders integrate themselves regularly into a certain sequence: (1) emotional shock with a latency phase; (2) loss of consciousness; (3) hallucinatory dream delusion; (4) lacunar amnesia. When awakening the subject may display temporary pithiatistic, physical disorders as well as occasionally chronic aftereffects in the shape of anxiety, insomnia, nightmares, etc. This clearly matches Charcot's description of traumatic hysteria, albeit that Charcot gave it a psychical explanation. Here, the role of emotion is only mentioned by way of an occasional element, in other words a minimal psychic input.

The German neurologists leave the mechanistic view of Oppenheim and acknowledge the psychic nature of the symptoms. Adolf Strümpell (1853-1925) is an important representative of this tendency which postulates the psychogenic element to explain the traumatic neurosis. In 1895 he introduces the notion of *Begehrungs-Vorstellungen* as being the conscious desire to escape the front and to ensure oneself of an army pension.[4]

In 1915 Max Nonne (1861-1959) posits that the symptoms of war neurosis are hysterical symptoms and therefore conferring with Babinski can be removed by hypnotic suggestion. His method is initially repudiated since it supposedly advocates a return to medieval mysticism, but as soon as the war neuroses become an epidemic (which makes massive hospitalization highly impracticable) Oppenheim's organic-etiological thesis is spectacularly disclaimed. The illness is now purely psychical. It notably concerns hysterical phenomena which can be cured by psychological means.[5] One even goes so far as to posit that the signifier war neurosis may be deleted in view of the evident equivalence with neuroses in peace-time. From this perspective it is not surprising that the Germans identify the French mental confusion as a hysterical delirium or a hysterical psychosis (compared with their tradition of hysterical twilight states). The physical disorders (pithiatism) are also designated as hysterical. In this, hysteria is synonymous with simulation or inferiority. The will is the dominant notion; war neurosis (war hysteria) is a *Willenskrankheit*.[6]

Both French and German neurologists and psychiatrists combine the study of war syndromes with the battle against simulation. Therefore, the conscious intention is just about the single acknowledged psychic factor that co-determines the clinical picture. This is a caricature of Freud's view of the neurotic symptoms as being psychically determined. In spite of the fact that the word unconscious turns up in numerous psychiatric texts, this is obviously a case of a refusal to accept the role of the unconscious. The not-wanting-to-go-battle is repressively handled in accordance with the principle that one is considered a malingerer as long as the organic determination has not been proved.[7]

Of all works on the traumatic neurosis which this epoch is abundant in, only those of the American psychiatrists and neurologists will have a certain future, notably in the newly born field of psychosomatic medicine. The First World War at any rate provides the long hoped for respect of the other medical subdisciplines.[8] The Anglo-American authors in their study of war neuroses attach a particular interest to the emotional shock and to the psychological and affective factors with the subject. The employed nomenclature strongly differs from that used by the French or the Germans. They particularly treat anxiety states, conversion hysteria, and *psychosomatic disorders*. The latter traditionally pertain to the domain of medicine but are attributed with a psycho-emotional origin.[9]

As war neurosis (traumatic neurosis in wartime) these disorders also get due attention in the then still limited psychoanalytical circles, in particular from Freud, Sandor Ferenczi (1873-1933), Victor Tausk (1879-1919), Karl Abraham (1877-1925), Ernest Jones (1879-1958), and Wilhelm Stekel (1868-1940).[10] Tausk and Ferenczi are the first analysts to go out on the warpath. On June the 7th, 1916 Tausk gave a lecture before the Viennese Psychoanalytical Society in which he explores the relationship of *war psychoses* (which occur less frequently than the war neuroses) with paranoia and melancholia. In his article from 1916 Ferenczi relates the war neuroses to the anxiety- and the conversion hysteria.[11]

In 1918 the Fifth International Psycho-Analytical Congress in Budapest is even initiated with a symposium on the war neuroses. Among the speakers are Freud, Ferenczi, Ernst Simmel (1882-1947), Abraham, and Tausk. Apart from official representatives from Hungary, Austria, and Germany there are also several high-ranking military physicians present at the symposium. In his introduction to the publication of some of the lectures Freud is to indicate that these official delegations were convinced by the lectures of the potential value of psychoanalysis for further research into and treatment of these war pathologies.[12] Particularly Freud and Jones in this respect emphasize that the research into these traumatic neuroses is still in its infancy.[13]

Just as Abraham, Ferenczi, and Simmel, Tausk too had direct experience with war neuroses. As a jurist, the latter in a certain sense occupies a unique position by approaching the issue of the experiences at the front line specifically from the angle of the phenomenon of desertion. Tausk distinguishes between seven categories of deserters, in which the hysterical and epileptical exceptional states are of particular interest to us.[14]

Ferenczi, Abraham, and to a lesser extent Simmel too, emphatically point out the blind spot with the neurologists, being the psychosexual determination of these war neuroses; the symptom is the fulfilment of an unconscious wish-fantasy.[15] In his survey of the literature on the symptomatology of war neuroses Ferenczi, with regard to the specificity of neurosis, stresses hysteria. He speaks of a museum of glaring hysterical symptoms and therefore of the classical Charcotian hysteria with the inclusion of the hysterical twilight states. Simmel emphasizes the presence of convulsive fits. Yet from the psychoanalytical quarter the motor disorders, more specifically the tremor and the paralysis, are emphasized. Charcot's elaboration of the traumatic paralysis gets its continuation here. Ferenczi develops two types: the conversion- and the anxiety hysteria (phobia).[16] Freud's theory on the acute hysteria, in which the hysterical deliriums took up a position of precedence, already seems far off.

Notes

1. In 1888, the *traumatische Neurose* was introduced by the German Hermann Oppenheim as a new label for the (neurological) disorders caused by railway accidents, which were till then described under the heading *railway spine* (J.E. Erichsen, 1866). As Oppenheim subscribes to a mechanistic view of (traumatic) neurosis—see Breuer —he will attempt to explain the war neuroses (*shell shock*) in an identical manner (organic).
2. See E. Showalter (1993), Hysteria, Feminism and Gender, in S.L. Gilman et al. (1993), *Hysteria Beyond Freud*, Berkeley, Los Angeles, London, University of California Press, p. 323.
3. As Showalter justly points out "The psychiatric theories that developed around war neurosis reflect the ambivalence of the medical establishment upon confronting hysterical behavior in fighting men. The first problem was in naming the disorder." E. Showalter (1993), p. 321. See also E. Trillat (1986), *Histoire de l'hystérie*, coll. Médecine et Histoire, Paris, Seghers, pp. 243-252.
4. E. Fischer-Homberger (1975), *Die traumatische Neurose*, Bern, Stuttgart, Vienna, Hans Huber Verlag, pp. 130-135.
5. J. Brunner (1991), Psychiatry, Psychoanalysis, and Politics during the First World War, *Journal of the History of the Behavioral Sciences*, 27, p. 353; E. Fischer-Homberger (1975), pp. 138-143.
6. E. Fischer-Homberger (1975), p. 145.
7. See J. Brunner (1991).
8. N. Lewis (1967), American Psychiatry from its Beginnings to World War II, in Arieti, S. (ed.), *American Handbook of Psychiatry*, vol. 1, Basic Books, New York, p. 12.
9. E. Trillat (1986), pp. 249-250 and 263-264. We shall return later to this future (psychosomatic medicine).
10. Stekel did not publish on war neuroses, but in his autobiography he gives an account of his experiences with war neurotics during the period 1914-1915. See. E. Gutheil (ed.) (1950), *The Autobiography of Wilhelm Stekel*, New York, Liveright, pp. 158-161.
11. V. Tausk (1916a), Diagnostische Erörterungen auf Grund der Zustandsbilder der sogenannten Kriegspsychosen, *Wiener medizinische Wochenschrift*, 66, pp. 1427-1433 and pp. 1456-1463; S. Ferenczi (1978[1916-1917]), Deux types de névroses de guerres (hystérie),

trans. from the German, *Œuvres complètes. Psychanalyse 2*, Paris, Payot, pp. 238-252.

12. The lectures of Abraham, Ferenczi and Simmel, together with an article by Jones, are published in one volume in 1919 under the title *Zur Psychoanalyse der Kriegsneurosen* and provided with an introduction by Freud. The English version is to appear two years later. Meanwhile, Freud gets the opportunity to explain his view on the war neurosis as an expert-witness during an official investigation into the electrical treatment of war neurotics in the clinic of Wagner-Jauregg. E. Jones (ed.) (1921), *Psycho-Analysis and the War Neuroses*, introduction by S. Freud, The International Psychoanalytical Library no. 2, The International Psychoanalytical Press, London, Vienna, New York; S. Freud (1955c[1920]), Memorandum on the Electrical Treatment of War Neurotics, *S.E.*, 17, pp. 211-215; K.R. Eissler (1986[1979]), *Freud as an Expert Witness. The Discussion of War Neuroses Between Freud and Wagner-Jauregg*, trans. from the German, Madison, Connecticut, International Universities Press.
13. S. Freud (1921[1919d]), Introduction in E. Jones (ed.), p. 2; E. Jones (1921), War Shock and Freud's Theory of the Neuroses, in E. Jones (ed.), pp. 44-59.
14. Each of the distinct categories is determined by the specificity of the desertion motive. V. Tausk (1975[1916b]), Contribution à la psychologie du déserteur, *Œuvres psychanalytiques*, Paris, Payot, pp. 129-156.
15. See E. Jones (ed.) (1921), part 2: Symposium held at the Fifth International Psycho-Analytical Congress at Budapest, September 1918, pp. 5-43.
16. S. Ferenczi (1987[1916-1917]).

6
Psychiatry, Psychoanalysis and Schizophrenia

Schizophrenia: a Product of Psychoanalysis?

1911 sees the publication of *Dementia praecox or the group of schizophrenias.*[1] In it the Swiss psychiatrist Eugen Bleuler (1857-1939) postulates that Kraepelin's dementia praecox is not one single mental illness but rather a collection of afflictions that have a certain characteristic in common namely, the *Spaltung* or the dissociation of the psychical functions. In this way he introduces the neologism schizophrenia as a better fitting description for what Kraepelin in 1893 presented as dementia praecox, i.e., an autonomous affliction which results in an overall, progressive and irreversible intellectual deterioration and which occurs mainly with young adults. A new name for an existing entity?[2]

Bleuler's description already gives rise to a suspicion of something different. This suspicion is confirmed by the work itself. Schizophrenia groups a collection of psychoses which develop now chronically—then by surges—which may stagnate at every stage and also re-enact every stage, although a complete return ad integrum is out of the question. The group of the schizophrenias therefore regroups, according to Bleuler, apart from the cases of dementia praecox—and here we select the diagnoses that are of interest to us—cases of manic-depressive psychosis, mania, melancholia, hysterical psychosis, amentia, hallucinatory paranoia, acute prison psychosis (Ganser syndrome), and also patients who before would have been diagnosed as hysterical.

The presence of a fundamental schizophrenic symptom (dissociation, ambivalence or autism) in his opinion is a sufficient argument to replace the former diagnostic categories by *schizophrenia.*

Bleuler replaces Kraepelin's evolutive criterion, typical of his classification system of disease entities, by a primary disorder of the psychical functions, the *Spaltung*, by which quite a number of acute states, such as acute confusion are absorbed. The repudiation of involution as an inherent criterion is framed in Bleuler's optimism with regard to the prognosis and the treatment of psychotic patients.

The primary *Spaltung* is ascribed to a primordial organical *Zerspaltung*, the morbid process. So schizophrenia is therefore a physiologically determined affliction of the personality. The primary symptoms give expression to this organic pathological process and among others include the acute confusion and all manners of somatic disorders. The secondary or psychogenic symptoms represent the reaction of the diseased psyche to the morbid process and constitute the actual, manifest clinical picture. When one describes Bleuler as a representative of dynamic psychiatry, one does so because of this innovative view, i.e., the taking into account of psycho(patho)logical mechanisms.[3]

The fundamental schizophrenic symptoms that make up the typicality of the affliction include the dissociation of the associations of ideas, the affective disorders (the ambivalence), and the severance of the relationship with the outer world (autism). Delusory states, hallucinations, illusions, and memory defects pertain to the category of additional symptoms which are insufficient to make up a diagnosis.

How does hysterical madness fare in this new group? Bleuler settles up with the distinct definitions it got over the past decades, ranging from deliria and delusory states over twilight states to confusion and chronic psychosis.

First, there is Charcotian hysteria. According to Bleuler, hysteriform fits in all possible variations just like other hysteriform symptoms often occur with schizophrenic patients. As an illustration Bleuler presents us with a female patient whose first epileptiform fit occurs after observing a similar fit. After ten years of true reproduction the fits disappear when she is transferred to another ward. If the disappearance of the symptoms after seclusion of the patient was the sign par excellence for Charcot's adherents that these symptoms were indeed hysterical, it is not capable of questioning Bleuler's diagnosis of schizophrenia.[4]

Second, there is psychiatric hysterical psychosis. Quite a substantial number of women who elsewhere are diagnosed as being hysterically psychotic, according to Bleuler, are indeed schizophrenic, in spite of the fact that their psychosis is the extension of the hysterical picture. Furthermore, he writes that as yet he has had no reason to use the diagnosis of hysterical psychosis. When a so-called hysterical patient becomes psychotic or deteriorates, she is not hysterical but schizophrenic.[5]

Third is the picture of hysterical twilight states and that of mental confusion or amentia that are perfectly compatible with a diagnosis of schizophrenia. Just as memory defects that for decades have been acknowledged as being typical of hysteria, they belong to the extensive gamut of additional schizophrenic disorders.[6]

The all devouring schizophrenia only ostensibly solves the differentiation problem between hysteria and schizophrenia. Every hysterical symptom may emerge on a schizophrenic basis; however, each schizophrenia symptom, within its definition, is, strictly speaking, aspecific since it may also occur—although not quite as prominently—with other afflictions. Bleuler, therefore, indicates that it is often difficult and virtually impossible for him to make the differential diagnosis with hysteria. Indications for hysteria are an affective autism, although comparable with what Charcot called *la belle indifférence* of hysterical patients, and also not being susceptible to the suggestion by the physician. An acute psychotic state automatically is indicative of schizophrenia.[7] It is not inconceivable that quite a fair number of troublesome patients in this way are labelled schizophrenic, a tendency which is to repeat itself with the emergence of the *borderline* in 1960.

Not only hysterical madness but also hysteria as such are devoured here by schizophrenia. Laruelle's *hypothetical* explanation of the recorded close similarity between hysteria and dementia praecox, namely that hysteria and dementia praecox are identical, is proclaimed as a *thesis* by Bleuler.

Bleuler's démarche is Kraepelinian. The introduction of schizophrenia is the result of a processing of Kraepelin's doctrine with psychoanalytical concepts.[8] In fact, Bleuler goes down in history as the psychiatrist who gave Freud's theory the floor within psychiatric circles hostile to Freud. And indeed, as far back as 1904 the group of Zürich, with Carl Gustav Jung (1875-1961) and Abraham, were to employ some of Freud's ideas in their study of psychosis. Initially Freud cheers on this sudden interest and he does so for several reasons. Particularly with regard to the study of the psychoses he expects important contributions from the psychiatric corner since their practice is chiefly populated by psychotics and his clientele is distinctly neurotic. Secondly the Zürich group enjoys quite a lot more esteem than the Viennese, although psychoanalysis in that period becomes the object of growing interest.[9]

Does this mean Bleuler is a Freud disciple? Bleuler's attitude with regard to psychoanalysis, just like his schizophrenia group, proves ambivalent. With the publication of the monumental work on schizophrenia Freud's real contribution remains restricted to a brief mention in the preface. The adopted psychoanalytical concepts have been stripped of every sexual tone. Exemplary of this is the neologism *autism* in substitution for Freud's autoerotism; the eros-element has been lifted from between the sandwich. Bleuler also passes over Freud's fundamental thesis which claims that not the organic substratum, but the unconscious is determinative for the human psyche and for the development of neuroses and psychoses. Bleuler may pay lip service to the mechanisms of the symptom formation as discovered by Freud, the affliction nonetheless remains organically determined.

The concept of schizophrenia therefore is the product of the (psycho)analytical discourse in the sense that it is repudiated. It is there, at the juncture of the acknowledgement of psychoanalysis, that we must recognize its fundamental denial. This denial will turn out to be far more efficient for the dissemination of a distorted type of psychoanalysis than any other strategy. For it defines Freud's theory in a user-friendly fashion by adopting crucial psychoanalytical concepts such as the unconscious, which becomes a psychical function, but providing them with innocuous contents. This makes for the psychologizing of psychoanalytical concepts by converting them into functions. It turns out to be a brilliant move since Bleuler's work is not only read on the European continent but is also and especially greedily devoured in America and obviously answers to an a-sexual demand for synthetic artlessness and clarity, i.e., one sole diagnosis.

The counter attack is launched. In 1911 (after ten years of almost complete silence on the subject of paranoia) Freud's Schreber study is published, a psychoanalytical contribution to the study of paranoia. In this study Freud discards both dementia praecox, to which Jung in spite of Bleuler's influence obstinately keeps clinging, as well as Bleuler's schizophrenia. He does so in favor of paraphrenia.[10] We quote Freud:

> I am of the opinion that Kraepelin was entirely justified in taking the step of separating off a large part of what had hitherto been called paranoia and merging it, together with catatonia and certain other forms of disease, into a new clinical unit —though "dementia praecox" was a particularly unhappy name to choose for it. The designation chosen by Bleuler for the same group of forms—"schizophrenia"—is also open to the objection that the name appears appropriate only so long as we forget its literal meaning. For otherwise it prejudices the issue, since it is based on a characteristic of the disease which is theoretically postulated—a characteristic, moreover, which does not belong exclusively to that disease, and which, in the light

> of other considerations, cannot be regarded as the essential one. However, it is not on the whole of very great importance what names we give to clinical pictures. What seems to me more essential is that paranoia should be maintained as an independent clinical type, however frequently the picture it offers may be complicated by the presence of schizophrenic features. ... It would seem to me the most convenient plan to give dementia praecox the name of "paraphrenia." This term has no special connotation, and it would serve to indicate a relationship with paranoia (a name which cannot be changed) and would further recall hebephrenia, an entity which is now merged in dementia praecox.[11]

In this Schreber study, Freud, for the first time, brings a theoretical specification of the distinction between paranoia and dementia praecox, which is extensively treated in a publication for the first time. To this end he makes use of his libido theory (the libido is a quantitative notion and refers to the psychical energy linked with the sexual drives).[12] Determinative for pathology are the fixation-points of the libido, the positions in the development of the libido where part of the libido remains. For paranoia Freud situates this in the stage of narcissism, for dementia praecox in that of autoerotism.

The pluriformity of the fixations, notably the possibility of different fixations, yields a possible explanation for those cases of psychosis in which both paraphrenic as well as paranoic elements are demonstrable. The Schreber case is a perfect example of this. The passive-feminine wish-fantasy to become the wife of God and the hallucinations Freud indicates as the paraphrenic elements. The offensive of homosexual libido (according to Freud the cause of Schreber's pathology), the mechanism of projection, and the delusory development constitute the paranoic elements.[13]

The specification of the relation between dementia praecox and paranoia finds its preparation in the correspondence with Jung (1906-1914). At the beginning of this correspondence Freud expresses the expectation that a fertile cooperation will plumb the depths of the distinction between dementia praecox, Jung's object of study, and paranoia or the paranoic element of dementia praecox. Ever more emphatically Freud opts for the signifier *paranoia* instead of *dementia praecox* in order to concentrate his study of the psychoses on it.[14]

The Differential Diagnosis Dementia Praecox-Hysteria

In 1902 Jung introduces Freud's theory at the Burghölzli clinic.[15] His monograph on dementia praecox, published in 1907, in which he repeatedly refers to Freud, gives the initial impetus to their intensive correspondence which is to last some six years, until Jung definitively stumbles over the matter of the sexual libido.[16]

Freud expects Jung's clinical observations to help him further elaborate his theory of the psychoses. Jung, who is confronted on a daily basis with psychotic patients, expects material on hysteria from Freud. What are the results of this exchange of case studies by two men who both on a clinical as well as on a theoretical level take up divergent points of departure, notably with regard to the relationship of paranoia, dementia praecox, and hysteria?

Jung's first letters already show that, in imitation of his master Bleuler and therefore in defiance of Freud's theory on hysteria, he employs a capacious concept of psychosis, i.e., that of dementia praecox. Throughout their further correspondence both Freud and Jung repeatedly come back to the specificity of hysteria and of presenile dementia. The exchange of cases, however, does not seem to help the correspondents in obtaining a well-founded knowing of the differentiation. Freud loses perspective of hysteria and for Jung the differences between dementia praecox and hysteria are fading since he practices psychoanalysis and is confronted with Freud's views.[17] How can we position this?

Freud's introduction to hysteria was already extensively discussed, but which part with regard to hysteria does Jung accept?

Jung joins the Bleuler staff in 1900 and two years later he

submits his medical dissertation on *occult phenomena*. The whole gamut of hypnotic pathologies extensively dealt with in previous chapters and classically linked with hysteria, is described.[18] Jung brings an exhaustive survey of the available literature on rare states and alterations of consciousness; Charcot's somnambulistic states are mentioned and so are Krafft-Ebing's hysterical delusions and psychoses. Following the descriptive bibliography there is an extensive report of numerous spiritistic seances of a female medium. Between the lines Jung himself pronounces on the diagnosis of hysteria.[19]

Another work dating from the same period confirms his caution with regard to the diagnosis of hysteria where hysterical symptoms are psychogenic and are notably determined by the subconscious (see Janet). Jung speaks of the Ganser syndrome in terms of hysterical psychosis or psychiatric hysteria. Hysteria to him, like to many other psychiatrists, seems like both a mental illness and a neurosis, depending on the manifest clinical picture of psychical or physical disorders. The hysterical (degenerative) disposition and the psychogenic symptoms remain typical.[20]

Contrary to Bleuler, Jung is interested in hysteria, although he does not share Freud's fascination with hysteria. Apart from a few enthusiastic reports of cases of severe hysteria with twilight states, his letters rather demonstrate an aversion to hysteria. Just as with any rule, this one also finds its proof in the exceptions. Or is it only *occult* hysteria, which may be called rare at the Burghölzli-Klinik, that is capable of charming Jung?

Early in 1908 Jung reports on a case of severe hysteria with twilight states in which he recognizes the perfect illustration to Freud's theory on hysteria. Similar inspiring and intelligent hysterical patients in his opinion are exceptional at the Burghölzli clinic. He persistently complains of his hysterical patients.

Jung's appreciation may undoubtedly be framed in what Charcot and Freud call the psychiatric view on hysteria and against which they react. The opposition between Freud's enthusiasm and Jung's aversion to the treatment of hysterical patients then yields—as it were—a German version of the double stand against hysteria in France, which we already amply reproduced by means of a historical reconstruction of the opposed views of the Charcot disciples and the alienists.[21]

Jung's typification of hysteria has a lot in common with Kraepelin's description of dementia praecox. This is evident from the correspondence, but can also be read in his monograph on dementia praecox. The fourth chapter, entitled "Dementia praecox and hysteria," sums up the analogies between both entities.[22] Jung is unsuccessful in his attempt to articulate any fundamental differences. Moreover, the occurence of dementia praecox is explained by means of some hypothetical, i.e., unknown toxin.

In this impossibility of indicating a fundamental difference between hysteria and dementia praecox on the basis of a comparison of clinical pictures, there lurks a diagnostic danger. It causes the accelerated correction and adjustment of an initial hysteria diagnosis in the direction of dementia praecox as well as to a loose use of the latter label. What are the indications for this? At the end of 1906 Jung writes that the concept of hysteria remains obscure in practice; numerous cases of mild hebephrenia are still unjustly diagnosed as hysteria.[23] In April 1907 he reports to Freud of often having cases which apparently convert effortlessly from hysteria into dementia praecox. And a few months later he proclaims that the differences between dementia praecox and hysteria are becoming blurred ever since he started analyzing both.[24]

Despite the fact that Jung gives great capacity to the picture of hysteria, i.e., notably leaves room for various delusory states, the diagnosis of dementia praecox lies far more within his reach than that of hysteria. The fact that this predilection does not so much typify Jung rather than the Burghölzli clinic is evident, for example, from Abraham's testimony.

After three years of registrarship under Bleuler, Abraham left Zürich at the end of 1907 in order to start up a private practice in Berlin. Some time later he writes to Eitingon that his formation in Zürich perhaps too often made him make the diagnosis of dementia praecox.[25] A confession of which the antecedents and the aftermath can be read in two articles published during this period: *Die psychosexuelle Differenzen zwischen Hysterie und Dementia Praecox* and *Über hysterische Traumzustände*.[26]

In the first article Abraham concludes with two fundamental points of difference between hysteria and dementia praecox which immediately allow us to characterize both. In dementia praecox there is a question of the destruction of the object love or the sexual transference and of the dissipation of the social and emotional effects of sublimation. In hysteria an excessive object love and an increased sublimation are in evidence. The dissipation of these final results of psychosexual development in Abraham's opinion indicates the relapse into an anterior stadium —that of autoerotism. With this, the constitution of dementia praecox is based on an inhibition of the psychosexual development, namely of the infantile auto-erotism that has not been transcended.[27] The cases that are supposed to corroborate this thesis do not convince however.[28] The fact that a substantial number of female patients fall in love with their physicians, who keep succeeding one another, is sufficient for Abraham to come to the conclusion that they are not capable of a real attachment to a person or an object. Freud, in the meanwhile, teaches that the fantasmic dimension is central in the object love and besides the attending physicians constitute the only objects available to the patients. Furthermore, it can be read in Abraham's article that "other patients for years on end nurture an imaginary love. This love only exists in their imagination."[29]

His article on the hysterical dream states is published two years later, an application of Freud's theoretical elaborations on the hysterical fit and on the day-dream. These states constitute a substitute for the forbidden autoerotic pleasure and are often accompanied with anxiety. The accompanying wishful fantasies are central. What a few years before still typified dementia praecox has suddenly become possible within a hysterical picture too. At the end of the article, however, Abraham still makes the link back to comparable states in dementia praecox.[30]

Bleuler's capacious schizophrenia group which avoids, among others, the differential diagnosis with the hysterical psychoses and rejects the role of sexuality, gains the suit. Initially Freud puts the signifier paraphrenia center stage. As a response is not forthcoming, he from then on rides roughshod over the issue of labelling. He speaks of the three narcissistic neuroses: paranoia, melancholia, and schizophrenia or dementia praecox. The latter two will continue to be used through and instead of each other in a Freudian definition.

Schizophrenia Overruns the World

After the First World War schizophrenia has an international breakthrough. It monopolizes the interest of psychiatrists and psychoanalysts who are to further elaborate on Bleuler's explanatory theory.[31]

A figure who separate from Bleuler makes his mark on this epoch, is the German psychopathologist and philosopher Karl Jaspers (1883-1969). His psychopathological writings, which mean to provide psychiatry with a general methodical basis, will determine the conceptual framework of modern-day German psychiatry.[32] In his *Allgemeine Psychopathologie*, published in 1913, he proposes, for the first time, a phenomenological approach of mental illnesses. As of yet, schizophrenia is only allocated a minor position in it because its definition at that moment still remains too vague in Jaspers' opinion.[33] Only after he is given the chair of philosophy at the University of Heidelberg (1921), does he sink his teeth into the subject of the *vital schizophrenic experience*. He does so surprisingly by means of a comparative pathographic analysis of four schizophrenics of a high spiritual level: Strindberg, Van Gogh, Swedenborg, and Hölderlin.[34] This study brings him to the juxtaposition of two types of schizophrenia: schizophrenia as an illness vs. the schizophrenic experience as a peculiarity of the psychic life. With this, Jaspers distinguishes between schizophrenia as a nosological category, which in his opinion and contrary to Bleuler's view is not determined by organic lesions, and schizophrenia as a *psychical process*. The comparison of both forms raises for him the topic about the position of schizophrenia in the world's cultures.

According to Jaspers, up until the eighteenth century, history has no examples of important public figures who could be typified as schizophrenic. Hysteria is allocated this role. For without hysteria neither the mysticism of the medieval cloisters nor lives such as that of Teresa of Avila can be explained. The fact that up until the end of the nineteenth and early twentieth centuries there is the question of hysterical mystics, one example being Janet's Madeleine, does not contradict this, considering the fact that these mystics are isolated and there is no question of any influence on their contemporaries. He concludes that the cultural influence of hysterics before the eighteenth century is comparable to that of present-day schizophrenics. To this he explicitly adds that the illness (schizophrenia vs. hysteria) must be clearly distinguished from the spirit of the epoch it incarnates. In this way he does not, in our opinion, indicate that hysteria used to be more prevalent than it is now, but he does posit that hysteria did have a higher degree of prevalence in the sense that the hysterical picture then expounded the spirit of the epoch or the prevailing discourse.[35] The incarnation of the spirit of our present-day era, which can be classed as intellectualistic and artificial, is what holds for schizophrenia. When we link this to Jaspers' thesis that hysteria adapts to every kind of environment and that it is extremely sensitive to imitation, we come to the conclusion that the schizophrenic picture might well be an adapted manifestation of hysteria.[36]

Apart from that, we would still like to point out that Jaspers, in contrast to Bleuler, in 1923 still mentions hysterical deliria and that in this connection he explicitly refers to the work of Freud and Breuer on the matter. He also emphasizes on more than one occasion the analogy between hysterical deliria and twilight states, described by Ganser in incarcerated persons (*Ganserschen Dämmerzuständen der Haft*).[37]

Notes

1. E. Bleuler (1950[1911]), *Dementia praecox or the Group of Schizophrenias*, trans. from the German, New York, International Universities Press. It may seem strange that it took nearly forty years for Bleuler's book to be translated into English. First of all it gives rise to the question as to just how well Bleuler's original work was actually known in America. Secondly the year 1950 is not that incidental after all, since the 1950s is the decade in which the psychotherapy of psychosis and in particular that of schizophrenia is made into an object of research.
2. Verification in several psychiatric textbooks reveals that the (possible) equivalence of both terms (dementia praecox and schizophrenia) is little questioned. The book of the French psychiatrist Jean Garrabé constitutes a rare exception to this. See H. Baruk (1967), *La psychiatrie française de Pinel à nos jours*, Paris, PUF, pp. 61-62; I. Gregory & D. Smeltzer (1977), *Psychiatry*, Boston, Little, Brown & Co, p. 22; M. Tsuang, et al. (1988), Schizophrenic Disorders, in A. Nicholi (ed.), *The New Harvard Guide to Psychiatry*, Cambridge, Mass., London, The Belknap Press of Harvard University Press, p. 259; J. Garrabé (1992), *Histoire de la schizophrénie*, coll. Médecine et Histoire, Paris, Seghers, p. 57.
3. Karl Birnbaum (1878-1950) who is to go down in history because of his innovative ideas regarding the pathogenesis of psychosis (structural analysis), emphasizes that Kraepelin's textbook is both synonymous with the apogee of clinical psychiatry and with the ultimate failure of its descriptive research method. In this perspective we can consider Bleuler's theory as the launch of a new psychiatric era. K. Birnbaum (1923), *Der Aufbau der Psychose*, Berlin, Springer Verlag. See also U. Peters (1984), *Wörterbuch der Psychiatrie und medizinischen Psychologie*, München, Vienna, Baltimore, Urban & Schwarzenberg, pp. 80 and 541-542; E. Vowinckel (1930), Der heutige Stand der psychiatrischen Schizophrenieforschung, *Internationale Zeitschrift für Psychoanalyse*, 16, p. 472.
4. E. Bleuler (1950[1911]), pp. 176 et seq.
5. *Ibid.*, pp. 286-288.
6. *Ibid.*, pp. 95-150.
7. *Ibid.*, pp. 321-322.

8. We would like to point out that Bleuler's use of the word schizophrenia dates back to 1906. P. Bercherie (1988), *Les Fondements de la Clinique*, Bibliothèque des Analytica, Paris, Navarin, p. 200.
9. S. Freud (1914d), On the History of the Psycho-Analytic Movement, *S.E.*, 14, pp. 26 et seq.
10. In 1912 Kraepelin introduces the endogenous dementias as a category in which the (small) dementia praecox subclass comes next to the new group of paraphrenias. Is Freud already aware of this latest development when he introduces paraphrenia? According to Laplanche and Pontalis he is; a general reference in the Schreber study could well be interpreted in that same direction. Neither Kraepelin's paraphrenia nor that of Freud find acceptance in German psychiatric circles, where the competition has already been decided. By 1913 Bleuler's doctrine is the work of reference in German-speaking Europe. P. Bercherie (1988), pp. 222-228; J. Laplanche & J.-B. Pontalis (1973), *Vocabulaire de la psychanalyse*, Paris, PUF, p. 301; S. Freud (1911c[1910]), Psycho-Analytic Notes on an Autobiographical Account of a Case of Paranoia (dementia paranoides), *S.E.*, 12, p. 75.
11. S. Freud (1911c[1910]), pp. 75-76. In 1913 Freud speaks of paraphrenia as the coordinating term for dementia praecox and paranoia. After 1917, however, he no longer mentions this innovation.
12. Freud first treats the libido development in his essays on the theory of sexuality from 1905. The further elaboration of this theory can be followed by means of the numerous notes and additions which have been introduced over the years. Freud will radically review his theory of the drive in 1920. An outline of the libido development: from autoerotism to object love over narcissism and the homosexual object choice, or put differently, from the partial drives over their clustering into a unit which is placed under the primacy of the genitals. Each stage of this development yields a potential point of fixation (disposition). S. Freud (1905d), *Three Essays on the Theory of Sexuality*, *S.E.*, 7, pp. 125-243.
13. Freud's analysis of the Schreber case is based on the latter's report on his own illness: D. Schreber (1973[1903]), *Denkwürtigkeiten eines Nervenkranken*, Frankfurt-am-Main, Berlin, Vienna, Ullstein.
14. The correspondence between Freud and Jung thoroughly differs from that between Freud and Fliess, more particularly in as far as the pres-

ence of the development of a theory is concerned. The evolution of Freud's theory cannot as easily be traced in it. The theoretical contributions are restricted to small paragraphs or succinct expressions of views with regard to a concise case study. W. Mc Guire (ed.) (1974), *The Freud/Jung Letters*, Princeton, New Jersey, Princeton University Press.

15. See J. Postel & C. Quétel (eds.) (1983), *Nouvelle histoire de la psychiatrie*, Toulouse, Privat, pp. 654-655.
16. C. Jung (1979[1907]), *The Psychology of Dementia Praecox*, trans. from the German, *C.G. Jung. The Collected Works*, vol. 3, London, Routledge & Kegan, pp. 70-98. So just like Bleuler, Jung refuses to acknowledge the importance of psychosexuality and with that the foundation of psychoanalysis.
17. See the letter from Jung of 4 June 1907 and the letter from Freud of 25 January 1908. W. Mc Guire (ed.) (1974), pp. 64 and 125.
18. It is worth mentioning here that in that very period Jung worked in the immediate vicinity of Janet.
19. C. Jung (1902), Zur Psychologie und Pathologie sogenannter occulte Phänomene, doctor's thesis, University of Leipzig. Thus his choice of subject for his dissertation already bears the seeds of his later theory, analytical psychology, of which the collective unconscious and the archetypical images are the central themes.
20. C. Jung (1903), Über Simulation von Geistesstörung, *Journal für Psychologie und Neurologie*, 2, pp. 181-201.
21. Charcot opposes the psychiatric view of hysteria, but he too does not escape the dichotomy of *good* vs. *bad* hysterics. A similar ambiguous attitude can be demonstrated in Freud's works by juxtaposing the case studies from the *Studies* against the Dora study and that of the young homosexual. J. Carroy-Thirard (1979), Figures de femmes hystériques dans la psychiatrie au 19e siècle, *Psychanalyse à l'université*, 4, 14, pp. 313-324; S. Freud (1905e[1901]), Fragment of an Analysis of a Case of Hysteria, *S.E.*, 7, pp. 7-122; S. Freud (1920a), The Psychogenesis of a Case of Homosexuality in a Woman, *S.E.*, 18, pp. 147-172.
22. C. Jung (1979[1907]). Jung distinguishes and compares the various emotional disorders, character abnormalities, intellectual disorders and stereotypes. For every disorder of dementia praecox he finds an equivalent in hysteria.

23. Letter from Jung of 4 December 1906. W. Mc Guire (ed.) (1974), p. 11.
24. Letters from Jung dated 17 April 1907 and 4 June 1907. *Ibid.*, pp. 39 and 64.
25. K. Abraham, letter to M. Eitingon of 3 March 1908. Quoted in J.-C. Maleval (1981), *Folies hystériques et psychoses dissociatives*, Paris, Payot, p. 281.
26. In the correspondence with Freud, Jung repeatedly complains of Abraham's so-called plagiarism, among others with regard to his article on the differences between hysteria and dementia praecox. This would mean that Jung agrees on the ideas propagated there, which strongly emphasize the sexual (libidinal) element. K. Abraham (1965[1908]), Les différences psychosexuelles entre l'hystérie et la déménce précoce, trans. from the German, *Œuvres complètes 1*, Paris, Payot, pp. 36-47; K. Abraham (1965[1910]), Les états oniriques hystériques, trans. from the German, *Œuvres complètes 1*, Paris, Payot, pp. 63-90; letters from Jung dated 19 August 1907 and 3 March 1908. W. Mc Guire (ed.) (1974), pp. 87 and 148.
27. See Freud's elaboration on dementia praecox in his Schreber study.
28. Maleval posits that the hospitalism, i.e., the effects of the institutional discourse, must be considered co-responsible for what Abraham calls the autoerotic retreat and the affective withdrawal. Abraham's typification of dementia praecox in his opinion can therefore be identified as the typical profile of patients that have been admitted into asylums and with that is aspecific. J.-C. Maleval (1981), pp. 235-236.
29. K. Abraham (1965[1908]), p. 43. Author's translation.
30. K. Abraham (1965[1910]), p. 87.
31. J. Garrabé (1992), pp. 83 et seq.
32. P. Bercherie (1988), p. 232.
33. This observation can still be read in the third, revised edition of this textbook. See K. Jaspers (1923[1913]), *Allgemeine Psychopathologie*, 3rd ed. revised and enlarged, Berlin, Heidelberg, Springer Verlag, p. 384.
34. K. Jaspers (1922), *Strindberg und Van Gogh*, Bern, Ernst Bucher. Discussed in J. Garrabé (1992), pp. 127-129.
35. The thesis that Madeleine Le Bouc was born in the wrong era is raised in the recent study of Cathérine Clément and Sudhir Kakar. P.

Janet (1926-1928), *De l'angoisse à l'extase I & II*, Paris, Félix Alcan; C. Clément & S. Kakar (1993), *La folie et le saint*, Paris, Seuil. A more interesting historical study on the subject of Madeleine is J. Maître (1993), *Une inconnue célèbre*, foreword by G. Lantéri-Laura, coll. Psychanalyse, Paris, Anthropos-Economica.

36. K. Jaspers (1923[1913]), especially pp. 237-238 and 231.
37. *Ibid.*, pp. 250-251.

7
The German Advance
Claude's Schizoses

Paraphrenia vs. Schizophrenia

Within the field of the psychoses, longer-lasting in France than in Germany, a battle rages between the work of the old Kraepelin and that of the newcomer Bleuler. After a brief struggle Bleuler's schizophrenias seize power in Germany while Kraepelin ventures a final sally from France with his paraphrenia group. It concerns two categories which, because of their dominant, respectively spectacular character exert a certain attraction on the dispelled concept of hysterical psychosis.

Paraphrenia fantastica, a subcategory of the paraphrenia group, gets exclusive attention in France during the interbellum period because of one single feature namely, the fantastic delusions. The clinical picture is furthermore characterized by multiple hallucinations and an increasing confusion and incoherence. The body is central. Apart from the delusions, the patient remains perfectly lucid. Because of this the paraphrenia fantastica is classified close to paranoia. Also typical is the fact that the delusory experiences remain latent longer, in other words the paraphrenic seems normal for a lengthy period of time.[1]

In this way, it is not in Germany but in France that paraphrenia (a signifier promoted by Freud in 1911) finds some response. A possible explanation for this foreign success may well be the concrete character of the concept as well as the fact that the

Germans now see their systematics personified elsewhere (in Bleuler). The paraphrenia episode at any rate concludes the exchange between the German and the French School which gave cause to the birth of modern-day psychiatry; the Germans and the French no longer borrow from each other.[2]

In spite of research undertaken by a number of authors, paraphrenia remains the designation for a limited group of spectacular cases—an ideal refuge for the spectacular hysteria?

The Official French Doctrine

During the 1930s texts emerge sporadically in France which bear evidence to a maintained clinical interest in hysteria and hysterical madness.[3] One of these contributions, which consists exclusively of case demonstrations, is noteworthy since the presenting psychiatrist, Capgras, still poses the generally considered superseded question of the existence of hysterical madness. The great master of that time, Baruk, however, cleverly presents his reactionary colleague with the general doctrine which is determined by the hysteria concept of Babinski and the schizophrenia group of Bleuler.

Capgras's onset sketches the tenor within French psychiatry:

> At the next congress in Brussels hysteria is the order of the day. Therefore, we felt it would be interesting to present to you a patient with a difficult diagnosis which opens the question of the connections between hysteria and schizophrenia, at least to those who still believe in the existence of a hysterical state of mind.[4]

After the presentation in which particular interest is paid to the imaginative delusion, Capgras concludes with the question of whether the slight confusion, despite the absence of dream images, does not permit to connect the clinical picture with the hysterical twilight states, of which—although they are now no longer mentioned—numerous examples used to be cited. His prudent question gets no shaded reply.

In the discussion Baruk raps him over the knuckles. He states that hysteria always shows itself from its neurological side and as a neurosis can be typified as somatic. Schizophrenic, on the other hand, is synonymous with mental; schizophrenia is a psychosis. An additional differential point is the fact that the hysterical disorder is always superficial and the schizophrenic disorder is always fundamental.[5] Baruk concludes his commentary with a warning. In his opinion there is no advantage in reanimating the old hysterical madness as this true proteus is, at the moment, virtually entirely fragmented into catatonia, dementia praecox, periodical psychoses, and other mental diseases. Now it may well be an indisputable fact that the category of hysterical madness was highly capacious and comprised quite a number of psychotic subjects. According to our observations it is also indisputable that a lot of hysterical subjects found shelter there.

However, Capgras does not capitulate:

> It is evident that when, as M. Baruk would wish, hysteria is reduced to a neurological syndrome (pithiatism) and all cases that are accompanied by the slightest mental disorder are extracted from it, the illness that I have just presented here can in no way still be connected with hysteria. Still it cannot be disputed that pithiatism is essentially neuro-psychical and is caused by a specific state of mind. Why would it not be possible then for this state of mind to give cause to neuropathic phenomena and psychopathic complications, twilight states in particular, or, by associating itself with another psychosis, add its own shades to the clinical tableau?[6]

His is a lone voice calling on psychiatric circles not to forget history and not to banish hysterical madness.

Baruk's option is obvious. Only a restricted hysteria picture based on the definition by Babinski can eliminate the difficulties connected with the differentiation between hysteria and schizophrenia. The basic premise is the strict division between physical and mental disorders, between neuroses and psychoses. The old *folie hystérique*, an amalgam of psychotic disorders, has rightly been fragmented and been made to disappear. When Baruk therefore uses the term *fausses schizophrénies* he can remain silent on the problematic cases of hysteria.[7]

That this division cannot be maintained to the hilt is already evident from his typification of hysteria. It *presents* itself as a physical affliction, i.e., mental disorders *seem* far off. This typification implies that the strict division between neuroses and psychoses shifts to a differentiation seized in terms of what generally prevails, i.e., physical or mental disorders. So for those who still accept hysteria, the difference remains vague. Therefore, it does not really come as a surprise that it is Baruk who announces and promotes the disappearance of the diagnosis of hysteria.[8]

Another, organically determined alternative for hysterical madness is presented under the heading of *psychical epilepsy*. This is specifically reserved for the dream- and confusional states, which are also situated within the group of the toxically determined states. We find the viewpoint in question voiced in a case presentation by Henri Claude (1869-1946) and others. Although the reporters of the case presentation are aware of the fact that the psychic significance of the symptoms with this patient is obvious and moreover accessible to the subject in question, they posit that the initial somatic condition (a masked form of psychical epilepsy) is primary.[9]

Schizoses and Hysterical Dissociation

Bleuler's theory is officially heralded in France, but not without a struggle, and is paid tribute to by the School of Claude among others. In 1926 Claude is supposed to have officially recognized schizophrenia at a congress.[10]

His contributions can be situated within the dynamical-biological perspective, which implies that Claude, just like Bleuler and the larger part of the psychiatrists, emphasizes dynamical processes but places these on a biological state of determination that he derives from the neurological theories of John Hughlings

Jackson (1835-1911). This English neurologist oriented himself on the basis of Herbert Spencer's evolutionist doctrine where morbid symptoms occur from the dissolution of the higher centers. The organo-dynamism of Henri Ey (1900-1977) is also indebted to Jackson. Both Claude and Ey assert themselves as opponents of Gaétan Gatian de Clérambault (1872-1934) who opts for a coherent classification system of the psychoses, proceeding from an essential, communal element—the *syndrome d'automatisme mental*—which is the natural result of the cerebral constitution. By the agency of the French psychiatrist-psychoanalyst Jacques Lacan (1901-1981), who was in school for one year (1928-1929) with de Clérambault, there is renewed interest in the history of the mental automatism after the 1970s. Incidently, Lacan's doctoral dissertation on paranoia (1932) closes the European debate on the psychogenesis of the psychoses.[11]

In the School of Claude, Bleuler's group of schizophrenias is replaced by the continuum of schizoses or *maladies par dissociation* in which neither hysteria nor hysterical madness are allocated an official position but to which, as will be shown, both do actually belong. The psychic dissociation (the schizoid constitution) remains the punctum saliens. As we have already noted, the Freudian démarche goes in the opposite direction. It is not the *Spaltung*, derived from the psychoses, but the hysterical *Spaltung* which for Freud constitutes the initial impulse to promote the condition of being divided as a fundamental characteristic of each subject. The aspecificity of the *Spaltung* is also one of the arguments which he put forward against the schizophrenia concept.[12]

Claude's continuum concept implies a gradual differential diagnostics. The schizoses are roughly subdivided into schizoidia, schizomania, and schizophrenia. Schizoidia in the first instance indicates a certain predisposition for schizophrenia.[13] Schizomania is a minor form of schizophrenia and is characterized by episodic surges. Schizophrenia, initially sharply distinguished from dementia praecox as a purely organic illness with the development of an encephalitis, is described as a psychogenic process which has its origin in an anterior schizoid constitution. Throughout the years Claude's nosology undergoes a further differentiation. Gradually, he relativizes the strict opposition between dementia praecox and schizophrenia.

Where does Claude place hysteria? He defines it as a diathesis which has its origin in a constitutional condition of the nervous system, the *nervosisme*. More specifically he defines hysteria as the capacity to isolate or fixate motor, sensitive, or psychic manifestations; this capacity exists outside of any wilful or conscious activity.[14] This fixation and dissociation are psychic processes which bring hysteria close to the schizophrenic dissociation.

Both hysteria and schizophrenia are organically determined and have a psychogenic development. Typical of hysteria is the temporary character of its disorders. From this assumption it follows that hysteria quite often evolves into schizophrenia, which brings it also very close to the schizoid constitution and schizomania. Analogies between both include dissociation, loss of contact with the outside world and autism. With this the distinction between hysteria and the schizoses is determined by way of the discrepancies between temporary and permanent disorder, superficial and profound autism, and partial and virtually total loss of any sense of reality. In this way all except a radical distinction with schizophrenia, schizomania, and schizoidia is established. When comparing the typification of hysteria with that of the distinct schizoses, it turns out to perfectly meet the requirements for the schizoid constitution, the precursor of schizophrenia.[15]

In 1937, Claude held an exposition on the relation between hysteria and schizophrenia before the *Société médicopsychologique* which still labels itself as the scientific center of French psychiatry. The ensuing discussion is highly instructive.[16] On the subject of whether or not to accept the reality of hysteria, notably its existence as an entity, the present forum was not unanimous. Still a compromise seemed possible in the shape of the assumption that hysteria is rather a reaction formation than an illness.[17] This implies that it is not worthy of a diagnosis. It is more of the order of the mechanism than it is a specific entity. In this way, hysterical phenomena may perfectly be fitted into schizophrenia, the reality of which nobody even questioned. Only Janet, who stresses the importance of the distinct form which the dissociation assumes in hysteria and in schizophrenia, sounds a cynical note:

> I thank M. Claude for the interesting way in which he has called to mind our old studies on the psychological dissociation in hysteria. While I was listening to him I wondered whether this was still 1937 or if M. Claude had succeeded, by some magical trick, in carrying us back to 1892.[18]

The policy directive is crystal clear; the study of hysteria is played out in favor of schizophrenia. Hysteria is only brought up again in psychiatric circles to either indicate or to specify its kinship with schizophrenia. Just how minimal its official contribution still is, is evident, for example, from the description of the *Schizose* by the German psychiatrist Peters; it is the synonym for the pseudoneurotic schizophrenia.[19]

Claude is the first French psychiatrist to procure psychoanalysis with an admission ticket to the psychiatric world. The first traces of the introduction of psychoanalysis become discernible during the second half of the 1920s, first by the creation, in 1925, of the *Groupe de l'Evolution psychiatrique* as the representatives of the new dynamical psychiatry which was not inimical to psychoanalysis. Their journal is *Evolution Psychiatrique*. In 1926 the *Société Psychanalytique de Paris* is formed. Many members of the Group become members of this S.P.P. The policy line of the Group is the confrontation of psychoanalysis and psychiatry within a liberal perspective. In concrete terms this implies the confrontation of psychiatrists with psychiatrists-psychoanalysts. It turns out to be a psychiatric attempt at the colonization of psychoanalysis.[20]

In a certain sense we can say that both the group of schizophrenias and the one of schizoses are the product of the analytical discourse. But in both cases it is in the capacity of apostate of the psychoanalytical theory. Claude may well take in psychoanalytically oriented psychiatrists; he does remain sceptical of Freud's teachings.

Notes

1. E. Kraepelin (1980[1912-1913]), *Les paraphrénies*, trans. from the German, presented by P. Bercherie and with a study of F. Bridgman, La Bibliothèque d'Ornicar?, Analytica no. 19, Paris.
2. The First World War is of course not unrelated to this change. See J. Garrabé (1992), *Histoire de la schizophrénie*, coll. Médecine et Histoire, Paris, Seghers, pp. 112-113.
3. The changeable popularity of hysteria can be measured by the frequency of psychiatric treatises on the subject; on the upgrade until 1900 (111 dissertations) and then downward to a virtual nadir in 1920 (13 dissertations). See J. Postel & C. Quétel (eds.) (1983), *Nouvelle histoire de la psychiatrie*, Toulouse, Privat, p. 541.
4. Capgras et al. (1935), Délire imaginatif, in *Annales médico-psychologiques*, 93, 2, p. 73. Author's translation.
5. In 1947 Baruk still presents the distinction between neuroses and psychoses in this way. Specifically, with regard to *folie hystérique* he posits that this is presently classed among the cyclic psychoses and hebephrenia (Baruk sought after periodicity in a lot of psychoses). H. Baruk (1947), *Psychoses et névroses*, Que sais-je?, Paris, PUF.
6. Capgras et al. (1935), p. 80. Author's translation.
7. H. Baruk (1956), Les fausses schizophrénies, *Evolution psychiatrique*, 21, pp. 15-21. The false schizophrenias which he sums up are the periodical psychoses (the former hysterical madness) and the mentally defective.
8. See Baruk's contribution at the congress in Brussels in 1921.
9. H. Claude et al. (1934), Troubles psychiques de type mystique, *Annales médico-psychologiques*, 92, 1, pp. 103-109.
10. See A. di Ciaccia (1982), Bleuler ou la psychanalyse apprivoisée, *Quarto*, 9, p. 56.
11. See D. Nobus (1993), In de schaduw van het fetisjisme, review, *Psychoanalytische Perspektieven*, 19-20, pp. 200-203; E. Roudinesco

(1986), *Histoire de la psychanalyse en France*, vol. 1, Paris, Seuil, pp. 121-123; J. Garrabé (1992), pp. 136-141.

12. This double use of the concept of *Spaltung* or dissociation is, considering the influence of both importers (Freud and Bleuler), possibly partly the cause for a certain confusion in the literature between hysterical and schizophrenic states or conditions. For, to the layman one and the same notion is postulated as a basis both for hysteria and schizophrenia.
13. The concept of schizoidia in fact originates from Kretschmer and is chiefly disseminated in France around the 1920s by Minkowski, who worked for a brief period under Bleuler. H. Scharbach (ed.) (1983), *Les états limites*, Conference of Psychiatry and Neurology of French Speaking Countries, Psychiatric Report, 27 June-2 July 1983, Paris, Masson, pp. 18-19.
14. With that Claude refutes Babinski's definition.
15. Only one study makes mention of hysteria as pertaining to the group of the schizoses. At any rate we believe to have demonstrated that the employed definitions of hysteria and schizosis do indeed give rise to this assumption. J. Postel & C. Quétel (eds.) (1983), p. 608.
16. H. Claude (1937), Rapports de l'hystérie avec la schizophrénie, *Annales médico-psychologiques*, 95, 2, pp. 241-246. Quite a number of prominent figures from home and abroad took part in this discussion: P. Janet, E. Kretschmer, E. Minkowski, H. Baruk. On top of this, we get to see here a cross section of the opinions on the relationship between hysteria and schizophrenia in a period when schizophrenia (still) has a strong foothold.
17. This assumption will press ahead and presently belongs to the most subscribed to (psychiatric) conceptions on hysteria.
18. H. Claude (1937), pp. 245-246. Author's translation.
19. U. Peters (1984), *Wörterbuch der Psychiatrie und medizinischen Psychologie*, München, Vienna, Baltimore, Urban & Schwarzenberg, p. 499.
20. E. Roudinesco (1986), vol. 1, Paris, Seuil, pp. 13-14 and 413-417.

8
General Developments

The rise and fall of hysteria as a clinical concept is more manifest in France than in Germany. The war vicissitudes are a particular illustration of this. Yet the trend towards less hysteria and more schizophrenia generally persists. It does so both on European and on overseas territory. Bleuler, who tends to sail under the psychoanalytical flag, follows after Kraepelin's international breakthrough. Notable in this is the fact that the notion of *schizophrenia* represents an ever-expanding group.[1]

An important overseas figure who makes original contributions to the further study of schizophrenia and who will strongly influence the development of American and British psychiatry is Adolf Meyer (1866-1950). This American psychiatrist of Swiss origin introduces *psychobiology*. This term covers an eclectic psychiatric doctrine which specifically emphasizes the influence of biological, sociological, and psychological factors of the personality. The nature of *stress* and the reaction of the individual to this constitute the basis for his novel conceptualization of mental disorders. Therefore, it is not astounding that schizophrenia here becomes a group of *reaction disorders*. One of the figures who is influenced by Meyer's thought is Harry Stack Sullivan (1892-1949). This founder of the dynamic-cultural psychoanalytical school will be the first in the United States to set up an institutional psychotherapeutical treatment for schizophrenics.[2]

And so the study of schizophrenia reigns supreme. Where miscellaneous states, situated between hysteria and schizophrenia are still discussed, this is done from an expanding concept of schizophrenia as will be evident from the nomenclature, e.g., pseudo-neurotic schizophrenia, hysterical manifestations within schizophrenia.

The refusal to continue to couple the signifier hysteria to psychic disorders implies the introduction of new signifiers in which schizophrenia serves as reference. Not only the clinical picture or the character features, but also the therapeutical chances of the patients determine the new labels.[3]

By the end of the Second World War *pseudoneurotic schizophrenia*, according to some to be a synonym for the schizosis or schizomania introduced by Claude some twenty years earlier, is in the ascendant.[4] The article by psychiatrists Paul Hoch and Phillip Polatin serves as a reference. The success of this new entity, however, will remain limited to the group around Hoch.[5] Hoch and Polatin class pseudoneurotic schizophrenia under schizophrenia, but position the clinical picture in between the psychoneuroses and schizophrenia. Besides that, they complain of the poor interest in the definition of the distinction between psychoneuroses and schizophrenia. Their purely descriptive definition comprises the schizophrenic (Bleulerian) mechanisms, the autism and the ambivalence, all of which are more distinctly present in the pseudoneurotic schizophrenia than in the (classical) psychoneuroses. There is also question of pan-anxiety, panneurosis and a chaotic psychosexual organization. This latter triad is to typify borderline pathology from the 1950s onward. The signifier borderline, by the way, already repeatedly emerges in this pre-borderline text.[6] The typically schizophrenic thought disorders are supposedly missing, but free association does produce problems. This is highly remarkable, Hoch and Polatin claim, since these patients are intelligent and verbally well versed. Another characteristic are the micropsychoses. These are brief, psychotic episodes, comparable to sudden downpours of rain where the traces disappear extremely fast after they finish. To summarize, it is the combination of a *benign* schizophrenia and a *malign* hysteria.[7]

This article indicates a certain sequence, i.e., how a certain clinical complex of symptoms shifts from psychoneurosis across apparently neurotic schizophrenia to borderline. Unsuspectingly, the authors provide numerous indications which strongly raise the suspicion that no schizophrenic but only hysterical patients are scrutinized here. One such indication is provided by one of their patients. Asked for any comments or thoughts on the destruction of the world, the patient simply replies, "I haven't yet, but give me time. It's an attractive idea." A second indication regards the occurrence of micropsychoses which is decisive to the authors in making their diagnosis. These psychotic episodes turn out to occur suspiciously frequently (are they induced?) during the disinhibitory natrium-amytal interview, in which the patient is administered a drug allowing him to speak freely, or rather to act on the suggestions of the interviewer.[8]

Two years later an article on the same clinical picture is published by American psychiatrist Douglas Noble.[9] The notion of psychosis is defined in a very wide sense; every acute anxiety fit, which need not be spectacular, is sufficient to make him speak of psychosis. The clinical labelling here too is shifting across hysterical psychosis and borderline state to the hysterico-schizophrenic illness up to the label *hysterical manifestations in schizophrenic illness*. In this, the author takes up a final point of view insofar as, in his opinion, the picture concerns hysterical reactions in the process of schizophrenic illness. In other words, the differential diagnosis between hysteria and schizophrenia is not questioned, but the boundaries of schizophrenia are scanned.

This démarche at that moment in time is more the rule than the exception. One wonders how hysterical symptoms and modes of reaction can be fitted into the schizophrenic process (which is generally assumed to have an anatomical basis). The answer is unequivocal; hysterical symptoms or mechanisms constitute an often temporary barrier against the advancing schizophrenic process. This installs a certain distrust toward so-called neurotic disorders. All too often they appear to disguise the true nature of the affliction, namely psychosis.[10] Additionally, this train of thought prompts the following assumption, explicitly phrased by Noble. He sees himself compelled to conclude to a continuum of disorders, ranging from hysteria to schizophrenia, with the inclusion of a hysterico-psychosis. The distinction between the latter and schizophrenia is obscure. The different orientation towards other people is one of the few usable indications.

As a consequence of this development, history too is reread. Countless patients, diagnosed as hysterical by the respective authors, are suddenly acknowledged as being textbook examples of schizophrenia. Particularly exemplary in this respect are the reinterpretations of Freud's study on the demonic possession of Christoph Haizmann.[11] For this case study indicates, in addition to the distinction between hysteria and psychosis, the issue of hysteria in the male.[12]

The fact that Freud's first patients and Anna O. are also "revisited" is an indication of just how far-reaching the redistribution of the area is.[13] Porot's observation that Charcot used a too capacious concept of hysteria, fits in with this development. And Veith's comment that a lot of Charcot's and Janet's patients were actually psychotic, pays lip service to one and the same idea.[14] With this we do not wish to categorically posit that all Charcot-patients were hysterical. Rather we do want to indicate that when the capacious hysteria entity is under siege or is criticized, this invariably occurs via the gateway of Charcot's major hysteria (currently called *folie hystérique*), i.e., one passes over the alienists, who unanimously subscribed to a hysterical madness. This latter episode has been utterly erased from memory.

Freud's official entry in North America, in 1909, cannot prevent his theory on psychoses from being disseminated and adjusted in a disfigured and censored version, first by his students and subsequently by the generation of Postfreudians.[15] A shining example in this respect is Paul Federn, who explicitly applies himself to the study of schizophrenia and who translates (Bleuler's) dissociation in terms of an ego deficiency—an impoverished ego.[16] This deficiency is coupled to the synthesis function of the personality and in this way is much more an echo of Janet's theory on psychic dissociation than an elaboration of Freud's view.[17]

By 1940, psychoanalysis is very popular in America. The promotion of the ego-deficiency and the maladjustment to reality are the major indicative factors for the theory and the praxis of the psychoses. Regarding the adjustment to reality, this trend ties in perfectly with the psychiatric view on psychopathology in general and on hysteria and schizophrenia in particular for isn't the mentally deranged patient estranged from reality? Where, within a psychiatric perspective, this initially only held for the psychoses, by 1940 this was also transferred to the neuroses. Ego analysts, too, adopted this social psychiatric criterion of illness. Exemplary in this respect is an article by the French psychiatrist Courbon on the relationship between hysteria and schizophrenia. In his article, the author tries to differentiate discrete schizophrenia and paroxysmic hysteria. His solution is that it concerns a total vs. a partial maladjustment to reality.[18]

The (Anglo-)American epoch had dawned and, in a second period, was to export its products to the European continent. The fact that the cult of the ego is a corruption of Freud's theory on *das Ich* is evident when one reads Freud's view. Instructive in this respect is an article from 1917, entitled *A Difficulty in the Path of Psycho-Analysis*. In it Freud dwells on three narcissistic blows which scientific research has made humanity undergo. The third is that the *Ich* (ego) is not master in its own house. Freud adds, "No wonder, then, that the ego does not look favorably upon psychoanalysis and obstinately refuses to believe in it."[19]

It is not just Bleuler's capacious schizophrenia concept that finds acceptance everywhere.[20] His optimistic view with regard to therapy gives cause to all manners of psychotherapeutical tours de force with schizophrenic subjects. The method of working of these therapists is generally inspired by the Freudian psychoanalytical technique which according to Freud is not applicable to psychotic subjects. By way of example we mention the American John Rosen—*direct analysis*—and the Swiss Marguerite Sechehaye—*réalisation symbolique*. British, more precisely Kleinian psychoanalysts, start treating schizophrenic patients from the 1950s on as if they were ordinary, i.e., neurotic patients.

Porot's comment on the results of these differing therapeutical tendencies again proves just how central a certain reality notion —which by no means is that of the "ill" patient—steers the therapy: "Without succeeding in modifying the schizophrenic structure of the personality, these methods sometimes allow a discernible re-socialization of the patient." In the sequel he specifies, "They [therapies] progress extremely laboriously and demand a considerable amount of time (up to several hours a day). In their present formats they can only be reserved for privileged cases."[21] The fact that hysterical patients, among others, feel it is incumbent on them to take up such an exceptional position is evident from the analysis of a few testimonies on the treatment of a female schizophrenic patient. In particular, we are referring to Renée (Sechehaye) and Mary (Berke).[22]

The force field of the hysterical fit is adopted by schizophrenia. At most they have a *Spaltung* in common. With this we come to another important influence of Bleuler's theory and his French counterpart Claude—a continuum view of psychopathology (see Noble).

After the Second World War all kinds of classifications which take psychic dissociation or the schizoid factor as their basis make their entry. They do so in psychoanalytical circles, too.[23] These classifications give shape to the quantitative line of thought which sees the field of psychic disorders as a continuum, in which the differentiation between the varying entities is expressed in terms of a plus and a minus.

In conclusion, a brief remark on the fragmenting of hysteria, in particular on the vicissitudes of its typically physical afflictions. We are referring here to conversion hysteria. This type of hysteria is kept out of the field of the psychoses but is drawn into the new capacious field of the *psychosomatic syndromes.*

Psychosomatic medicine, which manifests itself during the two world wars in America as a separate medical subdiscipline, owes its inception among others to the research into the typical war afflictions, i.e., the traumatic neuroses.[24] The American work of Franz Alexander is pioneering in this respect. The gateway to *psychosomatics* is conversion, for Alexander attempts to make a distinction between conversion and psychogenic somatic disorders. In his opinion conversion is the symbolic expression of a psychical conflict by somatic way. It traces the paths of the random nervous system or of the sensorio-perceptive system. The psychogenic somatic disorders, which do not symbolize a conflict, supposedly run along the autonomous nervous system. It is a reaction of somatic structures and functions to an ever recurring affective turmoil.[25] We could seize this distinction as lingually vs. non-lingually structured. Another gateway to indicate the difference is the absence in conversion of organic alterations.

Generally defined, the basis of psychosomatic medicine is the study of disorders and illnesses with the intention of disentangling its psychogenic background. The definition of the concept of *psychosomatic syndrome* is and remains, however, highly variable and the distinction with conversion is certainly not always maintained. The DSM classification, which is dealt with elaborately later, is no stranger to this in view of the fact that this classification lodges the conversion phenomenon with the Somatoform Disorders.

This may serve as background for the following observations. The successive slackening of the diagnosis hysterical conversion runs parallel with an increase of psychosomatic syndromes in the diagnostic field. Dalle, a rare French advocate of hysteria, in 1969, mentions an article by Brisset on the relation between hysteria and psychosomatic pathology in which the latter supposedly posits that in 1964 one comes across the major conversion hysteria even less than one comes across hysterical madness. He also refers to the American psychiatrist Grinker who during the

Second World War supposedly demonstrated by means of statistics that conversion hysteria is slackening in favor of psychosomatic afflictions.[26] To just what extent the signifier hysteria has been pushed aside in Europe by the psychosomatic affliction, can be measured by the fact that both general practitioners as well as psychiatrists use this term routinely to label symptoms which before would have been classed under hysteria. On that subject Van Hoorde says the following, "The confusion, which is now total, can best be illustrated by the things one learns in the media on psychosomatics. What struck me was that the term just as much as so many others has been given an allaying function, serves to cover the most various phobic, hysterical-conversive and anxiety neurotic complaints and in doing so serves one clear purpose namely, to rub out subjective responsibility."[27]

The relationship between the hysterical conversion symptom and the psychosomatic phenomenon is currently still problematic due to the lack of a worked-out theory. It is no coincidence that we are referring here to the conversion-*symptom* and the psychosomatic *phenomenon*. Within the Freudo-Lacanian psychoanalytical theory both are allocated a specific, *lingual* status, distinct from each other. It is not the aim of our work, however, to research this issue in depth.[28]

We conclude this psychosomatic interlude with Freud, who as far back as 1886, specifically with regard to hysterical paralysis, posited that hysteria perverts the laws of neurology and anatomy.[29] We can retranslate this to say that the hysterical body is a lingual body which is fragmented in accordance with the laws of the signifier and not those of anatomy. This distinction is usable for every hysterical symptom but in case of misrecognition it may lead to strange medical actions. The medical world needs little or no stimulus to proceed with action even in cases typified by vague or hard to grasp complaints; especially in those cases, the (possible) psychical or signifying dimension of the complaints is bearly recognizable when looked at through the medical eye. Examples of this? All kinds of aches (lower backache, headache) and the hyperventilation syndrome.

Notes

1. Just how influential Bleulers theory was in those days, is shown in the contents of some articles by psychiatrists-psychoanalysts, included in the *Internationale Zeitschrift für Psychoanalyse*, a journal set up by Freud. Some follow Bleuler rather than they do Freud. See, for example, A. von Endts (1924), Über Traüme von Schizophrenen, *Internationale Zeitschrift für Psychoanalyse*, 10, pp. 292-295.
2. U. Peters (ed.) (1984), *Wörterbuch der Psychiatrie und medizinischen Psychologie*, München, Vienna, Baltimore, Urban & Schwarzenberg, pp. 350, 438-439 and 548; M. Tsuang et al. (1988), Schizophrenic Disorders, in A. Nicholi (ed.), *The New Harvard Guide to Psychiatry*, Cambridge, Massachusetts and London, The Belknap Press of Harvard University Press, pp. 260-261; N. Lewis (1967), American Psychiatry from its Beginnings to World War II, in S. Arieti (ed.), *American Handbook of Psychiatry*, vol. 1, Basic Books, New York, p. 10.
3. See, for example, G. Bally (1930), Zur Frage der Behandlung schizoider Neurotiker, *Internationale Zeitschrift für Psychoanalyse*, 16, pp. 253-260. The author proposes a preparatory treatment for the neuroses with an expanded loss of the sense of reality, i.e., the latent schizophrenics.
4. Peters, for instance, puts pseudoneurotic schizophrenia, pseudoschizophrenic schizophrenia, schizosis, and schizomania on a par as synonyms. U. Peters (ed.) (1984), p. 396.
5. P. Hoch & P. Polatin (1949), Pseudoneurotic Forms of Schizophrenia, *Psychiatric Quarterly*, 23, pp. 248-276; P. Hoch et al. (1954), The Course and Outcome of Pseudoneurotic Schizophrenia, *American Journal of Psychiatry*, 111, pp. 337 et seq.; P. Hoch & J. Cattell (1959), The Diagnosis of Pseudoneurotic Schizophrenia, *Psychiatric Quarterly*, 33, pp. 17 et seq.; J. Cattell (1966), A Psychodynamic View of Pseudoneurotic Schizophrenia, in P. Hoch & J. Zubin (eds.), *Psychopathoplogy of Schizophrenia*, New York, London, Grune & Stratton, pp. 19-36.
6. In 1966 James Cattell writes that the following clinical pictures are

comparable to or related with pseudoneurotic schizophrenia: the borderline case, -patient or -state, latent schizophrenia, and ambulatory schizophrenia. Otto Kernberg, an internationally renowned authority on borderline pathology, explicitly classes the pseudoneurotic schizophrenia as described by Hoch and Polatin under the borderline pathology, which, from the 1960s on, is to become the new fashionable assembly group. J. Cattell (1966), p. 19; O. Kernberg (1975), *Borderline Conditions and Pathological Narcissism*, New York, Jason Aronson, p. 5.

7. This brings to mind an article by the German psychoanalyst Wilhelm Reich on hysterical psychosis in which he, faced with the dilemma "Are we dealing with hysteria or schizophrenia?" literally shuts up his female patient. His conclusion: Hysterical Psychosis. W. Reich (1927[1925]), A Hysterical Psychosis in «statu nascendi», *International Journal of Psycho-Analysis*, 8, pp. 159-173.
8. Possibly we already bear witness here to Hoch's interest in the research of pharmacologically induced psychoses. See P. Hoch (1967), Pharmacologically Induced Psychoses, in S. Arieti (ed.), *American Handbook of Psychiatry*, vol. 2, Basic Books, New York, pp. 1697-1708.
9. D. Noble (1951), Hysterical Manifestations in Schizophrenic Illness, *Psychiatry*, 14, pp. 153-160.
10. See, for example, E. Evrard (1958), Aux confins de la schizophrénie, *Acta Neurologica Psychiatrica Belgica*, 58, 5, pp. 356-371; J. Alves Garcia (1959), Les formes pseudo-névrotiques des schizophrénies, *Annales médico-psychologiques*, 117, pp. 25-45; P. Deniker & J. Quintard (1961), Les signes pseudonévrotiques dans les formes limites de la schizophrénie, *Encéphale*, 50, 3, pp. 307-323; D. Abse (1967), Hysteria, in S. Arieti (ed.), *American Handbook of Psychiatry*, vol. 1, Basic Books, New York, p. 290.
11. S. Freud (1923c[1922]), A Seventeenth-Century Demonological Neurosis, *S.E.*, 19, pp. 67-105; I. Macalpine & R. Hunter (1956), *Schizophrenia 1677*, London, Dawson; P. Racamier (1958), A propos de «Schizophrenia 1677» de I. Macalpine et R. Hunter, *Evolution Psychiatrique*, pp. 669-674.
12. The intended issue is the following. Hysteria in the male may well be officially acknowledged but it remains (also within Freudo-Lacanian circles) a dead letter since it is not studied. Together with Julien

Quackelbeen we are of the opinion that the theoretical clarification of male hysteria not only constitutes a crucial aspect of but even is the prerequisite for every study of the theoretical and clinical status of hysterical psychosis. As long as male hysteria remains a dead letter, its psychotic variant with male subjects can hardly be recognized as such.

13. See, for example, H. Ellenberger (1972), L'Histoire d'«Anna O»: étude critique avec documents nouveaux, *Evolution Psychiatrique*, 37, 4, pp. 693-717. Ellenberger mentions a certain Goshen who declares both Anna O. and all other patients from the *Studies on Hysteria* schizophrenic.
14. A. Porot (ed.) (1975), *Manuel Alphabétique de Psychiatrie clinique et thérapeutique*, Paris, PUF, p. 328; I. Veith (1965), *Hysteria*, Chicago and London, The University of Chicago Press, p. 250.
15. At the end of December 1908, Stanley Hall invited Freud to give a few lectures at the Clark University in Worcester, Massachusetts. Jung and Ferenczi accompanied him on this trip, which brought his theory a first official acknowledgement. The IPA (*International Psychoanalytic Association*) was set up in the following year with Jung as its chairman. E. Jones (1980[1953-1957]), *Sigmund Freud*, 4th ed., vol. 2, London, Hogarth Press, pp. 59-61.
16. Paul Federn (1871-1950) is one of the many Viennese psychoanalysts who left for America at the time of the *Anschluss*. After his demise, a collection of early articles on psychoses was published. P. Federn (1952), *Ego Psychology and the Psychoses*, New York, Basic Books.
17. See J.-A. Miller (1983), Schizophrénie et paranoia, *Quarto*, 10, pp. 18-38.
18. P. Courbon (1937), Hystérie, schizophrénie, pithiatisme et simulation, *Annales médico-psychologiques*, 95, 2, pp. 268-273. The author particularly appeals to war experiences with hysteria, hence the link with simulation.
19. S. Freud (1917a[1916]), A Difficulty in the Path of Psycho-Analysis, *S.E.*, 17, p. 143.
20. Sporadically, voices emerge which blame Bleuler (as well as Kraepelin) that the wealth of the classical clinic is wiped off the map by such an all-embracing category. This is one of the arguments which is to be used for the reintroduction of hysterical psychosis in the

sixties. (v.inf.)

21. A. Porot (ed.) (1975), p. 587. Author's translation.
22. M. Sechehaye (1947), *La réalisation symbolique*, supplement to the *Revue suisse de psychologie et de la psychologie appliquée* no. 12, Bern, Hans Huber Verlag; M. Barnes & J. Berke (1971), *Mary Barnes*, London, Mc Gibbon & Kee.
23. In British psychoanalytic circles, for instance, this advance is launched by Melanie Klein and Ronald Fairbairn. (v.inf.)
24. American Psychiatric Association (1944), *One hundred years of American Psychiatry*, New York, Columbia University Press, pp. 499-504; E. Trillat (1986), *Histoire de l'hystérie*, coll. Médecine et Histoire, Paris, Seghers, pp. 263-270.
25. F. Alexander (1950), *Psychosomatic Medicine: Its Principles and Applications*, New York, Norton; Th. Lidz (1967), General Concepts of Psychosomatic Medicine, in S. Arieti (ed.), *American Handbook of Psychiatry*, vol. 1, Basic Books, New York, pp. 651-652.
26. B. Dalle (1969), Syndrome hallucinatoire chronique et hystérie, *Evolution Psychiatrique*, 34, p. 356.
27. H. Van Hoorde (1988), Psychosomatiek. Veel vragen onder het mom van een bevestiging, *Rondzendbrief uit het Freudiaanse Veld*, 33, p. 13. Author's translation.
28. We would like to refer the interested reader to the pioneering labor of the French psychoanalyst Jean Guir with regard to the study of psychosomatic phenomena. J. Guir (1983), *Psychosomatique et cancer*, Paris, Point hors ligne.
29. Although Freud never explicitly wrote on the subject of psychosomatics, a rarely mentioned article does contain a fragment that sheds an interesting light on the matter. Freud distinguishes between "psychogenic" and "neurotic," i.e., functional disorders. The latter are determined by a toxic or physiological increase in the erotogenic factor. See S. Freud (1910i), The Psycho-Analytic View of Psychogenic Disturbance of Vision, *S.E.*, 11, pp. 211-218, especially p. 218.

Part Three

The 1950s to the Present

The Marginal Psychotic Existence of Hysterical Madness, The Numerical Diaspora of Hysteria

Introduction

In the 1960s the anti-psychiatry movement stirred up something in the world of all those people concerned with the human psyche. This does not mean to say that all were suddenly convinced of the freedom of the madman or madwoman. One of the implications, or let us more circumspectly speak of a parallel movement, is the generalized and rising criticism of the too comprehensive category of schizophrenia.

Within psychiatry this did not really reopen the road to classical nuancing and the clinical refinement of psychiatric nosology. The concern to recognize schizophrenia at an early stage, which already gave cause to pseudoneurotic schizophrenia and schizoidia, continues and results in the proliferation of a group of border states, i.e., the borderline pathology and more recently also the schizo-affective disorders. From the 1960s onward articles here and there are published on hysterical psychosis, a specific psychosis which supposedly distinguishes itself from schizophrenia by its transience and its curability.

Within Anglo-American analytic circles, beside established schizophrenia, borderline pathology or the borderline personality makes itself known; its actual, marginal but benign counterpart is the Multiple Personality Disorder (MPD), which emerges particularly in hypnotherapeutical circles. This development is grounded on the experience of exhaustive marathon sessions with apparently neurotic, but unanalyzable patients, i.e., a completely different impetus than that of the psychiatric borderline emancipation. Recently there is more and more talk in these analytical circles of narcissistic personality disorders.

Meanwhile, certain analysts continue to work at the development and application of an effective analytical therapy for psychotics, in particular for schizophrenic patients. In France Gisela Pankow shifts pioneering labor with her dynamical structuring, in America John Rosen practices direct analysis and in England Herbert Rosenfeld performs Kleinian analyses. All of them emphasize the necessity of an intensive and longer sustained therapy with the therapist in the role of a model to the patient.

Apart from that, in the 1960s the demise of hysteria had been confirmed by official sources. Important psychiatric textbooks and the statistical classification system DSM, which, especially since its third edition (1980), has become authoritative and is currently also the mandatory work of reference in psychiatry on the European continent, no longer mention hysteria. Hysteria has also virtually completely disappeared from the registers of the broad specter of psychoanalytic journals which subscribe to the IPA line.[1]

Note

1. Among others, the *International Journal of Psycho-Analysis* (U.S.A.), the *Nouvelle Revue de Psychanalyse* (France) and the *Revue Française de Psychanalyse* (France).

9
The Vanishing Act of Hysteria in the Psychiatric Field

The Diaspora of Hysteria and its Mad Variant

The publication of the first version of the *Diagnostic and Statistical Manual of Mental Disorders* (DSM-classification) in 1952 hastens the disappearance of hysteria; it is deleted from the Mental Disorders Diagnostic Manual, the precursor of the DSM, and replaced by the conversion symptom.[1] In this way, the trend which had started taking shape around the turn of the century, namely that the diagnosis of hysteria is made less and less frequently, is finally institutionalized. The second version of the DSM similar to the ICD-system (International Classification of Diseases) of the World Health Organization (the eighth edition is published simultaneously with the DSM-II), mentions hysterical neurosis and the hysterical personality again, but it is to be the final, deceptive rekindling before the ultimate fragmentation and with that also the vanishing of hysteria. The third DSM-edition in 1980 has permanently erased the regarding categories.[2] Currently the revised third edition, published in 1987, is still valid.[3] The fourth edition, initially planned for 1992 and now finally announced to appear in 1994, will contain an additional, psychodynamic axis. Although principally non-theoretical, the editors keep a close track of new trends and developments. New in the DSM-III-R, for example, are the schizo-affective disorders.

The inclusion of a new clinical entity doubtlessly reinforces its diagnosis, just as the deletion of a category makes for the diminution of that diagnosis. For almost every psychiatrist who follows the evolutions in his professional domain updates his diagnostic system, i.e., accords his diagnoses with the new or the revised classification system. The Dutch psychiatrist Rümke, one of the last great clinicians from before the DSM-generation, confirms that at the end of the 1960s the terminus technicus of hysteria gradually disappeared from psychiatry. Set against this he observes that the phenomenon of hysteria has certainly not died out yet, regardless of what one believes on the subject of hysteria. He mentions three categories: conversion phenomena, dream states or hysterical psychoses, and the hysterical character or degenerative hysteria.[4]

Hysteria, symbolically absent in the official psychiatric registers and already waning in the world of psychiatry, has almost completely disappeared from current psychiatric literature. Whoever, for instance, goes through the most recent annual volumes of the Dutch *Tijdschrift voor Psychiatrie* (Journal of Psychiatry), will indeed no longer find hysteria. A few notions from the DSM-III and DSM-III-R sporadically emerge. There is one single article on the conversion disorder and several on dissociation, that is evidently primary. Some authors even go so far as to say that conversion disorders are also of a dissociative nature, which is not in the line of the DSM. At any rate, a conversion disorder generally implies a dissociative problem.[5] From the viewpoint of Freud this observation could be read as the final "acknowledgement" of the splitting of the ego, or in the terms of Lacan, of the divided subject as subject of the unconscious. For Freud owes his discovery of the unconscious to hysteria and the Lacanian hysterical discourse (lingual social bond) with the divided (hysterical) subject as its agent is the discourse par excellence where the unconscious is concerned. Needless to say, there is no link to the Freudian hysterical *Spaltung*. In addition, it is not so much Freud's influence but that of Bleuler that can be demonstrated in the use of the notion of dissociation. The psychiatrists, who also seem to forget that the DSM primarily has been intended as a statistical instrument, persist in the exclusion of hysteria.[6]

The DSM, which is ironically renamed Diagnostic and Statistical Mania by the Belgian psychiatrist Vandereycken, is, roughly speaking, the indicative system in the psychiatric clinic. This American import is doing excellently both in the Dutch and the Belgian psy-market, while most certainly the latter can no longer pride itself in having a proper psychiatric tradition. German psychiatrists continue to be divided on the subject of what kind of nosology they should use. Will they adhere to the diagnostics that is oriented psychoanalytically, with the preservation of categories such as hysteria, or will they join the DSM-devotees? Up to now the former view held out.[7] In France the situation is somewhat different. There, too, the DSM-classification finds (general) acceptance; with a two to three year delay French translations of the DSM-editions are published. Still the French remain leaders in their dour resistance against the too-wide schizophrenia concept, which must share its fixed position with a number of typically French attainments. The French stick to a strict distinction between schizophrenia and the chronic hallucinatory psychoses.[8] Next to that there is also the French *bouffée délirante*, introduced by Magnan, which is still strictly separated in French psychiatry from the acute psychotic episodes within the frame of schizophrenia. Meanwhile, this exclusively French nosological entity (Brief Delusional and Schizophreniform Disorder in English) has been allocated a place within the international classification systems ICD and DSM, respectively under the headings Acute Delusional Reactions (ICD-9), and Brief Reactive Psychosis and Schizophreniform Disorder (DSM-III-R).[9]

Henri Ey is one of the psychiatrists who fought hard for the recognition of the *bouffée délirante* and against the expansion of the schizophrenia concept. As recent as 1975, Ey, being one of the last of the French clinical heavyweights (after him there is the DSM-generation and/or the biological psychiatrists) opposes what he calls the superficial clinicians, who classify far too many disorders as psychosis or schizophrenia. With these numerous psychiatrists the old hysteria à la Charcot disappears in the realm of psychosis. Hallucinations and hallucinatory delusory states in Ey's opinion are compatible with the diagnosis of hysteria, when they meet certain requirements. A clear regression to fantasmic wishful thinking must be discernible in it. These regressions do bring hysteria close to psychosis, from which it cannot always be distinguished. Hysterics do not only fabricate false organic, but also false mental illnesses according to Ey and in this way make a mockery of nosography by their ingenious yet morbid aptitude for falsification and for an unauthentic and delirious existence. He stresses the imaginary significance of hysteria, which in his view is the neurosis of the desire, the imagination, psychoplasticity and psychological automatism. The latter indicates a strong influence of the ideas of Janet's. Ey is clearly still permeated by the doctrine of the Salpêtrière, where the action of suggestion and the pregnancy of the picture indeed took center court. In this way, Ey stresses the false and the *as if* character of hysterical phenomena in general and of hallucinations in particular. The latter can be situated in his theory on the hallucination as being a perception without object (a typical psychiatric view of hallucination). It reminds us of the notion of pseudo-hallucination, i.e., a hallucination accompanied by "insight." The subject knows it is a perception without object.[10]

Since the DSM-classification is officially a non-theoretical collection of clinical disorders, two different conclusions can be drawn from the observation that the proffered clinic changes.[11]

Either one can assume that entities disappear as time elapses or even cease existence under the influence of certain social developments, while other, new entities take their place. To those who might consider invoking the prophylactic function of analytic theory for the occurrence of neuroses as an important factor, it should be said that this function can be described as anything but unequivocal, let alone that it would constitute an incontestable datum. For Freud himself felt compelled with time to thoroughly review his initial optimism in this matter.

This earliest view we find, for instance, voiced with Kortmann. The author proceeds from the observation that a shift is taking place in current psychopathology which he takes to be an exchange. Narcissistic, identity, and borderline disorders come to take the place of the neurotic disorders. This substitution, according to Kortmann, is the consequence of the fact that the father and mother roles are no longer unequivocal, which evokes a pathogenic confusion within the child. Instead of focusing on the need to clarify these roles, he orients himself rather to relieving the ego-wounds that have been found within the patient and he does so in the shape of what can be called orthopaedic therapeutical methods.[12] From this angle, hysteria is at any rate Victorian and borderline up to date.

Or, departing from a view of psychopathology which is disconnected from the phenomena as such, one may proceed from a number of invariant structures, which are actually positions of the subject, which go and express themselves differently according to space and time (the context).

Those of us who share the latter basic assumption, ask ourselves the following question anyhow: what has happened to hysteria in this classification system which calls itself non-theoretical and has been drawn up for the benefit of statistical processing but unexpectedly has a meteoric international rise as a textbook and in generalized diagnostic usage? Officially hysteria has been fragmented into, among others, the Conversion Disorder and the Dissociative Disorders. The physical and the mental have notably been (arbitrarily) separated. As far as hysteria is concerned one is referred in the first instance to the latter group which also comprises the Non-Specified Dissociative Disorder, apart from the Multiple Personality, the Psychogenic Fugue, Psychogenic Amnesia, and Depersonalization.[13] When we read up on the diagnostic criteria of the Conversion Disorder in the DSM-III-R, old characteristics of the hysterical phenomena are found to emerge, just as a charitable attitude with regard to the issue of simulation.

The authors who still occupy themselves with the problem of

conversion, disagree on the efficacy of a psychotherapeutic treatment of such disorders. Some refer to poor motivation, others stress the efficacy of hypnosis. In this way Hoogduin and others refer in their recent article on the treatment of conversions with hypnosis, to Charcot's observations on traumatic paralyses, yet without even once mentioning the word hysteria. Another conclusion is that the conversion disorders apparently occur more in women than in men. If they are observed in men they are generally soldiers in wartime; the traumatic neurosis has been brainwashed.[14]

So much for the clinical picture of hysteria which corresponds with axis I of the DSM-III-R.[15] Under the personality disorders of axis II we find the hysterical personality under the label of *histrionic*. The publishers substituted hysterical with histrionic because of the charged connotation of the first adjective.

Hysterical madness, in its Freudian definition, is not explicitly indicated but we most definitely find it under the Brief Reactive Psychosis and the Factitious Disorder with Psychological Symptoms.[16] The Schizophreniform Disorder includes, among others, the longer lasting brief reactive psychoses, i.e., reactive psychoses lasting more than two weeks. This gives rise to the suspicion that hysterical madness may lurk in this category too.

And so the rich clinical arsenal from around the turn of the century turns out to be fragmented into categories that are numerically distinct from each other. The "diaspora" of hysteria and its mad variant?

The Statistical System Directs Trends in Psychopathology

What happened to the Charcot-hysteria or the severe hysteria from Freud's *Studies* by the 1990s? This question was already dealt with in the previous chapter up until the 1950s. There we specifically talked about the expanding schizophrenia concept and its border scans in the exemplary shape of pseudoneurotic schizophrenia.

The DSM-system officially deletes hysteria from the list and replaces it by an amalgam of numerical disorders. These disorders emancipate themselves as distinct diagnostic labels and additionally as new or resurrected nosographical entities. Moreover, we dare posit the thesis that hysteria should also be suspected in the categories which, over the past years, with the wave of criticism for schizophrenia, have come under psychiatric scrutiny and thus have been re-included in the DSM. In particular we refer to the multiple personality and the borderline personality disorder.

With the resurgence of the usage of hypnosis, started in the 1960s, and especially evident in America, Charcotian manifestations of hysteria re-emerge. In this way certain authors indicate that with the current bloom of hypnosis the number of ascertained hysterical fits is also on the upgrade.[17] Other typical hypnotic pathologies, in fact all dissociative disorders including the multiple personality par excellence, are every bit as present.[18] Another remarkable observation is the growing attention, especially in hypnotic circles, for the category of the Post Traumatic Stress Disorders (in the DSM part of the Anxiety Disorders or the neurotic anxiety- and phobic-states). These disorders are more and more linked presently to the dissociative disorders.[19] So it seems that although many believe that the Freudian theory on the role of sexual traumata in the etiology of neuroses, especially hysteria, definitely belongs to the past, the (f)actual fragmentation of the neuroses in the DSM classification is not able to prevent the *nachträgliche* resurrection of the (old) affinities between the respective fragments.

The multiple personality was included for the first time as a separate category in the third edition of the DSM in 1980; this was done under the label of the Dissociative Disorders. It is described there as rare. In recent years, however, the number of American and Canadian studies on this disorder has been piling up. The DSM-typification is purely descriptive, which cannot be said as readily for other publications. These incorporate a certain more explicit view of the personality. It is not difficult to imagine that this causes quite a bit of confusion considering the fact that the authors sometimes neglect to specify in which sense they are using the concept. The various authors hammer away more at the specificity of the affliction than make the link with hysteria, a link which the DSM does not neglect. Moreover, the feature amnesia, a typically hysterical characteristic lacking the DSM-description of the multiple personality is to be added to the DSM-IV.[20] When the multiple personality is classified with the existing entities, one rather opts for borderline or psychosis; a few authors draw the link with the notion of hysterical psychosis, that will be discussed later.[21]

In the ongoing discussion concerning the status of the multiple personality, borderline or psychosis, the Dutch psychiatrist Derksen, for example, chooses psychosis. The Multiple Personality Syndrome (MPS) is a psychotic organization of the personality in which various personalities fend off psychotic decompensations.[22] Van der Hart and Boon—for their part—link the MPS to the Münchhausen syndrome and the Münchhausen syndrome by proxy which, together with the Ganser syndrome, have been classified with the Factitious Disorders in the DSM. The Münchhausen syndrome, named after the figure and the fantastic tales of Baron von Münchhausen and described for the first time by Aher in 1951, is typified as the exaggerated, made up, and possibly self-produced pathological phenomena which, in view of their credible presentation, cause numerous hospitalizations and medical interventions. In the by proxy syndrome, described for the first time in 1971 by Meadow, the Münchhausen syndrome is expressed via a substitute, namely the child.[23]

The Belgian psychiatrist Megens posits that where the multiple personality is studied in psychiatric circles, it vanishes under psychotic disintegration states or borderline pathology. In his opinion history is even being rewritten, since quite a number of authors insist that the prevalence of this pathology so far has been underestimated. Here again history turns out to be lurking under the veil of amnesia, at least where learning something from the history of hysteria is concerned. From Megens' literature survey we extract the following frequently mentioned characteristics from the MPS: conversion phenomena, brief psychotic decompensations, inhibited-disinhibited antagonism between ego and alter-ego, incest or sexual violence during childhood, more than average intelligence, and protracted therapy (hypnosis!) with a good prognosis.[24]

The account of the case history and treatment of Sybil, published by Schreiber, is an American exception to the rule.[25] The book tells of the analysis of Sybil, lasting eleven years, by the psychiatrist-psychoanalyst Wilbur, who subsequently requested Schreiber as a journalist to publish the course of the cure in all its facets as a novel. Wilbur, who is convinced of the diagnosis grand hysteria, actually did consult history and came out with a good deal more than the sheer descriptions of the American psychiatrist Morton Prince.[26]

According to Wilbur, Sybil's various *selves* are nothing other than personified unconscious formations that are in competition with each other, which, in fact, take us back to Freud's studies on hysteria. For Breuer and Freud spoke of a splitting of consciousness in terms of distinct psychic states. By the way, in 1923 Freud comes back to the issue of multiple personalities. He regards them purely as ego-fragmentations that are attributable to over-intense, over-numerous, and incompatible object identifications.[27] Freud ascribes the de-doubled or dual personalities to no other but a psychic reality. This is in contrast to Janet who explicitly refers to the formation of a second personality. The splitting or dissociation of the personality, as postulated by Janet, makes multiple personalities plausible, as his clinical works as well as their present reappraisal indicate. Van der Hart, for instance, states that Janet's original dissociation theory again plays an important role in the study of the dissociative disorders and symptoms that are back in the spotlight after a century of neglect.[28]

Both with regard to the splitting of consciousness and the role of traumata in the anamnesis of psychiatric disorders (two concepts which are currently finding acceptance in psychiatry),

Freud's theory on the subject is forgotten. It might perhaps pose too strong an invitation to re-question the now widely accepted assumption that Freud's theory has become obsolete.

In this way, it is not that surprising that Freud and Breuer's early female patients, Anna O. being the first, are currently not so much recognized as multiple personalities but rather as schizophrenic or borderline. The honor of being the patron of the multiple personalities has not been reserved for the hysteric Anna O.

Still, the multiple personality remains a highly controversial diagnosis outside the United States. It is very often classified as an American fad, an artifact of hypnotherapists who are hardly or not at all aware of the fact that sub-personalities are induced during trance.[29] A number of these studies do acknowledge the repetitive character of the epidemic, but here too its coupling to hysteria is neglected.

The first bloom period of the multiple personality is situated in the second half of the nineteenth century. Then too the issue was presented to the public at large by way of vulgarizing works. One of the most popular cases is the American Mary Reynolds, a case of dual personality first described around 1815 and re-edited in 1889 by Weir Mitchell. Another well-known American is Miss Beauchamp, described by Morton Prince in 1906. Janet was one of the first to systematically carry out experiments with such subjects.[30]

One century later the number of ascertained de-doublings is simply sensational. One such spectacular case, for this is the way that the public presentation of this case study is announced, is Billy Milligan, blessed with no less than twenty-four personalities.[31] The fact that the number of fragmentations knows no upper limit, whatsoever, is evident when, in 1987, the autobiography of Truddi Chase is published, to which this lady brings the story of her 92 personalities.[32]

In our first chapter we briefly indicated that the twentieth century is to become that of the personality. Now the second axis of the DSM, that of the *personality disorders*, voices and stimulates another tendency that experiences less criticism than the multiple personality. Among psychiatrists and all kinds of other psy-workers there is an obvious rise in interest in certain personality disorders. Particularly the borderline and the narcissistic personality, both first mentioned in the DSM-III, are presently in vogue. In this the order of mentioning is not at random. Meanwhile there has been a lot of psychiatric research into the borderline patient but preciously little into the narcissistic patient, a notion which is causing a furor in psychoanalytic circles. Borderline, used here as a descriptive label, is still proving its validity within psychiatry but is being downgraded for the narcissistic disorders which supposedly are more easily treatable. The differentiation with regard to other personality disfunctions, such as the histrionic or hysterical and the anti-social personality disorders, does not turn out to be smooth sailing all the way, which is already made abundantly clear by a quick comparison between the DSM-typifications.

Notwithstanding the fact that the DSM-III borderline concept is descriptive, it does encourage colored typifications. An excerpt from such a typification, based on the DSM, from 1980:

> Because of their appearance and behavior, borderline patients are found less attractive than the others ... since their behavior seems ill adapted to the clinical interview. They do things which disturb the interview, ask questions beside the point, get up from their chair or change chairs or simply refuse to answer questions. They behave in a predominantly quick-tempered fashion in which they express their anger on numerous occasions and also against their interlocutor. They argue, are unstable and sarcastic, they make demands without tact or any respect, in an attempt to manipulate the interviewer. While giving hostile comments, they act with the intention of fulfilling their wishes as if they were special patients who constitute the exception to every rule.[33]

The Dutch psychiatrist Hummelen confirms the unfavorable disposition regarding the borderline patient, an attitude which in our opinion remarkably contrasts with a certain affectionateness with regard to the multiple personality. This brings to mind the aforementioned classical dichotomy between *good* and *bad* hysterics. Hummelen's critical research into the use of the diagnosis of borderline reveals that this descriptive label, at least in the Netherlands, is often used as a legitimization for the rejection of a patient.

> Some authors see in the group of patients which simultaneously meets the criteria of all of these three concepts [DSM-III, Gunderson and Kernberg] the *real* borderline patient and speak of a prototypical borderline. It seems that in doing so one loses sight of the fact that every borderline concept is a diagnostic construct and the fact that borderline patients only exist in the mind of the diagnostician.[34]

Here we come to the distinction between the *object* of research and the *subject* of the researcher. Descriptive systems such as the DSM inevitably sanctify the conviction that the object of research is quite separate from the observer.

The descriptive borderline personality is only one aspect of the borderline specter. The concept of borderline became a controversial issue from the 1950s onward and this also in French psychiatry (*états limites*). It has also widespread in the Netherlands and Belgium. This happened despite continuing confusion on the psychiatric use of the concept; i.e., does it refer to the labelling of a patient, of a morbid entity or is it a diagnosis which refers to a nosographical category?[35]

Between fifteen and forty percent of residential and ambulant psychiatric patients are given this label in America. The ratio would be just as representative for Europe. On what circumscription is this diagnosis based and how rigorous is it applied, is something that is rarely mentioned.[36] Therefore, it is hardly surprising that the number of borderline patients is noticeably increasing and particularly unruly patients (those who are not easily pigeonholed) are brought together by it. If they do not fit into definition number one, there is still definition number two, number three, etc.

Within psychiatric circles, borderline (a notion which is ultimately allocated the position of a residuary category within any nosology, but which is soaring now in its exacted singularity) emancipated itself from the psychotic corner. It converts from an individual into a group status at an early age. With this, borderline nestles itself next to or above notions such as pseudoneurotic schizophrenia, latent schizophrenia and pre-psychosis, in which the neurotic symptoms supposedly represent a defense against the rise of psychosis, but continues to officially maintain a position in between psychosis and neurosis. Stronger than notions like pseudoneurotic schizophrenia, borderline implies a continuum concept of psychopathology. Considering the fact that borderline is given the most varied definitions, the presence of mad hysteria, in view of its proteiformity and sensibility to environmental factors, can be more than surmised.[37] The already mentioned shift within the diagnostic field strengthens our suspicion in this matter; neurosis is inclined to vanish altogether in the face of the multiplication of the borderline states.[38] This presence of hysteria we sense more emphatically in the psychoanalytic emancipation of borderline and of the narcissistic disorder, which will be discussed later.

Notes

1. Both textbooks are published by the American Psychiatric Association, the standard bearer of American psychiatry. See I. Veith (1965), *Hysteria*, Chicago, London, The University of Chicago Press, p. viii.
2. In the presentation of the third version of the classification system the editors posit that the neurotic disorders have now been distributed over the affective, the anxiety, the somatoform [conversion hysteria], the dissociative [dissociative hysteria] and the psychosexual disorders. A detailed comparison of the DSM-classification and the ICD-system on the subject of neurosis can be found in: P. Tyrer (1989), *Classification of Neurosis*, Chichester, New York, John Wiley &

Sons.

3. American Psychiatric Association (1987), *Diagnostic and Statistical Manual of Mental Disorders. Third Edition Revised*, Washington.
4. H. Rümke (1973[1967]), *Psychiatrie III*, Amsterdam, Scheltema & Holkema, pp. 137-138. An important observation is that Rümke is of the conviction that Sechehaye's famous schizophrenic patient Renée suffers from development hysteria.
5. The fact that the definition of the relationship between conversion and dissociation is dependent on the used DSM-version is evident from an article by Watson who bases himself on the DSM-II. The author concludes that conversion and dissociation correlate reversely. C. Tilleskjor & C. Watson (1983), Interrelationships of Conversion, Psychogenic Pain and Dissociative Disorder Symptoms, *Journal of Consulting and Clinical Psychology*, 51, 5, pp. 788-789.
6. See H. Van Hoorde (1992), *Psychiatrie en Psychoanalyse: Scheiding van Tafel en Bank?*, Pegasos series no. 9, Ghent, Idesça, p. 74.
7. W. Vandereycken (1989), review, *Tijdschrift voor Psychiatrie*, 31, Books 2, pp. 18-19.
8. B. Dalle (1969), Syndrome hallucinatoire chronique et hystérie, *Evolution Psychiatrique*, 34, pp. 339-358; J.-P. Tachon & F. Raffaitin (1983), A la recherche d'un langage commun, *Information Psychiatrique*, 1983, 59, 6, pp. 787-802.
9. J. Postel (ed.) (1993), *Dictionnaire de psychiatrie et de psychopathologie clinique*, Références Larousse, Paris, Larousse, pp. 90-92.
10. H. Ey (1973-1975), *Traité des hallucinations*, vol. 2, Paris, Masson, pp. 874-895.
11. With regard to this atheoretical nature, Tachon and Raffaitin adopt the following statement: "Chase theory and it returns at a gallop." J.-P. Tachon & F. Raffaitin (1983), p. 801.
12. F. Kortmann (1981), Van neurose naar borderline pathologie, *Tijdschrift voor Psychiatrie*, 3, pp. 151-162.
13. For the comparison between the DSM-II and the DSM-III, see: American Psychiatric Association (1980), *Diagnostic and Statistical Manual of Mental Disorders. Third Edition*, Washington, Annex C.
14. Also usual at the time under Charcot, the application of hypnosis here comprises primarily the suggesting away of symptoms (the symptom oriented treatment). Only in the second instance is the time-honored hypno-cathartic method (Breuer) or the exploring treatment used. C. Hoogduin et al. (1990), Behandeling van conversies

met hypnose, *Tijdschrift voor Psychiatrie*, 32, 7, pp. 450-461.

15. The DSM-system is a multi-axial system. Axes I, II and III constitute the official diagnostics of the DSM, axes IV and V are optional. Axis I comprises the clinical syndromes, axis II the developmental and personality disorders, axis III the physical and affective disorders, axis IV the severity of the psychosocial stress and axis V a global evaluation of the functioning of the patient over the year preceding the disorder.
16. See also H. Van Hoorde (1984), De hysterische psychose, nosologische struikelsteen en eerherstel?, *Psychoanalytische Perspektieven*, 6, pp. 45-57.
17. T. Caldwell & R. Stewart (1981), Hysterical Seizures and Hypnotherapy, *American Journal of Clinical Hypnosis*, 23, 4, pp. 294-298.
18. See, for example, J. Kaplan & H. Deabler (1975), Hypnotherapy with a Severe Dissociative Hysterical Disorder, *American Journal of Clinical Hypnosis*, 18, 2, pp. 83-89.
19. See, for instance, J. Bloch (1991), *Assessment and Treatment of Multiple Personality and Dissociative Disorders*, Sarasota, Professional Resource Press; D. Spiegel (1991), Dissociation and Trauma, in A. Tasman & S. Goldfinger (eds.), *American Psychiatric Press Review of Psychiatry*, vol. 10, Washington, American Psychiatric Press, pp. 261-275; D. Sakheim & S. Devine (eds.) (1992), *Out of darkness: Exploring Satanism and Ritual Abuse*, New York, Lexington Books, Macmillan.
20. Some recent literature on the subject: F. Putnam (1989), *Diagnosis and Treatment of Multiple Personality Disorder*, London, Guilford Press; C. Ross (1989), *Multiple Personality Disorder*, New York, John Wiley & Sons; C. Ward (1989), *Altered States of Consciousness and Mental Health, a Cross-Cultural Perspective*, London, Sage Publications; R. Aldridge-Morris (1989), *Multiple Personality. An Exercise in Deception*, Lawrence Erlbaum Ass. Ltd. Publishers; J. Carroy (1993), *Les personnalités doubles et multiples*, Psychopathologie-Epistémologie/Histoire, Paris, PUF.
21. See K. Seeman et al. (1984), Fantasized Companions and Suicidal Depressions: Two Case Reports, *American Journal of Psychotherapy*, 38, 4, pp. 541-557.
22. J. Derksen (1986), *Structurele diagnostiek van psychische stoornissen: neurosen, borderline, psychose*, Baarn, Nelissen.

23. O. van der Hart & S. Boon (1990), Het Münchhausen-syndroom «by proxy» en de relatie met de dissociatieve stoornissen, *Tijdschrift voor Psychiatrie*, 32, 1, pp. 54-5.
24. J. Megens (1985), De multipele persoonlijkheid, een literatuuroverzicht, *Tijdschrift voor Psychiatrie*, 27, 5, pp. 301-310.
25. F. Schreiber (1973), *Sybil*, New York, Warner.
26. Prince (1854-1929), a pioneer of American psychopathology, set up the *Journal of Abnormal Psychology* in 1906. He worked in the same vein as Janet and used the experimental method. M. Prince (1913 [1906]), *The Dissociation of a Personality*, London, Longmans Green.
27. S. Freud (1923b), *The Ego and the Id*, *S.E.*, 19, pp. 30-31.
28. O. van der Hart (1991), review, *Tijdschrift voor Psychiatrie*, 33, Books 1, pp. 21-22.
29. This can be interpreted in the same way as Charcot's so-called cultural hysteria and hypnotism; hysterics meet the desire of the master therapist or arouse his desire to know. See L. Israël (1976), *L'Hystérique, le sexe et le médecin*, Paris, Masson; J. Lacan (1991[1969-1970]), *Le Séminaire, Livre XVII, L'envers de la psychanalyse*, edited by J.-A. Miller, Paris, Seuil, p. 36.
30. H. Ellenberger (1970), *The Discovery of the Unconscious*, New York, Basic Books, pp. 126-141.
31. D. Keyes (1982), *Billy Milligan, l'Homme aux 24 personnalités*, trans. from the English, Paris, Balland, discussed in J. Attié (1982), 24 personnes en une, *L'Ane*, 7, p. 26. The scenario of the book is comparable to that of Sybil; Keyes is the reporter and a Dr. Caul the hypnotherapist.
32. T. Chase (1987), *When Rabbit howls*, New York, Dutton.
33. H. Scharbach (ed.) (1983), *Les états limites*, Conference of Psychiatry and Neurology of French Speaking Countries, Psychiatric Report, 27 June-2 July 1983, Paris, Masson, pp. 74-77. Author's translation. This typification is attributed to Perry and Klerman. J. Perry & G. Klerman (1978), The Borderline Patient, *Archives of General Psychiatry*, 35, pp. 141-150; J. Perry & G. Klerman (1980), Clinical Features of the Borderline Personality Disorder, *American Journal of Psychiatry*, 137, 2, pp. 165-173.
34. J. Hummelen (1990), De bruikbaarheid van de diagnose borderline, *Tijdschrift voor psychiatrie*, 3, p. 150.
35. For a critical historical reading of the borderline as a Postfreudian

and contemporary issue, see F. Leguil (1979), Etats-limites et naufrage de la clinique, *Actualités Psychiatriques*, 8, pp. 75-78.

36. See our comparable comment on the multiple personality.
37. Some authors link the psychotic episodes within a borderline personality disorder to hysterical psychosis. See A. Lotterman (1985), Prolonged Psychotic States in Borderline Personality Disorder, *Psychiatric Quarterly*, 57, 1, pp. 33-46.
38. This same idea is formulated by Maurey, who judges the danger of "psychotising" severely neurotic patients to be highly realistic. G. Maurey (1977), A propos de ce qui suit, *Etudes Psychothérapeutiques*, 28, pp. 77-79.

10
Hysteria Re-enters Psychiatry as a Distinct Psychosis

A New Old Category is Born

Oddly enough, articles on a *new* old category emerge here and there in these barren times for hysteria. From the 1960s on psychiatric studies are published in dribs and drabs in the Anglo-American countries and in Europe on *hysterical psychosis*, a so-called specific psychotic structure which would supposedly split itself off from the schizophrenia group. Its clinical typification surprisingly often reveals strong similarities with those of the dissociative disorders from the DSM. This trend in the margin which feeds on the nostalgia for the nosographical wealth of the last century and the criticism of the far too expansive schizophrenia concept, continues up to the present but remains situated in the margin of the psychiatric goings-on. The authors fully go in for inbreeding which, as the ancient Egyptians already experienced, does not make for a good quality product. By merely appealing to each other, they need not, as it were, bother with a more profound theorization.

In view of the fact that the framework, more specifically the discourse in which something suddenly appears, is never accidental or without significant effects, we use the word group *hysterical psychosis* as something novel here. The numerous references to *folie hystérique* and/or *hysterisches Irresein* of some hundred years ago are not unimportant either, but on no account do they allow us to use the two together and instead of each other. It is, therefore, a *new* old category.

Hysterical Psychosis as "Bouffée Délirante"

In France, the honor of having first reported on hysterical psychosis accrues to Follin. In 1961, he publishes, together with his colleagues Chazaud and Pilon, a clinical article (comprising several case fragments) on the *hysterical psychoses*. It comprises no historical research nor any theoretical elaboration. Noteworthy is the descriptive plural form.[1] In 1962, de Boucaud and Demangeat make their presence felt from one and the same reference to Régis and Chaslin. In the cases put forward by them the confusion and the acute oneiric delusion are central. They also use the plural form and they speak of rehabilitation. Accordingly, the authors believe they must restore something, an idea which is less outspoken in Follin.[2] The latter uses scraps of Postfreudian terminology. As will be evident further on, this influence must be especially attributed to Chazaud, who calls himself a psychiatrist-psychoanalyst.

Follin and colleagues study a picture that is psychotic, comprising both hysterical and psychotic phenomena and, just like borderline of which there is no mention in the article, comes somewhere between hysteria and psychosis. For their clinical typification (fragmentation of the personality and realization of ego-emancipations) they call on Chaslin.[3] To Freud and Janet they claim that the hysterical phenomena as described by them have now been included in the frame of schizophrenia or, more restricted, within that of the acute, sub-acute or periodic *bouffées délirantes*. Their effort takes on the shape of an attempt to safeguard the position of the hysterical psychoses within the category of the *bouffées délirantes aiguës*. This means that the hysterical psychoses come next to schizophrenia within the group of the psychoses. Quaintly enough the English summary of their contribution speaks of *psychotic hysteria*, which causes the emphasis ostensibly to fall upon hysteria, at least when we assume that the choice for certain signifiers also implies a certain stand with regard to the status of the distinction between hysteria and psychosis. This second element concerns the question of whether both are situated on one and the same continuum or whether they are separated from each other by a faultline. The fact that any theoretical foundation whatsoever is wasted on these authors is evident from Chazaud's later publications on the hysterical psychoses, which he does not distinguish at any point from hysteria. On the contrary, one of his case studies he describes as a *grand hysteria.* Any terminological strictness is alien to him as well. As he holds less to words than to things, according to Chazaud, he is prepared in 1981 to trade in hysterical psychosis for *hysteroid psychosis.* Is it just a matter of minimizing the share of hysteria? Not that he wishes to exclude any other possibilities in doing so; *madness, delusion* or even *pseudopsychosis* are every bit as eligible as long as the picture remains separate.

> There was no question of *psychotizing* hysterics, but of offering those patients afflicted with this variety of psychosis the possibility of escaping from the *psychiatric over-alienation* of a false (and prevailing) schizophrenic attribution and of specifying the position to be held in order to withdraw them from this.[4]

Despite these noble intentions some criticism is due here. The fact that the rigorous application of a theoretical frame is the only solid way to escape a schizophrenic attribution does not seem to get through to the author.

Rather than pinning himself with the label of psychiatrist or analyst, we find patchworker to be more applicable. From his concern to save a certain picture from the pool of schizophrenia, he helps himself to scraps of theory and well-sounding labels to assume some level of authority. It escapes his notice that, because of this, his exposition is rendered void and loses credibility. The fact that he can neither properly gauge the extent of the criticism of the psychoanalyst Maleval with reference to his patchwork style (as at least is evident from his reply in which as yet he makes some conceptual concessions) confirms the caliber of this psychiatrist.[5] His sole merit consists in having indicated the prevalence of hysteria within the typically French *bouffée délirante*. That this is and was an adopted or a shared opinion may be shown from other references.[6]

In 1983 Chazaud publishes his by then twenty-year-old view again in a work on schizophrenia, paranoia and hysteria.[7] The signifier hysteria which looks attractive in the title is suddenly replaced in the book by hysterical psychosis. Although he does not indicate that he wishes to class all hysterics under this denominator we, in the meantime, know better.

The Reactive Hysterical Psychosis

Hirsch and Hollender set the American ball rolling in 1964. Their two articles on hysterical psychosis, respectively published in 1964 and 1969, are frequently quoted as pioneering articles. Their first contribution is worthy of this acclaim since it is the first to raise the subsequently repeatedly confirmed discrepancy between the praxis situation and the official doctrine as it is revealed in the journals. The second contribution, however, is no more than a listing of possible symptoms. The theoretical lacuna, which was already evident in the first article, is not given a content there either.[8]

So what is surprising is the fact that these psychiatrists based the importance of their first article on an observed discrepancy between day to day praxis and psychiatric theory. Before 1964, allegedly no specific study on the picture of hysterical psychosis was published in spite of its frequent clinical-diagnostic usage, as is shown from their inquiry within psychiatric circles. Hysteria therefore is obviously not as rare as is officially proclaimed.

Their description of hysterical psychosis:

> It is a state marked by a sudden and dramatic onset, temporally related to a profound upsetting event or circumstance. Its clini-

> cal manifestations include hallucinations, delusions, depersonalization, and grossly unusual behavior. Thought disorders, when they occur, are usually sharply circumscribed and very transient. Affectivity, if altered, is changed in the direction of volatility and not flatness. The acute episode seldom lasts longer than one to three weeks, and the eruption is sealed off so that there is practically no residue. The disorder is encountered most often in persons referred to as hysterical characters or hysterical personalities.[9]

The tableau of this clearly reactive hysterical psychosis, as is shown by the second article, may be the result of at least three distinct processes. The three thus selected types are: (1) hysterical psychosis as culturally sanctioned behavior, the transcultural aspect; (2) hysterical psychosis as (psychical) ersatz for the (somatic) conversion, a pseudopsychosis; and (3) true hysterical psychosis.

The first type was supposedly suggested to them by Langness. Basing himself on the first article by Hirsch and Hollender, this author professes that hysterical psychosis is being cross-culturally used in order to accomodate hard to classify forms of psychopathology. It is a residual category. In spite of this general and, in our opinion, usable conclusion to further investigate the status of so-called hysterical psychosis, Hirsch and Hollender believe that these non-autochthonous hysterical psychoses should be isolated in a separate pigeonhole. With this, they indicate that Langness produces nothing on *the* hysterical psychosis, but instead on one single type of hysterical psychosis. It is remarkable that Langness too refuses to define hysteria and psychosis and to situate hysterical psychosis within a psychiatric frame of reference. The already mentioned description of hysterical psychosis suffices as (an absolute) referent.[10]

This brings to mind the psychiatric tirade against Janet where not the elaboration of a theory but experimental research is important for the progress of psychiatry as a science. So the same tendency is present here and, if not a consequence, is an artifact of the rise of biological psychiatry, which, with the discovery of the psychopharmaca in the 1950s, has been constantly given hefty injections. A descriptive DSM-classification will obviously do for the biological psychiatrists, for the explanation of the syndromes is organically determined. The emphasis, observed here, on the description and repudiation of any theory, is fully understandable in the knowledge that *The American Journal of Psychiatry* is the official mouthpiece of The American Psychiatric Association; the latter organization introduced the DSM-classification.

A second, double trend of which Langness's article is a product, concerns the epidemiological and the transcultural tendency. Over the last few years it has become a psychiatric necessity to go looking for Western psychopathology outside of the typically Western civilization model and to go and study culturally bound *syndromes*.[11] The World Health Organization especially concerns itself with the first of these necessities. This kind of labor aiming at the prevention and control of the illness is lodged under social psychiatry which studies the role of the environment in the outbreak of disease. In 1975 for instance, a pilot study on schizophrenia was published. There too the main concern turns out to be a standardized, symptomatological approach; has schizophrenia got an identity of its own?[12]

The second type of hysterical psychosis is the psychic counterpart of the classical somatic conversion hysteria. Just what actually constitutes the distinction here with the real psychosis? The tableau is identical so that the authors now make use of mechanisms. In type two there is no question of an erased but rather of a fortified repression. Classically, it belongs under the dissociation but is actually part of the conversion phenomena. In old DSM-terms this type belongs both to dissociative and to conversion hysteria. This kind of classificatory difficulty can be read as an artifact of the artificial splitting up of hysteria into conversion and dissociative hysteria. Ultimately, every hysterical phenomenon must be provided with the epithet conversion or dissociative.[13]

Because they keep hammering away at true psychotic behavior, which automatically implies the existence of a falsehood, Hirsch and Hollender open the gates for labels such as pseudopsychosis and simulated psychosis. Such an interpretation constitutes the point of departure for the study of the Americans Bishop and Holt, who, in 1980, declare the hunt open for psychosis simulators, who have supplanted those of the organic disorders. The French contribution of Le Roux and Rochard takes a much more nuanced stand on the issue of pseudopsychosis. They use pseudopsychosis more in the sense of moments within a hysterical neurosis with a psychotic style.[14]

The third category then is the actual hysterical psychosis where the coping-mechanism fails, the ego-levees collapse and the ego is washed over by a temporary disruption. The authors refer to Freud's second article on the neuropsychoses of defense. This allows us to make the following remark. The contrast between type two and type three can be summed up as an antagonism between a reinforcement of the typically hysterical defense on the one hand and a failure of that same defense on the other. In one and the same clinical picture we find the two sides, as distinguished by Freud, of the wish-fantasy. The authors agree on a behavioral continuum commencing with the hysterical or histrionic character (a future DSM-notion) and finishing up with hysterical psychosis. This assumption, in our opinion, implies that the types can perfectly succeed one another from somatic across psychic conversion to hysterical psychosis. Since the distinction with schizophrenia is not theoretically founded either, this entity may supplement or complete the line without any problems. This implication too seems to pass by those who study hysterical psychosis in a theoretical vacuum.

Psychosis is the Sole Entity that can still take the Adjective Hysterical

Striking in all these publications, both American and French, is the absence of any theoretical frame. None of the just mentioned authors transcend the descriptive level, or succeed in conveying anything more than subjective impressions of so-called hysterical psychoses. Why, for example, the signifier *hysterical psychosis* and not *hysteria* is used, is not even touched upon. In view of the fact that virtually all other articles appeal to these French and American pioneers and scarcely surpass their level of theorizing, the marginality of this concept of hysterical psychosis, which—in its ambiguity—is unusable and non-specific, does not seem such a bad thing after all.

Anyway, Hirsch and Hollender find response with other Anglo-American psychiatrists who concur with them on the *Hirsch and Hollender paradigm* and who flesh it out further. What it does not create is a platform for discussion with regard to the theoretical status and the impact of this so-called hysterical psychosis. Martin, for example, applies their description on problematic, in particular *symbiotic* marriages. Hysterical psychosis could, in this interpretation, be the final way out of such a marriage. Psychosis appears as a temporary adjustment mechanism to certain living conditions. Separation and individuation are the problems with which these women are dealing.[15]

Cavenar and colleagues, in turn, speak of the neglected role of psychodynamics, which they concretize as the importance of sexual proposals. The authors conclude that hysterical psychosis is not reserved for hysterical personalities; in other personalities, however, there is no question of sexual causes. In 1972, Hollender already came to a comparable conclusion.[16] In this connection we can note that the picture of hysterical psychosis is not the only thing being detached from hysteria. The DSM-tendency towards the uncoupling of syndromes and personality disorders has as a consequence that conversion and dissociative disorders are also losing their official link with hysteria, again as a consequence of the DSM-doctrine.

Spiegel and Fink for their part wish to contribute their descriptive mite in a differential diagnostic fashion. Hysterical psychotics, in their opinion, can be hypnotized, schizophrenics cannot. They appeal to Freud and Janet and forget they were speaking of hysteria.[17] Fourteen years later Spiegel, together with the Dutchman van der Hart, is to publish an additional study on the therapeutical use of hypnosis in cases of hysterical psychosis, which, according to van der Hart, ties in closely with the non-typical psychosis (DSM-III-R) but which, because of its reactive character, should better be called reactive dissociative psychosis. This time the Dutch psychiatrist-hypnotherapist Breukink (1860-1928) is taken as a referent and every explicit link with hysteria has disappeared, although Breuer, Freud, and Janet are reviewed.[18]

Already in 1971 (eight years earlier than Spiegel), Siomopoulos attempted, on the basis of the description of Hirsch and Hollender, to distinguish schizophrenia from hysterical psychosis. His point of departure was the element which phenomenologically creates most confusion of all, the delusional-hallucinatory experience. He came up with the following differences: in hysterical psychosis the delusions are rectifiable and the hallucinations (pseudohallucinations?) are rather thoughts than perceptions.[19]

In 1985, Gift and others conduct an empirical study and come to the conclusion that none of the examined patients meet all the requirements as stipulated by Hirsch and Hollender, i.e., the criteria that can be distilled from the above description. They conclude that, no matter how interesting the concept may be, it has become obsolete after twenty years.[20] Such a frontal attack is to elicit a rebuff. In their reply Hollender and a certain Pattison have it in for the descriptive rigidity of Gift, who indeed is of the belief that only clinical phenomenology, i.e., the descriptive level, can offer operational criteria and make a further verification of the concept possible. For in their reply to the comments of Hollender and Pattison, Gift, and Strauss stress their DSM-inclination.[21] In our opinion, this talking across each other skirts the essence of what is central here. None of the parties involved is on to the fact that not one or another entity, but the goodwill of the observer—what we call his unconscious desire—is under discussion here. Not one description of a pathology can describe the individual patient or the subject which presents himself or herself with his or her pathology. For each subject is typified differently by his singularity, something which Charcot attempted to obviate by supplementing his type-hysteria with the numerous *formes frustes* or crude forms. This means that the allocation of a descriptive diagnosis is always an attribution; the observer recognizes something. It is not so much the description but rather the observer who is a determinant for the diagnostic process.[22] And the fact that hysterics perfectly know how to captivate the desire of the observer, is something which Charcot already experienced. The same comment also applies to the DSM-classification—a problem which the editors believe to have obviated by building in various axes, to the effect that several diagnoses not only become possible but are also plausible. Even then, however, the question remains as to the kind of subjective selection the observer carries through in objectifying the patient seated before him. The fact that the negative conclusion of Gift, who explicitly goes out to find the hysterical psychosis as introduced by Hirsch and Hollender, has been anticipated for so long, is an exemplification of the fact that one keeps reinforcing what one preliminary acknowledges. The recognition is a function of a preceding acknowledgement; each finding is a finding back.

According to the American group, hysterical psychosis is essentially a coping-mechanism, notably a reaction formation to a reality factum that is unbearable to the subject, which under no pretext can be called specific. In this, none of the members of the group mention the article by Richman and White, who study hysterical psychosis within the domestic circle and who supply us with interesting elements. The anxiety related to aggression, death, and actual object loss is central in the case fragments reported by them. The symptoms are family syntonic; the hysterical psychosis is the acting out of a family fantasy. Feelings of guilt are overpresent, just as are primary and secondary gain through sickness. The latter constitutes a first feature of hysterical psychosis. The four remaining are the acute onset, the absence of schizophrenic thought disruptions (the disrupted responses are to be related to the eliciting situations or they represent a tidal wave of associations), the object relation which is qualitatively and quantitatively different from schizophrenia, and the quick recovery. These authors have obviously spent more time listening to their patients, but they too attest to a harrowing lack of a basic theoretical frame.[23]

Hysterical psychosis in America is often used as a synonym for reactive psychosis, which is indeed a DSM-notion. This substitution speaks for itself, in view of the reactive typification of hysterical psychosis. The more capacious label, by the way, was already suggested in Cavenar's article. Important to this substitution is the disappearance of the explicit reference to hysteria, despite the fact that the premorbid personality is generally identified as hysterical.[24] With this, the American status of hysterical psychosis is on the same level as the French status, notably that of the *bouffée délirante.*

This neutralizing movement does not prevent certain psychiatrists from "reinventing" hysteria in a posterior movement. In this way, Steingard and Frankel proclaim that the *hysterical or brief reactive psychosis* is a repository for various disorders and psychopathologies. Their aim is to order this amalgam. On the basis of a very limited number of cases they thus identify the *brief reactive psychosis associated with dramatic dissociation*, which is clinically typified by hallucinations, conversion- and dissociative disorders, high suggestibility and therefore curable by means of (auto-)hypnosis. The exemplary case study has, as it were, been plucked straight out of Freud's book on hysteria.[25]

In the Scandinavian countries, too, the hysterical psychosis is given the status of reactive psychosis, although this label has a specific tradition there. The psychogenic, constitutional or reactive psychoses are considered as a separate clinical entity, which is detached from manic-depressive psychosis and schizophrenia. Especially Strömgren is an advocate for this group-entity, which is situated along the lines of Jaspers' way of thinking. Essential to the clinical typification is that these psychoses have been elicited and along their course are influenced by a trauma, hence the label of reactive psychoses. They are subdivided into affective psychoses, confusional psychoses and paranoid psychoses, respectively determined by situational conflicts, traumata that influence the perception of the environment, and traumata that affect the self-image. The hysterical psychoses, according to Refsum and Astrup, essentially come under the *confusional psychoses*, characterized by disorders of consciousness, which brings to mind the German tradition of twilight and confusional states. When Refsum and Astrup posit that hysterical psychoses are not always accompanied by alterations of consciousness, their clinical illustrations show that in those cases it concerns hysteria tout court. So the notion of hysterical psychosis here covers a broad specter.[26]

Hysterical psychosis is introduced, both by Follin as well as by Hirsch and Hollender, as a specific category in order to differentiate within the clinical group of the psychoses.

The Swiss Besso, the first psychiatrist who is able to present a comprehensive literature survey, comes to the following conclusion in his study of the relationship between hysteria and schizophrenia, in which he ultimately adopts the clinical notion of hysterical psychosis from Follin and company:

> And so we see that hysteria, long considered as the «neurosis par excellence» and as the best indication for a classical analysis, is more and more rich in structural psychotic elements, and following naturally from this, demands an extremely toilsome treatment; schizophrenia on the other hand, often considered as more or less inaccessible for therapy because of the absence of transference movements, these days appears on the scene with the best understanding of the determining mechanisms and can be approached better by means of psychotherapeutical techniques.[27]

With this, Besso confirms the increase of psychotiform hysteria, parallel to a theoretical evolution which favors the study and treatment of schizophrenia. Although he does not connect both observations that hysteria, in a manner of speaking, dresses after the latest fashion in psychiatry he does warn against too easy and too fast a conclusion to psychosis. And although he mentions the notion of hysterical psychosis, he does so in the first instance as a typification of the severe hysteria and not, like Follin, as a diagnostic label.

In this sense we can adduce Besso as one of the few psychiatrists who is careful not to act and implement too strictly the accepted psychosis paradigm and thus to become the advocate of hysteria, which does keep acquiring more and more psychotic features.

The fact that his warning goes unheeded is evident among others from the absence of this article in the already thin bibliography of the contributions on hysterical psychosis after 1969. Follin, as well as Hirsch and Hollender, remain the only permanent diagnostic benchmarks. Considering the increasing number of articles which mention the frequency of hysterical psychosis, it seems to us that hysteria in psychiatry is only given some measure of attention within the psychosis paradigm and by virtue of this is also given some right to exist. The fact that this right to exist only regards the intuitive clinical typification, while the ultimate diagnosis follows the official titling (reactive psychosis, psychogenic psychosis or *bouffée délirante*) proves the hysteria phobia of the psychiatric doctrine.

Hysterical Psychosis Lays both Claim To and Salves the Sick Spot of the Differential Diagnostics

Parallel to the entry of hysterical psychosis, a call is heard from the clinical psychiatric practice for more clarity on the differentiation between hysteria and schizophrenia. This cry particularly hails from psychiatrists who still acknowledge hysteria and who also give proof of a certain theoretical interest.

Numerous clinicians feel cornered between the theoretical assumption of a rigid distinction between neurosis and psychosis, i.e., hysteria and schizophrenia, on the one hand and a clinic which turns out to be comprising more and more clinical miscellaneous states, on the other hand. The fact that the new labels to tag these miscellaneous states (e.g., borderline and hysterical psychosis) are mere salve on a festering wound is shown from the doubts that each time accompany the discussion of the case fragments.

Even if the continuum concept which allows for the location of the entities between hysteria and psychosis is acknowledged and followed up, it does not solve the unease of the diagnostician and the therapist.

We stop for a brief while to call on the few hysteria adepts that still exist. In 1956 a clinical contribution is published in France on the differentiation between hysteria and schizophrenia. Although its main concern is the frequent evolution from a hysterical to a schizophrenic pathology, it presents a case of severe chronical hysteria, which, in spite of the repeated psychiatric diagnosis of catatonia, remains labelled as hysteria. Determinative, according to the authors, is the absence of real suffering, plus the fact that none of the material is offered gratuitously but only on demand. Therefore, they by no means preclude a further schizophrenic evolution.[28]

In 1964, the Brits Mallett and Gold mention the pseudoschizophrenic hysterical syndrome, a hysterical syndrome which brings to mind schizophrenia because of its severity. Although all described patients are classed as hysterical in the end, each of them is at least once diagnosed as schizophrenic over the course of their lengthy history as residential patients. This generally was the case after an acute episode of inaccessibility or after a long period of unsuccessful treatment. What is striking in the clinical observations is the recurrent use of psychopharmacal drugs after the schizophrenia diagnosis; the authors emphasize and describe the action of these psychopharmacal drugs as ranging from inefficient to pernicious. The only positive result is the curtailment of the acute episode. Apart from that the poor therapeutical results and the escalation of the problems into suicide attempts do not look good either. Five out of the thirteen considered cases take these attempts to an ultimately successful result. It should not be excluded in our opinion that there is a question here of a successful *passage à l'acte* as a lethal final point of a drawn out *acting out*. The patients in question in their complaint rather express the absence of a desire to live than a desire for death. The sketched picture also does not differ from what is currently given as the typification of the borderline patient.[29]

Five years later an article by Cottraux and others exemplifies how, from a restrictive definition of hysteria, one is almost compelled to introduce a borderline state. The authors claim to be certain of their diagnosis of hysteria, but when typical psychotic symptoms such as delusions and hallucinations emerge, they get stuck in a rut since hysteria is classically subdivided into the hysterical personality and the somatic conversion symptoms, and is determined in a Freudian sense by a conflict between the ego and the unconscious drives. For the delusions and hallucinations settle in as a consequence of a conflict between ego and reality, which supposedly is typically psychotic. In the absence of a theory on hysteria which explains the above constellations—the assumption of simulation does not explain the authentic anxiety either—the authors opt for the notion of hysterical psychosis.[30]

The Canadian Sirois, too, places the issue of hysteria center stage. Why does one hysterical patient become psychotic and the next does not? Thus this is a question as to the choice of symptoms. Anna O. and Dora go as the respective type examples. Sirois is the only psychiatrist who bothers to accurately read up on the Freudian references. All previous authors restrict themselves to a single quotation, adopted from Freud's second article on the neuroses of defense, in which there is a question of the overwhelming of the ego. Sirois, however, gets bogged down in hysterical psychosis as a radical failure of the defense, i.e., Freud's view in Manuscript K. Sirois is driven by the question of the symptom choice. After a forceful onset, the article lapses into the "promoting" of the borderline hysteric. Psychosis does not pertain to the standard construction of hysteria, but is reserved for the less cultivated patients.[31] We also observe this movement in other authors who still hold aloft the banner of hysteria. The seemingly psychotic forms of hysteria become, generally from the toilsomeness with which some measure of therapeutic result is attained, identified with primitive hysteria.[32]

Aubin, Bruno, and Giudicelli have the same thing wrong with them. These authors attempt to theoretically underpin an intuitively clinical distinction between psychotic hysteria and schizophrenia. Since they appeal too much to distinct and fragmentary theoretical references (adopted from psychoanalysis) and attempt to bring matters into line with each other, the result is more confusing than it is solidly founded. Rather than proceeding from one particular theoretical frame and situating the clinical manifestations of hysteria under discussion within that frame, they stick theoretical concepts, which more often than not appear out of the blue, to their clinical typifications.[33] With this, they exemplify a certain usage of psychoanalytic theory within psychiatric circles that are still seeking theoretical support outside of biology. In this usage, which is more the rule than the exception, the clinical picture is canonized and is adorned with a few loose psychoanalytic notions. These are void, since the underpinning psychoanalytic view of the psychism is not taken into account. On top of that this is framed within what Eitingon labelled the colonization of psychoanalysis by psychiatry.[34]

Just how little rigorous signifiers such as psychoanalysis and psychoanalyst are used is exemplified by Kovess who, in a survey into the use of the diagnosis hysteria among French psychiatrists, effortlessly classifies psychiatrists who have not had their training analysis, among the analysts. His results confirm the already intimated trends. An explicit distinction is made between the hysterical personality and hysterical neurosis and psychosis. Hysteria is pre-eminently the hysterical personality or the hysterical character. Conversion by no means implies the diagnosis of hysteria, and particularly the differential diagnosis with regard to psychosis poses problems.[35]

What is to be Concluded?

Hysteria is no longer an illness, but a personality or a character disorder. The conversion phenomena and the somatic disorders only occupy a minor position within the hysteria picture. The psychotic episodes and the depressive syndromes keep on winning ground. With that, hysteria à la Charcot has made its comeback, although it re-emerges onto the scene in a contemporary guise and with a contemporary signifier. Hysterical psychosis signifies hysteria as a mental disorder. As such it claims its place within the prevailing psychosis paradigm of which the borderline disorder delineates the boundaries. Garrabé posits that the emergence of hysterical psychosis, which we have not heard the last of yet, together with the interest in for example paranoia, is a reaction to the comprehensiveness of schizophrenia. Both are non-schizophrenic forms of psychosis.[36] The company to which hysteria belongs has also changed into that of theoretically neutral psychosis categories, i.e., psychogenic or reactive psychosis vs. the *bouffée délirante*. An even more general denominator under which hysterical psychosis is sometimes discussed, is that of the functional psychoses, i.e., those psychoses without a (as yet) demonstrable organic etiology.[37] Each of these diagnostic labels belongs to an official category.

The renowned psychiatrist-psychoanalyst Kammerer takes an exceptional position. He stresses his rejection of the diagnosis of hysterical psychosis in favor of the *psychose délirante aiguë* in a hysterical subject. What is exceptional is that he does so from the thesis that a subject is not necessarily lumbered with one and the same structure for the term of his natural life. The psychic structure may be altered, either temporarily or permanently, among others by organogenetic factors. This thesis perfectly meets the DSM-view which makes the combination of a hysterical personality with a brief reactive psychosis plausible. The difference with the latter lies in the theoretical assumption of the reversibility of the psychic structure, which Kammerer nonetheless does seem to nuance in the assumption that the acute delirious psychoses are reserved to subjects ridden with a *psycho-allergy.*[38]

In order to explain the syndromal reversal (from neurosis to psychosis), certain American authors adduce that the somatic disorders (one rather tends to speak of psychosomatic disorders than of conversion phenomena in the United States) have become suspect. Besides the admission facilities for psychotic patients, as well as the way in which mental disorders are regarded, have considerably improved, among others through the agency of the media. Mental illnesses offer a more tempting perspective than the classical neurotic disorders. With hysterical psychosis, therefore, malingering eternally linked with hysteria also makes its entry anew. This results in a distinction between true hysterical psychosis and pseudopsychosis, which is either or not equated with psychic conversion. Both the importance of the imitation of clinical pictures and thc alienating role of psychiatry are acknowledged and indicated, but things never quite get beyond a fraternal warning against simulators and a caution not to underestimate or neglect the effect of psychiatrization, which tends to give rise to erroneous schizophrenia diagnoses. Why certain subjects are more psychiatry-sensitive, and which mechanism props the imitation and the psychiatrization effect, are questions that are not asked. As far back as 1911 this is exactly where Freud placed the identification mechanism. For, in February 1911 Freud writes a letter to the Swede Bjerre in which he comments on the latter's successful analysis of a case of paranoia. That same day, he writes a letter to Jung in which he comes back to Bjerre's case study in the following wording, "It seems to be a case of hysterical paranoia, something which, I tend to think, actually exists, identical in form to real paranoia, but reducible because it is based on identification with a genuine paranoiac."[39]

The usage of hysterical psychosis is just as little unequivocal as that of the borderline. In the former case the differentiation with regard to schizophrenia is still raised, but that with regard to borderline is carefully avoided. Not that the assumption of one label excludes the usage of the other. The emergence of a notion such as borderline hysteria leads the way of compromise and confirms the hypothesis that quite a substantial number of hysteria patients find accommodation within the borderline group.

Despite the phenomenal number of pages devoted to the typification of hysterical psychosis and the differentiation of hysteria and schizophrenia, the usefulness of the psychiatric results seems minimal, for lack of a rigorous use of a theoretical frame of reference.[40] The (feeling of) malaise remains. But how are things with the contribution of the psychoanalysts?

Notes

1. S. Follin et al. (1961), Cas cliniques de psychoses hystériques, *Evolution Psychiatrique*, 26, pp. 257-286. Fourteen years before, Follin published the elaborate version of one of these case studies under the label of oneiric psychosis: S. Follin (1947), Une psychose oniroïde de culpabilité (aspects cliniques de la sociogenèse des troubles mentaux), *Evolution Psychiatrique*, 12, pp. 61-95.
2. N. de Boucaud & T. Demangeat (1962), Les psychoses hystériques: une tentative de réhabilitation, *Journal de médecine de Bordeaux*, 139, 8, p. 962. Nine years after the event de Boucaud, together with a few colleagues, again brings the theme of hysterical psychosis into the psychiatric limelight: N. de Boucaud et al. (1971), Psychoses délirantes aiguës et structure hystérique, in *Comptes rendus du Congrès de Psychiatrie et de Neurologie de langue française, Caen, 5-10 juillet 1971*, Paris, Masson.
3. Chaslin, together with Régis, belonged to the group surrounding Séglas, which particularly studied mental confusion. Chaslin's work is characterized by an emphasis on description, the lack of a theory on pathogenesis, and a mistrust of nosographical categories. (v.sup.)
4. J. Chazaud (1981), A propos du concept de «psychose hystérique», *Information Psychiatrique*, 57, 1, p. 51. Author's translation. There he takes up his part again from the article from 1961, for which he awards Follin with the mastership.
5. J.-C. Maleval (1981), *Folies hystériques et psychoses dissociatives*, Paris, Payot; J. Chazaud (1981).
6. See, for example, P. Bail (1967), Les moments psychotiques de

l'existence hystérique, doctor's thesis, University of Paris.

7. J. Chazaud (1983), *Hystérie, schizophrénie, paranoia*, Domaines de la psychiatrie, Toulouse, Privat.
8. S. Hirsch & M. Hollender (1964), Hysterical Psychosis, *American Journal of Psychiatry*, 120, pp. 1066-1074; S. Hirsch & M. Hollender (1969), Hysterical Psychosis: Clarification of the Concept, *American Journal of Psychiatry*, 127, 7, pp. 909-915.
9. S. Hirsch & M. Hollender (1969), p. 909.
10. L. Langness (1967), Hysterical Psychosis: The Cross-Cultural Evidence, *American Journal of Psychiatry*, 124, 2, pp. 143-152.
11. See, for example, W. Tsoi (1973), The Ganser Syndrome in Singapore: A Report on Ten Cases, *British Journal of Psychiatry*, 123, pp. 567-572; A. Mikhial (1973), Exotic Syndromes, *Foreign Psychiatry*, 2, 3, pp. 55-84; M. Benadiba et al. (1980), Quelques problèmes particuliers posés par la pathologie mentale des transplantés nord-africains, *Annales médico-psychologiques*, 138, 1, pp. 88-94; M. Weller (1988), Hysterical Behaviour in Patriarchal Communities: Four Cases, *British Journal of Psychiatry*, 152, pp. 687-695.
12. World Health Organization (1975), *Schizophrenia: a Multinational Study*, Public Health Papers no. 63, Geneva, World Health Organization.
13. By way of example we refer to the discussion on the nature of the (hysterical) hallucination and to the discussion regarding the status of pseudodementia. See, for example, G. Asaad & B. Shapiro (1986), Hallucinations: Theoretical and Clinical Overview, *American Journal of Psychiatry*, 143, 9, p. 1090; F. Mc Kegney (1967), Auditory Hallucinations as a Conversion Symptom: A Theoretical Proposal with Two Case Illustrations, *Comprehensive Psychiatry*, 8, pp. 80-89; F. Mc Kegney (1987), Hallucinations as Conversion Symptoms, letter to the editor, *American Journal of Psychiatry*, 144, 5, p. 696; G. Asaad & B. Shapiro (1987), Hallucinations as Conversion Symptoms. Drs. Asaad and Shapiro Reply, letter to the editor, *American Journal of Psychiatry*, 144, pp. 696-697; P. Liberini et al. (1993), What is the Incidence of Conversion Pseudodementia, letter to the editor, *British Journal of Psychiatry*, 162, pp. 124-125.
14. E. Bishop & A. Holt (1980), Pseudopsychosis: A Reexamination of the Concept of Hysterical Psychosis, *Comprehensive Psychiatry*, 21, 2, pp. 150-161; A. Le Roux & L. Rochard (1984), Contribution à

l'étude des rapports entre névrose hystérique et psychose schizophrénique, *Annales médico-psychologiques*, 142, 7, pp. 975-988.

15. P. Martin (1971), Dynamic Considerations of the Hysterical Psychosis, *American Journal of Psychiatry*, 128, 6, pp. 745-748.
16. J. Cavenar et al. (1979), A clinical Note on Hysterical Psychosis, *American Journal of Psychiatry*, 136, 6, pp. 830-832 M. Hollender & Ch. Welles (1972), Hysterical Psychosis, *Journal of the National Association of Private Psychiatric Hospitals*, 4, 3, pp. 36-38; M. Gelder et al., *Oxford Textbook of Psychiatry*, 2nd ed., Oxford Medical Publications, Oxford, New York, Melbourne, pp. 202-214.
17. D. Spiegel & R. Fink (1979), Hysterical Psychosis and Hypnotizability, *American Journal of Psychiatry*, 136, 6, pp. 777-781.
18. O. van der Hart & D. Spiegel (1993), Hypnotic Assessment and Treatment of Trauma-induced Psychoses, *International Journal of Clinical and Experimental Hypnosis*, 41, 3, pp. 191-209: O. van der Hart et al. (1993), From Hysterical Psychosis to Reactive Dissociative Psychosis, *Journal of Traumatic Stress*, 6, 1, pp. 43-64.
19. V. Siomopoulos (1971), Hysterical psychosis: Psychopathological Aspects, *British Journal of Medical Psychology*, 44, pp. 95-100.
20. T. Gift et al. (1985), Hysterical Psychosis: An Empirical Approach, *American Journal of Psychiatry*, 142, 3, pp. 345-347. The authors place the American hysterical psychosis next to the European reactive psychosis and emphasize the cross-cultural aspect.
21. M. Hollender & E. Pattison (1986), Why no Cases of Hysterical Psychosis?, letter to the editor, *American Journal of Psychiatry*, 143, 8, pp. 1070-1071; T. Gift & J. Strauss (1986), Drs. Gift and Strauss Reply, letter to the editor, *American Journal of Psychiatry*, 143, 8, p. 1071.
22. Cf. Hummelen's comment with regard to the diagnosis of borderline.
23. J. Richman & H. White (1970), A Family Review of Hysterical Psychosis, *American Journal of Psychiatry*, 127, 3, pp. 280-285.
24. See, for example, J. Weiss & J. Rhoads (1979), Brief Reactive Psychosis: A Psychodynamic Interpretation, *Journal of Clinical Psychiatry*, 40, 10, pp. 440-443; J. Modestin & K. Bachmann (1992), Is the Diagnosis of Hysterical Psychosis Justified?, *Comprehensive Psychiatry*, 33, 1, pp. 17-24.
25. S. Steingard & F. Franckel (1985), Dissociation and Psychotic Symptoms, *American Journal of Psychiatry*, 142, 8, pp. 953-955.

26. J. Anderssen & H. Laerum (1980), Psychogenic Psychoses, *Acta Psychiatrica Scandinavica*, 62, pp. 331-342; H. Refsum & C. Astrup (1982), Hysteric Reactive Psychoses: A Follow-up, *Neuropsychobiology*, 8, pp. 172-181.
27. L. Besso (1969), Contribution à l'approche psychodynamique du problème des rapports entre l'hystérie et la schizophrénie, *Archives Suisses de Neurologie, Neurochirurgie et de Psychiatrie*, 105, 1, p. 126. Author's translation.
28. C. Müller et al. (1956), Hystérie ou schizophrénie, *Encéphale*, 45, pp. 256-266.
29. S. Gold & B. Mallett (1964), A Pseudoschizophrenic Hysterical Syndrome, *British Journal of Medical Psychology*, 37, pp. 59-70. For an elaborate discussion on the Lacanian concepts *passage à l'acte* and *acting out*, we refer to an article by J. Quackelbeen (1988), Eduquer contre le passage à l'acte, analyser l'acting out?, *Scientia Paedagogica Experimentalis*, 25, 2, pp. 29-41.
30. J. Cottraux et al. (1969), La notion de psychose hystérique, *Journal de Médecine de Lyon*, 50, pp. 959-965.
31. F. Sirois (1977), La psychose hystérique, *Acta Psychiatrica Belgica*, 77, p. 225.
32. See, for instance, M.-D. Bruno & G. Maurey (1979), L'hystérique délire toujours, *Etudes psychothérapeutiques*, 38, pp. 287-292; M.-D. Bruno (1979), L'hystérique délirant, doctor's thesis, University of Paris.
33. B. Aubin et al. (1977), Schizophrénie et/ou hystérie, *Etudes Psychothérapeutiques*, 28, pp. 81-90; S. Giudicelli (1986), Hystéries et psychoses, *Evolution Psychiatrique*, 51, 3, pp. 639-669.
34. E. Roudinesco (1986), *Histoire de la psychanalyse en France*, vol. 1, Paris, Seuil, p. 412. This reproof was specifically addressed to the French group *Evolution Psychiatrique* but unfortunately made itself generally valid. (cf. Chazaud's patchwork method).
35. V. Kovess (1982), Le diagnostic de l'hystérie: enquête auprès de psychiatres français, *Information Psychiatrique*, 58, 10, pp. 1239-1250.
36. J. Garrabé (1981), Monopsychose?, *Information Psychiatrique*, 57, 1, pp. 45-46.
37. See, for example, R. Kendell (1988), Other Functional Psychoses, in R. Kendell & A. Zealy (eds.), *Companion to Psychiatric Studies*, 4th

ed., Edinburgh, Churchill Livingstone, pp. 362-371.

38. Th. Kammerer & R. Wartel (1986), Dialogue sur les diagnostics, in R. Gori et al. (eds.), *La Querelle des diagnostics*, coll. Cliniques, Paris, Navarin, pp. 68-71.

39. J. Chazaud & A. de la Payonne-Lidbom (1988), A propos d'une correspondance récemment découverte entre Freud et Bjerre, *Frénésie*, 5, p. 109; W. Mc Guire (ed.) (1974), *The Freud-Jung Letters*, Princeton, NJ, Princeton University Press, p. 391, letter of 12 February 1911. From an earlier letter to Jung, dated 4 April 1909, it is evident for that matter that Freud already spoke at an earlier stage of the imitation of psychotic disorders. Additionally, we refer to the chapter on Charcot in which the mechanism of the imitation was extensively discussed.

40. A recent example of how little transferable the results of such an approach are, is provided by M. Steyaert. The work of this French psychiatrist is, however, highly interesting from a clinical point of view, since he provides the reader (by means of recurring themes and clinical fragments) a well nuanced picture of the hysterical delusion and by the same token also exemplifies the singular relation of the hysteric to knowledge and to the master figure. M. Steyaert (1992), *Hystérie, folie et psychose*, Paris, Les Empêcheurs de penser en rond.

11
Psychoanalysis, too, Renounces Hysteria

Hysteria Falls into Disrepute with Postfreudian Psychoanalysis

The most important work of Otto Fenichel (1898-1946), a German psychoanalyst who went into exile to America, is *The Psychoanalytic Theory of Neuroses.* It is recorded as one of the few generally accepted psychoanalytic textbooks and, certainly during the 1940s and 1950s being the heyday of American psychoanalysis, an important work of reference. In his so-called bible of the neuroses Fenichel, who was known as an analyst who (still) referred to Freud, devotes a surprisingly small number of pages to hysteria, which was, after all, the cradle of Freudian psychoanalysis.[1] In it hysteria becomes anxiety hysteria and conversion hysteria is reduced to a conversion syndrome, i.e., a historic symptom constellation which is determined by repressed experiences from the past of the hysterical person(ality). Under conversion we find a recital of possible symptoms. Next to the classical somatic conversion phenomena Fenichel distinguishes the hysterical hallucination, the hysterical dream state, and the disorders of the consciousness or hypnotic disorders.

The theoretical framing proves to be a mild rehash of Freud's original theory in which a clear-cut shift is revealed in the use of concepts. The multiple personality in Fenichel's opinion, for example, is the acme of the multiple hysterical identifications, which he defines as based on identical etiological needs. In the same context Freud spoke of an identification on the basis of a certain communality. With regard to the hysterical hallucination Fenichel argues that it was a perception at the time of the repression. This is in contrast to the schizophrenic hallucination—a substitute for a lost perception. The disorders of consciousness too, as well as the daydreams acted out in the dream states, he owes to repression, without further reasoning the singularity of this repression.

A second impoverishment with regard to Freud's theory (apart from the impairment to his theory) is connected with the elimination of the element of particularity or singularity. Freud always stressed the overdetermination of every unconscious formation. In his view, every dream or symptom has more than one single meaning and each of these (possible) meanings can only be discovered through the associations of the patient. Hence, the meanings of a symptom are always dependent on the patient and are always singular. Now, in Fenichel's work every conversion symptom gets its fixed interpretation, which, just like Jung's dream symbolics, goes against the particularity of every unconscious formation, whether a symptom or a dream.

In the chapter on character disorders Fenichel's choice is explicit. The ego, which is determined by the character and the personality, is the new research area. In his opinion this area implies the broadening of the theory of Freud which in essence is a theory on the unconscious. Still, it is indebted to Freudian psychoanalysis in view of the fact that the importance of the study of consciousness was only demonstrated via the roundabout way of the unconscious. Causes for the development of this ego-psychology are the resistance analysis and the increasing number of personality disorders. Just how massively the character or the ego replaces the unconscious, is evident from its description where character reflects the historic development of the individual.

Concerning the psychoses, apart from manic-depressive psychosis there is only the question of schizophrenia, which is extensively discussed. This confirms the supposition that the Postfreudians have not so much disseminated Freud's teachings rather than Bleuler's schizophrenia. Neither paraphrenia nor paranoia are mentioned and hysterical psychosis or amentia as well as the reactive psychotic episodes come under the schizophrenic episodes of brief duration according to Fenichel. And this notwithstanding the fact that Freud has always juxtaposed amentia against schizophrenia. The borderline cases (the schizoid character disorder and the schizophrenia mitis or ambulant schizophrenia) are also discussed under the heading of schizophrenia. They testify to a psychotic disposition.

In Fenichel's work we observe a number of distinctly anti-Freudian theses, which at that moment had already swamped the American market. In this way he appeals when possible to organic-physiological backgrounds and places emphasis on the ego and on the self-consciousness. The distinction between neurosis and psychosis is founded on the basis of their relation to reality; both the schizophrenic and the neurotic regress as a consequence of a conflict between ego and reality. The profoundity of the regression is what determines the difference. Additionally, it must be said that the neurotic adheres to reality whereas the schizophrenic breaks with reality. The reading of Freud's articles from 1924 shows that this elaboration is a violation of his final statements on the relation of neurosis, respectively psychosis, to reality. The minimal conclusion which can be drawn from these articles is that both with neurosis as with psychosis the relation with reality has been disrupted and that this disruption cannot be seized by means of the typification partial vs. total disruption.[2]

Within Fenichel's own analytic doctrine, but in a broader sense also within the Postfreudian psychoanalysis in general, both hysteria and mad hysteria are allocated a highly restricted and measured position. Hallucinations and dream states barely just fit into the hysteria picture, acute psychoses by definition come under the heading of schizophrenia.[3]

The ego- and the self-doctrine, parallel to the development of the object relations, are the American trendsetters. From the

1950s the official psychoanalysis, the one directed by the IPA, that is, is dominated by the development of *ego-psychology*. American Postfreudian psychoanalysis becomes a psychology of the ego. This psychology bases itself on a thorough reinterpretation of Freud's second topical representation of the psyche, elaborated in his writing of 1923 on the ego and the Id.[4] As Milton Klein puts it, "Psychoanalytic ego psychology is a psychoanalytic theory attempting to mate a new ego and an old id."[5]

James Strachey, editor and translator of Freud's works in English (the Standard Edition), lays down the foundation for this new interpretation. Heinz Hartmann (1894-1970), Ernst Kris (1900-1957) and Rudolph Löwenstein are the leading figures within this ego-psychology during the 1950s.[6] They pass as orthodox Freudians. In substitution for the omnipotence of the unconscious they are to rethink, rationalize and synthesize Freud's metapsychology proceeding from the model of experimental and cognitive psychology and afford the autonomous ego the dominant position. This ego has little to do any more with the Freudian ego from the second topical representation of the psyche. With the allocation to the ego of a synthesis function, it acquires a different status and by the autonomous position it is granted within the concept of the psyche it is also awarded a position which deviates from Freud's. With this, Freud's comment with regard to the third blow to the universal narcissism of man very specifically applies to these Postfreudians. This is confirmed by the fact that the crucial concept of the unconscious has virtually disappeared altogether from psychoanalytic nomenclature.[7]

Notions such as ego-strength and self-consciousness apply as basic concepts of this type of psychoanalysis, which also presses ahead in the other departments of the IPA. The study of the narcissistic and the borderline disorders, as well as the problems with hysterical patients, perfectly fit into this ego-policy.

Those who are fixated on the developmental disorders of the ego and who employ a deficient view of psychopathology cannot hear the unconscious speak. For, the unconscious is only there for those who listen out for it.

The notion of object relation too, never used by Freud and strongly criticized by Lacan in the 1950s, has become self-evident and entwined with the concept of transference to such an extent that it virtually wipes out the latter. The relation of the ego with the objects in the outer world is central and the development level of these relations is a measure for the degree of adjustment of the ego. Of course there is hardly any question of psychic reality and of the subject as a subject of the unconscious.[8]

Suddenly it becomes clear why hysteria is being kept out of this psychology. Freud owed his discovery of the unconscious and of psychoanalysis to his hysterical patients to whom he opened his ears and by whom he let himself be instructed. In keeping at bay the discourse or the speaking of the unconscious, hysteria is automatically kept off, too. The Postfreudians no longer listen, but are guilty of ego-building; the deficient ego of the patient is patched up by the mature ego of the analyst.[9] A typical example is the fact that they have some difficulty adopting a non-interpretative attitude, which to them is equal to doing nothing for the cure. The question of the hysteric is not central, but their model-knowledge with the own strong ego as a referent.

In this way, the hysterical question is nipped in the bud and the hysteria rigidifies. This is a first logical consequence which ends up in new diagnoses—that of the borderline and of the narcissistic disorder.[10] In his critical analysis of the theory of Bergeret, Demoulin reorients his view by the position taken by fellow analysts regarding the psychoanalytic notion of the borderline. First of all, that of Leguil, who asserts that the borderline is the neurotic who puts up a fight against normalization where psychoanalysis degrades itself to the level of normative therapy. Then there is Silvestre who specifies that what is at hand is hysteria which has become unanalyzable by the orientation (turned orthopaedic) of psychoanalysis. We can also refer here to a statement from 1984 from the current leading figure among the

Lacanian psychoanalysts, Jacques-Alain Miller.

> ...is [it] not a necessity that the psychoanalyst has forgotten about the unconscious, which already made his practice «grow pale», in order to only be able to greet the present-day forms of hysteria under the heading of «borderline»?[11]

A second implication is that hysterical patients seek other therapists to question, particularly the sympathetic schizophrenia therapists, a minority within the IPA.

When we go through the last twenty annual volumes of *The International Journal of Psycho-Analysis*, it appears that extremely few articles indeed have been published on hysteria.[12] At the International Congress for Psychoanalysis in 1973 a panel discussion was dedicated to hysteria. It turns out, among others, that quite a large number of psychoanalysts define hysteria as a defensive mechanism to keep primitive, psychotic, and non-sexual anxieties at bay and under control. Hysteria notably becomes primitive, psychotic, and asexual, i.e., a return to the psychiatric view of hysteria from before Freud.

> We can understand why, for example, psychoanalysts claim not to find hysterics any more in their consulting rooms: patients may be hysterics but *since the theory looks for something else, it also finds something else*. One could take this even further: we can turn around, look at the cases of hysteria treated by Freud, and maintain that they were in fact more disturbed, borderline patients.[13]

A warning which by then had already been a fait accompli for a long time.

The borderline and narcissistic disorders are respectively defined as disorders of the ego and as disorders of the self. For the borderline therapy is directed at improving ego functions, for the narcissist at self-esteem through the mirror transference. With that, first of all, the already precarious distinction between the ego and the self has been broached.[14] Secondly, there is the delineation of the borderline with regard to the psychoses and with regard to the neuroses which yields problems. Depending on the author and the pertaining definition of the category either one or the other side of the differentiation is emphasized.

The Briton Kohon is one of the few to criticize the just described theoretical swing-round, an impoverishing definition of Freudian psychoanalysis. More specifically, he criticizes the desexualization of Freud's theory on the neuroses, namely that the neurotic conflict is generally defined as a conflict between actual sexual impulses and Freud's psychosexuality degenerates into mere genitality. In spite of the fact that the ego- and self culture have blown across from America to France, according to Kohon, French analysts have less problems in finding hysterical patients than their Anglo-American colleagues. One such author, for example, is de Mijolla who mainly directs himself against his English speaking colleagues, who only sparsely make use of the signifier of hysteria.[15] Within the French strongholds of the IPA these critical comments are situated in the margin.

Benign Schizophrenia and Malign Hysteria

If hysteria initiated the analytical process, it also, by the same token, delineated its boundaries. The hysterical population may have depleted over the years, but it continues to play tricks on analysts. In Postfreudian circles there has been a marked tendency over the last couple of decades to emphasize the curability of schizophrenia and the unanalyzability of hysteria.[16] Dora and to a lesser extent Emmy von N. have become the type examples of this unruly hysteric. As the mentioning of Dora could already make us suspect, the comments particularly refer to the relationship between the analyst and the (one being) analyzed, notably to the handling of the transference in the cure, which is one-sidedly reduced to the object relations of the patient. The general tendency in typifying the hysterical object relations goes from oedipal to pre- or pseudo-oedipal. These object relations, more precisely their so-called oedipal or preoedipal character, are so central that the diagnosis is adjusted accordingly. As Satow points out:

> In fact, the expanding interest in the preoedipal period may be the reason that many therapists today claim that they are getting more and more borderline patients and fewer and fewer neurotics (i.e., hysterics).[17]

The unruly hysterics become the borderlines, as is evident from the reinterpretation of the cases from Freud's studies on hysteria. Another clue in that direction is the tardiness and the hesitation of the analysts to take on the treatment of borderline patients. In spite of the fact that they make up the large majority of the clientele, they are certainly not sought-after patients for they refuse to work in the cure. And here, too, the hallmark of the authenticity of hysteria (the hysteric demands, even orders the other to work) is no longer recognized under this refusal to work.[18] This adjustment does not work in the reverse way. In the face of the sometimes thaumaturgical healings of schizophrenic patients, one does not rethink the diagnosis as a possibly severe form of hysteria.

Hysteria has fallen from grace. The balance of the inherently dual attitude towards hysteria, which we already mentioned several times, proves to be tilting towards the rejection of hysterical patients. Contrary to this is the therapeutic interest of the analysts in schizophrenia, which sometimes takes on the air of a furor sanandi, and is more highly thought of. With this, the *bad hysteric* is opposed against the *good schizophrenic*.[19] With the treatment of the latter still some credit can be gained:

> The psychoanalyst can thus turn the psychotic into his professional ideal ... To cure a psychotic, there is a creative effort which complies with the noblest of objectives of science and medicine.[20]

The negative stance with regard to hysteria is amply demonstrated in an article by Zetzel on the population of the so-called good hysterics, out of which she distills the true hysteric, ready for analysis. This ideal hysteric—Zetzel's article, classed as the ultimate hysteria reference, exclusively speaks of women—is characterized by a genital oedipal situation, while the lowest of the four categories distinguished by her, are typified by a pseudo-oedipal and a pseudogenital symptomatology. These hysterical patients are hardly or not at all suited for analysis. Other authors express this division as genital as opposed to oral hysteria, or oedipal vs. preoedipal hysteria, depending on the dominant mode of the object relations and the profoundness of the regression to fixation points in the ego development. The female patients who meet the requirements of this ideal model are rare. Malign hysteria, of which the defense mechanisms demonstrate analogies with those of the psychotic and the borderline groups, now rules the roost. The fact that the description of this last group shows considerable similarity with the aforementioned psychiatric typification of the borderline patient gives rise to the suspicion that quite a substantial number of these unruly hysterics are labelled elsewhere with the diagnosis of borderline.[21]

That others act upon Zetzel's typification can be read, for example, in Stewart's report of an analysis of a hallucinating hysteric, a rare contribution, by the way, from the *International Journal of Psycho-Analysis.* Stewart locates his woman patient between levels three and four, notably with the virtually unanalyzable, and labels her as a hysterical, depressive character.[22] Kohon mentions this case study as an example of a hysterical woman who did not come out of the first, i.e., the phallic-oedipal stage of the female oedipus complex.[23] Stewart's way of typifying his woman patient suggests that he thinks that those, like him, who still dare commence an analysis with this kind of "minor" female patients should really be showered with flowers.

At two distinct moments during the treatment, the behavior of his patient (more particularly the sudden introduction of drawings) reminds Stewart of two testimonies of a psychoanalytic treatment of a "schizophrenic" woman patient. It concerns the bestsellers *The Hands of the Living God* and *Mary Barnes*, two examples of creative treatments of clearly hysterical patients.[24] In his report Stewart does not elaborate on these references, i.e., the role of the model, but he seems unmistakably enchanted by the comparability of these three female patients. He emphasizes his own perseverance and creativity in conducting this difficult cure. In our view, the transference is cultivated in such a way that numerous *acting outs* are the consequence. It is clear that his woman patient is instructing *him*. And as a good hysteric she does not fail to rub his nose in it.

An important merit of this article, therefore, is that it indicates that the analyzability of the female patient is rather a subjective matter than an objective factum expressible in terms of object relations. More precisely, it shows that the analyzability is a function of the position taken up by the analyst on whether or not he allows himself to be "seduced" into analysis.

The Insidious Rise of the Hysterics within the Psychosis Paradigm

In 1988 Frosch proposes to drop the ambiguous term of borderline personality and to introduce the *psychotic character*. His argument originates in the fact that generally the notion of neurosis is used as a reference in defining the notion of borderline. As the notion of borderline is ambiguous, he relinquishes it. Proceeding from the alternative of the psychotic frame of reference, he opts for the psychotic character. He does not, however, place psychotic character with reference to the notion of psychosis.[25]

So Frosch strongly opposes certain early authors who, in imitation of Freud, take neurosis as the basic model for psychosis and borderline. The group of patients he has in mind is characterized by the perennial threat of fragmentation, i.e., of dissolution of the self. It concerns weakly structured personalities who decompensate at the slightest shortcoming. He puts this fragmentation before the *splitting*, a mechanism postulated by Kernberg (the American basic author for psychoanalytic borderline) as being innate to the borderline. In view of the fact that quite a number of patients stay outside of psychosis their whole life and if they should land in it they sojourn there only briefly, Frosch does not emphasize the clinical picture but rather the psychotic process. This process is responsible for the impression these patients leave upon their environment: chaotic, disorganized, and unstable.[26]

This article is symptomatic of the prevailing malaise in the psychoanalytic field where the hard-to-manage transference was the cause for the introduction of the borderline (first as a tentative indication). It resulted in novel, adapted forms of the analytical therapy. And oddly enough, borderline-studies are uncommonly unanimous on this particular therapeutic point. However, there is a supporting theory constructed around this that ossified the issue. Since the patients in question prove to find benefit from an energy wrecking, supportive therapy they become captives of this new label. The settled hysterics are encaged within a boundary-paradigm that continues to gain in purport.

This brings to mind Pontalis' lament on the altered psychoanalytic situation. He asks himself whether the analyzed or the analysts have changed but formulates no reply. The answer, however, is already contained in the question and has all to do with the part of transference and the theory on the relationship between the analyzed and the analyst, i.e., the mirror transference in which the analyst does not hold up the mirror of language before the analyzed, but assumes the position of mirror himself. The fact that this lamentation ends in the observation that Freud's hysterics can now effortlessly pass as borderlines, renders further commentary superfluous. The hysterics of the past have become the borderlines of the present.[27] The introduction of narcissistic disorders further delineates the development of events. The borderlines sweep into the realm of psychosis, notably that of Freud's narcissistic neuroses. There they become the so-called benevolent clones of the psychotic patients.

Quaintly enough, hysteria in this new domain suddenly turns out to be attractive again to some as the hysteric reveals herself as a model-schizophrenic patient giving quite a number of new therapies the light of life. With respect to this, Zarifian brings a sublime anecdote with the thaumaturgical healing of schizophrenic patients by means of hemodialysis. It is obvious that most schizophrenic patients were in fact hysterics. Furthermore, it again proves that hysteria not only lends itself to the realization of the desire of the physician in attendance but also to that of the analyst.[28]

From the 1950s psychoanalysts develop not only adapted forms of therapy for borderlines but also for schizophrenics. Every single one of them prides himself on his psychosis speciality. It is our belief that each of these therapists has quite a fair number of hysterical patients among their clients.

A leading figure who performed pioneering labor in treating schizophrenic patients is Gisela Pankow. After her psychiatric training under Kretschmer, she came to France in 1950 to present her analytic psychotherapy with psychotics, which yields surprisingly good results. Meanwhile, she has many articles to her credit that particularly testify to a marked therapeutic concern, explicitly concentrated on schizophrenic patients. Her theory, which in her first works she borrows from Freud and in her later efforts also from Lacan, can, in fact, hardly be attributed this status. Her therapeutic actions are more intuitive than they are theoretically founded (see Chazaud), which, of course, raises the question as to the transferability of such a method.

According to Pankow, there are two paths open for the study of psychosis: (1) from the outside, which contributes to the development of psychiatric nosography and (2) from the inside which consists in taking the patient by the hand in order to accompany him in his descent into hell (a reference to the highly popular regression mechanism). She opts for the latter, thus forsaking her neuro-psychiatric training and responding to what her patients have taught her. In spite of the fact that she calls herself an analyst, her psychiatric training determines the diagnosis.[29]

The track which Pankow covers with the schizophrenics, the

dynamic structuring of the body image, proceeds from the fragmentation, in order to arrive, via the recognition of the body image, at the acceptance of a unisexual body. A second step is the sexualization. This method, which distinguishes two essential steps, is entirely analogous to the therapy for borderline patients, as proposed by the French borderline specialist Bergeret. In a first instance the patients are brought up to the classical-neurotic, i.e., the genital-oedipal level, from where in a second instance a classical cure can be initiated.[30]

Pankow is one of the few who operate within the psychoanalytic field and yet simultaneously distinguishes *hysterical psychosis*. The difference between nuclear and peripheral psychosis, to which schizophrenia and hysterical psychosis respectively belong, is formulated in terms of disorders of two functions that actually make up the two levels of the body image. The first function of the body image concerns the body as a spatial structure, as a form or Gestalt. *Le corps vécu* or *le corps ressenti* then comprises, next to the body as a formally discrete unity, the body as an inhabited spatiality. The second function of the body image is the level of *le corps reconnu*, the level of the psychic sexualization. The initial diagnosis is based on a verification of the prevalence of these functions in the patient. In so far as both functions have been afflicted or destroyed, we are dealing with schizophrenia; if the affliction or the destruction only applies to the second function, it is hysterical psychosis which is present. The two phases of the dynamic structuring of the body image for psychosis then take the restoration of both functions as their objective. In this way the treatment, conducted via trial and error, can ultimately open up the path for a classical cure.[31]

Her view of hysterical psychosis is interesting, in particular where she brings in the father. Typical of this category, says Pankow, are the weakness and the perversion of the father. The way in which she describes the failure of the father, as well as the perverse connotation, bring to mind Freud's first theory on hysteria in which the father is allocated a similar role by the patients themselves, and which Freud questions in the end. The invalidated father is taken seriously again by Pankow although now she acknowledges this notion not for hysteria but for hysterical psychosis.[32]

A second figure, mainly popular in America, is John Rosen who during the 1950s developed *direct analysis* for the benefit of schizophrenic patients. In the description of his method his slight analytic-theoretical rigidity rings through. He describes his method as a psychological technique for the treatment and healing of psychotic patients. His *furor sanandi* can be measured by the introduction to his work in which he states that against the encountered excessive phenomena he observed his own incompetence and sometimes felt frustrated. However, thanks to his work, desperate cases have transformed themselves. These people have been cured and were able to take up their place in society again. He writes that, when one more other healing comes about as a consequence of the publication of his book, he will be able to say that the effort has been worthwhile.[33]

Rosen employs a quantitative distinction between neurosis and psychosis (the one is simply much more pathologic than the other) and he takes Freud's theory as a model for psychosis. The manifest contents of psychosis in his view is an unfinished nightmare in which the desires are camouflaged in such a way that the patient does not wake.[34] The role of the therapist is to make the patient wake up by unveiling the real content of the psychosis. One means to this is the direct, notably naked interpretation. This often yields spectacularly quick results which sometimes turn out to be of brief duration, however. The role of the therapist is concentrated on the building up of the patient's weak ego with the strong ego of the therapist. In this way, the therapy results in an identification with the therapist. The position of the therapist, in Rosen's view, is comparable with that of the mother figure.

Both Pankow and Rosen work much more intuitively than they do from a rigorous theoretical frame. This is demonstrated in their inability to properly gauge both the efficiency and the inefficacy of their interventions. Typical of their method is the supporting, ego-oriented attitude which at the same time is also strongly directive. The therapist functions as a model. Their desire to cure drives them to the installation of a massive transference which ultimately yields spectacular, yet often merely temporary results. The variability of these results, attained with exclusively so-called psychotic patients, brings us to ask the question as to the efficiency of the method and also with regard to the diagnosis of hysteria or schizophrenia. In our view this is a central point which, however, is treated only minimally both by Pankow and Rosen. The analogy with Stewart's case study, in which there is question of hallucinatory hysteria, after all, is patent.

A third figure we wish to mention is the psychiatrist-psychoanalyst Herbert Rosenfeld (1910-1986), who was part of Melanie Klein's first group of students. Rosenfeld mainly studied adult cases of borderline and of schizophrenia, with a preference for confusional states.[35] With Rosenfeld we again find ourselves in the pigeonhole for model patients which we already came across with Charcot, Janet, and others. Hysterics are promoted to model patients. Rosenfeld's publication on the analysis of Mildred, first presented in 1947 at the British Psychoanalytical Society, is historically of greatest importance. It notably regards the first publication of a successful therapy with an adult psychotic woman within the Kleinian tradition, i.e., the first *psychosis under transference*.[36] A rereading of the Mildred case, however, shows that there is no question of schizophrenia here, but on the contrary of a severe hysteria, which some would probably label as hysterical psychosis. Among the female schizophrenia patients who were made into a paradigm, we furthermore count Renée of Marguerite Sechehaye, Suzanne of Marion Milner, and Mary Barnes of Joe Berke.[37]

Up to now it appeared that, within IPA circles, the rejected hysteria does not just simply come back and sneak into the analytic session under the guise of a new reality, i.e., the hysterical psychosis. The rising psychiatric star of hysterical psychosis as yet has no counterpart in psychoanalysis.

Before concluding, we are still left with an excursion into the Freudo-Lacanian field, on the look-out for the so-called hysterical psychosis.

The Revaluation of an Ancient Nosological Category

The often implicitly used psychosis paradigm is not only a tributary of American ego-psychology, it also indicates the major impact of Melanie Klein's theory (the so-called ultra-orthodoxy) within psychoanalytic circles.[38] For a long time this impact is restricted to the British Commonwealth, not in the least by the grim polemic which went on for years between Anna Freud and Melanie Klein.[39]

Within the ontogeny of the child Klein presupposes a psychotic stage, which she is later to formulate as a psychotic position —the schizo-paranoid phase.[40] Fixation in this stage is determinative for schizophrenia and paranoia. In this view, psychosis is a developmental fixation. The influence of her theory results in the general assumption of a psychotic nucleus or a psychotic part in every individual. The Bleulerian *Spaltung*, which has a sequel in Fairbairn's schizoid factors, is replaced by a psychotic nucleus which is either or not kept well hidden and kept at bay by neurotic defensive mechanisms.[41] This nucleus is almost a metaphor for the repressed material, for the unconscious truth that has been kept at bay.

This kind of assumption favors the sudden and acute psychotic upsurges with hysterical patients:

> These days, the prevalence of a psychotic nucleus in a neurosis makes the analyst, insofar as he is mobilizable at all, recede far less than do the ossified and rigid defensive mechanisms.[42]

That not a single personality remains spared of psychosis is evident then from the following commentary by Bergeret:

> No basic structure of personality is able in practice to continue to act as pure or perfect; a hysterical-neurotic structure, for example, may demonstrate slight psychotic defensive mechanisms of the derealization type in order to guise its structural deficiencies.[43]

And so the analysts choose for acute psychotic moments and against the rigidified personality disorders. Does a new turn in the psychoanalytic clinical field present itself with this, in imitation of the psychiatric interest in hysterical psychosis?[44] The articles on psychotic moments in hysterical patients that have sporadically emerged over the past decade are as yet insufficient to confirm this hypothesis. Nonetheless, it does remain conspicuous that certain psychiatrists like referring to Freud's early studies on hysteria in order to subscribe to the existence of a hysterical psychosis, while the psychoanalysts as yet reinterpret Freud's initial studies on hysteria as borderline or schizophrenic. What is certain, however, is that the few articles on psychotic episodes in hysteria base themselves on psychiatry. In this respect several authors make use, for example, of the psychiatric label of *bouffée délirante*. Another influence (the articles mainly originate in French quarters) is the work of Jean-Claude Maleval on *folie hystérique*.[45] The numerous studies by this author, most of which were collected under the title of *Folies hystériques et psychoses dissociatives*, are meant as a rehabilitation of hysterical madness (*la folie hystérique*). Maleval, a psychologist by training, mainly takes Lacan's theory as a basis.[46] Lacan's theory establishes a radical fracture between neurosis and psychosis.

It should be said that both structures (neurosis and psychosis) actually are juxtaposed for the first time by Freud, although his continuing development of theory on the psychoses maintains the neuroses as its model.[47] After Freud the neurosis paradigm is virtually completely replaced by the paradigm of psychosis. In either case this amounts to analogous reasoning. With Freud the theory of neuroses and psychoses is based on a neurotic foundation, with the Postfreudians on a psychotic one. Only a rigorous distinction between neurosis and psychosis, without ultimately taking either as a model for the other, may offer an outcome to the multitudinous impasses to which this gives rise. Here is where Lacan's revision of the structural foundations of neurosis and psychosis with the introduction of a radical distinction between both (in the 1950s) is situated.[48]

Lacanian psychoanalysis acknowledges the prevalence of psychotic phenomena in hysteria, notably a type of hysteria which may display psychotic features, but hardly pays it any specific attention. This does not, however, mean that the difference between hysteria and psychosis is not questioned.[49] The one main exception to this rule is precisely Jean-Claude Maleval, who has turned *folie hystérique* from a touchstone into a diagnostic referent. Having proceeded from the Lacanian terminology and insights Maleval first brought about the rehabilitation of this Prefreudian category. Initially, he does not attribute a specific structure to so-called hysterical psychosis, but pleads for the reintroduction of ancient categories. First, we encounter *folie hystérique* or hysterical madness, in which the hysterical delusion is allocated a central position as a symptom.[50] Later on Maleval speaks of *hystérie crépusculaire*.[51] In this twilight hysteria the hysterical delirium gets the preponderant position. Ultimately this enterprise may be criticized, since he extracts a signifier from its discourse and introduces it into another discourse (psychoanalysis) without taking into account the immediate implications of this. Notions such as psychoanalytic nosology may, therefore, raise some eyebrows, since, after all, it is not the illness but the subject who is the object of study of psychoanalysis.

Maleval perseveres in his search for a mechanism that explains the specificity of hysterical madness. He introduces new notions to delineate mad hysteria from psychosis. He proposes, for example, *verbal hysterical illusions*, which he opposes to verbal psychotic hallucination. This démarche finally tends to promote hysterical madness both as a specific form of hysteria, and as the paradigm of neurotic madness in general. For he opposes neurotic delirium, determined by the mechanism of rejection (*rejet*) to the psychotic delusion determined by the foreclosure.[52] In this way, he haphazardly splits up hysteria and neurosis in general into an ordinary form and a mad form. The difference is implicitly determined by a (psychical) deficiency. By sticking to the notion of an imaginary deficiency, typical of hysterical madness, he introduces the deficient character of so-called hysterical psychosis via a back entrance. For the typification of hysterical psychosis he follows, in fact, the psychiatrist-psychoanalyst Perrier. The latter demonstrates in a dramatic fashion the extreme fragility of certain patients, as well as their predisposition to regression through the absence of a narcissistic imago.[53] The emphasis of an imaginary deficiency or a certain fragility immediately brings to mind the imaginary register, being the register of the image, of the identification, and of the narcissism, which is also the register to which the ego-psychologists submit. The assumption of an imaginary deficiency, moreover, ties in close with the view of, for example, Kammerer who speaks of a psycho-allergy.

When someone like Maleval, who knows the history of hysterical madness intimately and has discussed it at great length, ultimately proves to be disseminating the views of someone like Janet—in spite of the fact that he claims to be proceeding from the Lacanian theory on the subject—there is quite a lot of work that urgently needs to be done. Neither hysterics nor psychotics are any the better off with a theory that subscribes to a deficiency view on pathology. This criticism does not prevent, however, that the honor of having reopened the issue of hysterical psychosis is due to Maleval. The fact that his pioneering labor has remained relatively undiscussed within Lacanian circles (the references are generally tinted negatively) as well as the fact that hysterical psychosis has virtually always been a non-topic in these circles, constitute an invitation to clearly delineate theoretically the position of madness in hysteria.

Notes

1. O. Fenichel (1945), *The Psychoanalytic Theory of Neuroses*, New York, Norton; E. Simmel (1946), Obituary Otto Fenichel, *International Journal of Psycho-Analysis*, 27, pp. 67-71.
2. S. Freud, Neurosis and Psychosis (1924b[1923]), *S.E.*, 19, pp. 149-153; S. Freud (1924e), The Loss of Reality in Neurosis and Psychosis, *S.E.*, 19, pp. 183-187.
3. O. Fenichel (1945), mainly pp. 216-235 and 415-452. Fenichel divides the neuroses into the traumatic and the psychoneuroses which, to start with, is a non-Freudian division. Under the psychoneuroses we find the following categories: anxiety hysteria, conversion, organ neurosis, obsession and compulsion, the pregenital conversions, perversions and impulse neuroses, depression and mania, and finally schizophrenia.
4. S. Freud (1923b), *The Ego and the Id*, *S.E.*, 19, pp. 12-66. The topical representation of the psyche elaborated here (Ego, Id and Super-Ego) under no circumstances replaces the first one (unconscious, preconscious, consciousness). And despite the fact that Freud explicitly elaborates the mutual relations between the distinct psychical systems, there is no evidence that he would favor the instance of the ego.
5. Milton Klein (1983), Freud's Drive Theory and Ego Psychology: A Critical Evaluation of the Blancks, *Psychoanalytic Review*, 70, 4, p. 505; R. Jaccard (ed.) (1982), *Histoire de la psychanalyse*, vol. 2, Paris, Hachette, pp. 283-288.
6. P. Kaufmann (ed.) (1993), *L'apport freudien*, Paris, Bordas, p. 621.
7. S. Freud (1917a[1916]), A Difficulty in the Path of Psycho-Analysis, *S.E.*, 17, p. 141-142.
8. For the purpose of clarity we should add here that we make a statement on the general use of the notion of object relation. For there are several psychoanalytic theories that place the object relation center stage. For a critical discussion of a number of leading tendencies (including that of the British School and that of Otto Kernberg) we refer to: O. Sternbach (1983), Critical Comments on Object Relation Theory, *Psychoanalytic Review*, 70, 3, pp. 403-421.
9. This concept was already introduced by James Strachey: J. Strachey (1934), The Nature of the Therapeutic Action of Psychoanalysis,

International Journal of Psycho-Analysis, 1934, 15, pp. 127-159.

10. C. Demoulin (1984a), Critique de la théorie de Jean Bergeret, *Quarto*, 15, p. 58.
11. J.-A. Miller (1984), Liminaire, *Ornicar?*, 29, p. 6. Author's translation.
12. Some four articles, including one on a hallucinatory form of hysteria.
13. G. Kohon (1984), Reflections on Dora: the Case of Hysteria, *International Journal of Psycho-Analysis*, 65, p. 79, italics by the author.
14. J. Derksen (1989), Over het ego en zelf bij borderline- en narcistische stoornissen, *Tijdschrift voor Psychiatrie*, 31, Books 2, pp. 8-13.
15. A. de Mijolla (1986), Du prudent usage des notions d'«hystérie» et d'«hystérique» en psychanalyse, *Revue Française de Psychanalyse* 3, pp. 891-904.
16. L. Besso (1969), Contribution à l'approche psychodynamique du problème des rapports entre l'hystérie et la schizophrénie, *Archives Suisses de Neurologie, Neurochirurgie et de Psychiatrie*, 105, pp. 115-144; E. Eskelinen de Folch (1984), The Hysteric's Use and Misuse of Observation, *International Journal of Psycho-Analysis*, 65, pp. 399-410.
17. R. Satow (1979), Where has all the Hysteria gone?, *Psychoanalytic Review*, 66, 4, p. 469.
18. J.-A. Miller (1984), p. 6.
19. This dual attitude, in which the desire of the analyst is unmistakably present, can already be demonstrated in early analytical publications. See W. Reich (1927[1925]), A Hysterical Psychosis in «statu nascendi», *International Journal of Psychoanalysis*, 8, pp. 159-173.
20. O. Flournoy (1974), Les cas-limites: psychose ou névrose?, *Nouvelle Revue de Psychanalyse*, 10, pp. 123-124. Author's translation.
21. E. Zetzel (1968), The so-called Good Hysteric, *International Journal of Psycho-Analysis*, 49, pp. 256-260.
22. H. Stewart (1977), Problems of Management in the Analysis of a Hallucinating Hysteric, *International Journal of Psycho-Analysis*, 58, pp. 67-76.
23. G. Kohon (1984), p. 81.
24. M. Milner (1969) *The Hands of the Living God*, London, Hogarth Press; M. Barnes & J. Berke (1971), *Mary Barnes*, London, Mc Gibbon & Kee.
25. The draughtsmen of the DSM classified the borderline under the

heading of the personality disorders in order to secure the distinction with the psychoses. This implies that the introduction of the category of the psychotic character (Frosch claims that he wishes to capture the cluster that is common to all borderline concepts) pushes clinical diagnostics even more into the direction of the psychotic nucleus.

26. J. Frosch (1988), Psychotic Character versus Borderline, *International Journal of Psycho-Analysis*, 69, 3, pp. 347-357 and 4, pp. 445-456.
27. J.-B. Pontalis (1974), Bornes ou confins?, *Nouvelle Revue de Psychanalyse*, 10, pp. 5-16.
28. E. Zarifian (1986), Un diagnostic en psychiatrie: pour quoi faire?, in R. Gori et al. (eds.), *La Querelle des diagnostics*, coll. Cliniques, Paris, Navarin, p. 79.
29. Pankow left the dissident Société Française de Psychanalyse (Lacan) and joined the French division of the IPA in 1961.
30. We find the same with Rosen, who will be discussed later.
31. G. Pankow (1969), *L'homme et sa psychose*, Paris, Aubier-Montaigne; G. Pankow (1977), *Structure familiale et psychose*, Paris, Aubier-Montaigne; G. Pankow (1981[1956]), *L'être-là du schizophrène*, Paris, Aubier-Montaigne.
32. G. Pankow (1973), L'image du corps dans la psychose hystérique, *Revue Française de Psychanalyse*, 37, 3, pp. 415-416.
33. J. Rosen (1953), *Direct Analysis*, New York, Grune & Stratton. With his direct analysis John Rosen develops a treatment which ties in with the theoretical viewpoints of Paul Federn, one of the Postfreudian psychoanalysts who have launched into the elaboration of a theory on the psychoses, but who exclusively relies on the imaginary armature of the ego.
34. Those who do not subscribe to a radical fracture between psychosis and neurosis (a position which, ultimately was taken by Freud, too) often emphasize the analogy between the psychosis and the dream.
35. H. Rosenfeld (1965), *Psychotic States*, London, Hogarth Press.
36. H. Rosenfeld (1947), Analysis of a Schizophrenic State with Depersonalization, *International Journal of Psycho-Analysis*, 28, pp. 130-139; D. Tuckett (1989), A brief View of Herbert Rosenfeld's Contribution to the Theory of Psychoanalytic Technique, *International Journal of Psycho-Analysis*, 70, pp. 619-625.
37. M. Sechehaye (1947), *La réalisation symbolique*, supplement to the

Revue suisse de psychologie et de la psychologie appliquée no. 12, Bern, Hans Huber Verlag; M. Sechehaye (1950), *Journal d'une schizophrène*, Paris, PUF; M. Milner (1969); M. Barnes & J. Berke (1971).

38. We derive the term ultra-orthodoxy from: P. Bercherie (1988), *Géographie du champ psychanalytique*, Bibliothèque des Analytica, Paris, Navarin, pp. 74-82.
39. See, for example, Ph. Grosskurth (1987[1986]), *Melanie Klein*, Cambridge-Massachusetts, Harvard University Press.
40. Melanie Klein (1946), Notes on some Schizoid Mechanisms, *International Journal of Psycho-Analysis*, 27, pp. 99-111. Already in 1940 Fairbairn introduced the schizoid position as determinative for schizophrenia.
41. R. Fairbairn (1974), Les facteurs schizoïdes dans la personnalité, *Nouvelle Revue de Psychanalyse*, 10, pp. 35-55. In this article, first published in 1952 and constituting the revision of an article from 1940, the author arrives at a classification of some four schizoid states. This classification totally comprises the most various kinds of psychopathologies; apart from somnambulisms, fugues, dual and multiple personalities, even the intelligentsia find a place in it. The search for any indication as to hysteria however remains fruitless.
42. A. Green (1974), L'analyste, la symbolisation et l'absence dans le cadre analytique, *Nouvelle Revue de Psychanalyse*, 10, pp. 231-232. Author's translation.
43. J. Bergeret (1974), Limites des états analysables et états-limites analysables, *Nouvelle Revue de Psychanalyse*, 10, p. 108. Author's translation.
44. E. Laurent (1988), Limites de la psychose, in GRAPP, *Les Psychiatres et la psychanalyse aujourd'hui*, Paris, Navarin, pp. 88-93.
45. J.-C. Maleval (1981), *Folies hystériques et psychoses dissociatives*, Paris, Payot. Of the analysts which call upon this work, we mention L. de Urtubey (1985) and A. Jeanneau (1974, 1985, 1990).
46. Here and there in French psychiatry his ideas find some response. See, for example, J. Postel (ed.) (1993), *Dictionnaire de psychiatrie et de psychopathologie clinique*, Références Larousse, Paris, Larousse, pp. 234-235: "folie hystérique"; M. Steyaert (1992), *Hystérie, folie et psychose*, Paris, Les Empêcheurs de penser en rond, p. 39; I. Le Goe-Diaz (1988), La dépersonalisation, in *Encyclopédie Médico-*

Chirurgicale, *Psychiatrie*, 37125 A10, 6, pp. 4-5.

47. P. Bercherie (1988), pp. 158-159.
48. See, for example, J. Lacan (1977[1957-1958]), On a Question Preliminary to any Possible Treatment of Psychosis, *Ecrits. A Selection*, trans. from the French by A. Sheridan, New York, Norton, pp. 179-225. In this article, Lacan heavily criticizes the postfreudian theorization on the subject of psychosis and proposes the concept of *foreclosure* (*Verwerfung*) as the fundamental mechanism that distinguishes the structure of psychosis from that of neurosis.
49. We mention a few authors (all Lacanian psychoanalysts): P. Lemoine (1973), A. Cordié (1976), C. Demoulin (1984), C. Léger (1984); M. Rouanduano de Maeso (1986); S. Basz et al. (1986).
50. J.-C. Maleval (1981). In his afterword to the Spanish and the Portuguese translations, Maleval cautions the reader by way of two remarks. The first concerns the notion of imaginary deficiency: it is not sufficient to seize the structure of hysterical madness. The second remark nuances the importance of the hysterical delusion, which is implicitly appointed a privileged position. J.-C. Maleval (1985a), Postface aux éditions en langues espagnole et portugaise de «Folies hystériques et psychoses dissociatives», *Cahiers de lectures freudiennes*, 6, pp. 87-91.
51. J.-C. Maleval (1985b), Les hystéries crépusculaires, *Confrontations psychiatriques*, 25, p. 91. According to Maleval the honor for the introduction of the signifier twilight hysteria falls to R. Wartel. Here a German psychiatric term (*Dämmerzustände*) is rehabilitated, but this time not by means of an explicit reference.
52. J.-C. Maleval (1983), Les illusions verbales hystériques, *Cahiers de lectures freudiennes*, 2, pp. 53-72; J.-C. Maleval (1985b). Maleval mentions the notion of rejection for the first time in 1979, in an article on Freud's case study of the Wolf Man. J.-C. Maleval (1979), A propos de la symptomatologie «limite» de l'homme aux loups, *Etudes psychothérapeutiques*, 38, 4, mainly pp. 267-270.
53. J.-C. Maleval (1981), mainly p. 112; F. Perrier (1968), Structure hystérique et dialogue analytique, *Confrontations Psychiatriques*, 1, pp. 101-117. Perrier himself refers to Follin's article from 1961.

Conclusion

At this point we resume the multi-layered structure of the material with which a hysterical subject writes his or her history, as made explicit in the introduction. In this gesture we test this representation, which we derived from Freud, with regard to its fertility concerning the historiography of hysterical madness. Consequently, we shall distil from this historiography two lessons which bring us a supplementary, Lacanian reading of this representation and are integral for the study of the distinction between hysteria and psychosis. In the last instance we shall then return to the relationship between psychiatry and psychoanalysis, the two disciplines which are interwoven in a specific manner in this work.

A Freudian Representation of the Hysterical Material

The threefold Freudian stratification of the hysterical material, so we said, can be found in the material we use to write the history of hysterical psychosis. We put this to the test.

The first ordering, the *linear-chronological* one, in the first instance, delineates itself in the succession of the different chapters which, each on its own, bring us in a chronological sequence, a cross section of a certain period of time. The limitation of the respective periods, which always constitutes a choice and therefore is arbitrary, was inspired by general tendencies, apparent in the psychiatric and psychoanalytic literature on the matter. This gives us an outline of the life story of hysterical madness. This account starts with the general acknowledgement of the very existence of hysterical madness within the distinct psychiatric schools and the heyday of the study of the major neurosis and the hysterical fit within the frame of neuropathology in its ongoing development. The Freudian discovery and revelation of the action of unconscious psychical processes in the creation of hysterical symptoms and the introduction of psychoanalysis there unmistakably mark a breaking point with respect to the positions taken by the psychiatrists and the neuropathologists. With the turn of the century, the signifier hysteria—and with it hysterical madness—vanishes into the margin of the psychiatric field, where new signifiers have come to set the tone. The marginality of the differential diagnosis with the then distinct psychoses, being mental confusion, manic-depressive psychosis, dementia praecox, and schizophrenia, as well as the study of the war neuroses, lead the way to new ways of accomodating of hysterical madness. After the Second World War the enthusiasm for psychotherapy with psychotics is an indirect cause for the revaluation of the ancient hysterical madness, which then led a marginal existence in the land of psychosis while the numeric diaspora of hysteria pushed on internationally. With this, the initial promising future of the major hysteria seemed to have ended in a minor key.

Apart from the diachronic dimension of the historiography we distinguish, in the second instance, the linear-chronological ordering within each of the distinct themes. These themes are the recurrent clinical accents in the typification of hysterical madness.

We shall clarify this statement. The history of hysteria—in general and that of hysterical madness in particular—impels the conclusion that each phenomenon may settle itself into the picture of hysteria, respectively that of hysterical madness. Did not Charcot discover a new hysterical symptom day after day? Did not the alienists unanimously emphasize the protean nature of hysterical delusion and hysterical madness? In spite of the fact that in this way we see the number of clinical themes expand to a mass which can neither be taken in or be articulated, hysteria itself supplies us with an argument which permits the reduction in the number of typifications. We are referring to its fashion-consciousness. Just what phenomenon, analogous to the street scene, determines the picture of hysteria at any given moment, is inextricably linked with the ruling master discourse. In this way there is always the question of a dominant phenotype, mediated by the attention the hysteric is able to capture. Since we sought to describe hysterical madness in the psychiatric and the psychoanalytic field of operation, we shall restrict ourselves to the tendencies in vogue in these domains over the years. This does not imply that all hysterics also follow psychiatric and psychoanalytic fashions. Nowadays, too, we still find a stray Charcotian hysteria every now and then.

That is why we restrict ourselves here to the clinical accents that are both recurrent and which at a given moment over the considered 130-year period tie in with one or another fashionable trend in the world of psychiatry or that of psychoanalysis in which hysterics move. In succession this yields the hysterical fit, modelled after the epileptic fit; the deliriums and dream states, the clinical picture of which assumes that of the organically determined toxic states and hallucinoses; the dual or multiple personalities as well as the twilight states that copy the hypnotic state; mental confusion linked with—among others—the clinical pictures determined by a physical trauma; and finally the states of depersonalization and the acute psychotic episodes that use schizophrenia and borderline as their model. What is striking is the permanent presence of alterations of consciousness and brief, hallucinatory delusory states (cf. the Freudian elaboration of the hysterical deliria and the amentia or mental confusion). The clinical emphasis falls on the temporary nature of madness. Chronicity tends more to be linked with the personality.

The second stratification is the *concentric ordering* of each theme around a pathological nucleus. In this, each stratum is characterized by a certain degree of resistance, that increases as the primally repressed nucleus is approached. Each theme stretches out across the various strata.

How does this ordering present itself in the material that lays before us? The way in which the distinct clinical accents within hysterical madness become minor traits, i.e., the way in which the clinical picture is being typified is a measure for the amount of resistance against the approach of the nucleus. Every author either implicitly or explicitly presents his view of hysteria which, as we saw, was always twofold and therefore gave away a certain subjective division. He or she who writes about hysteria is both fascinated and at the same time shocked by it.

What we are saying here is that the degree to which the subject of the clinician, the researcher, i.e., the master figure, or still the accidental partner of the hysteric—the one writing about hysterical madness—emerges from the respective typification or—to the contrary—is being kept meticulously out of that typification in order to disappear under the cloak of objectivity, is an indicator of this concentric ordering. Recurrent signifiers (attributions), for example, include the suggestibility, the compliance, the infantility of hysteria or precisely its non-hypnotizability, its steadfastness. Another example is the way with which the importance of sexuality is dealt. Therefore, it is not the clinical description, but everything surrounding it—notably the framing and the way in which it is dressed up that is different for every clinician. This is what determines the stratum or the strata across which the theme has distributed itself.

What remains for us to render explicit is the *dynamic* stratification. This is the most important and most fertile layeredness Freud found very hard to represent. In approximative terms Freud spoke of a logical zigzag line from and to the nucleus, of a tree structure—of lines with various nodal points where two or more wires converge. In short, he meant to cast the complex logic which the development of symptoms seems to imply and the overdetermination of the hysterical symptom into a sort of representation. What Freud posited there on the hysterical symptom also holds for hysterical madness.

For the articulation of this final ordering we must refer the reader to the unabridged script, more specifically to the intervening, anticipating and recurring moves that are made in it and in which are certain, but by no means all determinants indicated and elaborated.

And then there is the *nucleus*, the elusive and impalpable traumatic nucleus, the instigator of the multiple stratification that does not stop not writing itself but does cause writing. We are referring here to what it takes to incite writing about hysterical madness, more specifically to what directs the research: the desire to constitute a knowledge with respect to hysterical madness or the not-wanting-to-know. It has everything to do with the way the hysterical subject constitutes a master, animated by a desire to know. With this, our personal subjective effort is affected and may be acknowledged. We are referring here to a structural lack which time and again cranks up the continual solicitation of the hysteric for a knowledge concerning his or her fundamental division. Those who, like Freud, allow themselves to be instructed by hysterics, approach this enigmatic nucleus closest of all. The nucleus, however, may only be encircled by approximation at the best of times. The final word never gets spoken and every encounter by definition is a failed one.

The Status of Hysterical Madness and the Function of the Subject

The fact that the vicissitudes of hysterical madness are inextricably interwoven with those of hysteria as such, is one constant which can be pointed out in the over one hundred year history of hysterical madness. With this, it has emerged that hysterical madness is in fact much rather the problem of mad, i.e., seemingly psychotic hysteria. The history of the (moving) encounters between hysteria and madness, however, is extremely informative on more than one score to those who are willing to lend an ear. In this respect we briefly mention two lessons.

A first lesson of history deals with the civil status which falls to hysterical madness. Does it, as history seems to indicate, essentially regard a historic statue or is a permanent symbolic status due her? We can demonstrate that the way in which history is read yields a radically different answer to the question as to the civil status. If one takes history as what it pretends to be, namely an objective factual account, then both hysteria and hysterical madness pertain to the murky past of psychiatry. If, however, one takes history beyond what it pretends to be—namely as a string of tales and testimonies out of which every tiny trace of subjective fascination is carefully kept out—then hysteria and hysterical madness prove not to be so easily dismissable as just temporary phenomena. This is where the path opens itself to us to propose the constant presence of both (their symbolical status) as an alternative to the historical statue. The elaboration of this status as well as the question of whether hysteria or hysterical madness lay claim to a status that is distinct from each other, we must leave unanswered here. When employing the diagnosis of hysteria or hysterical madness, a symbolic acknowledgement or rather a recognition within the lingual register is conferred upon it. In that case listings in diagnostic classification systems and the allocation of a position within the gamut of psychopathological afflictions constitute official indicators of this acknowledgement. Within this angle the generalized, official absence of the two (this absence is more outspoken for hysteria than for hysterical madness) is a fateful sign which indicates that currently they are assigned hardly any right of existence or any dimension of reality. Among others we can link this with their absence from the descriptive DSM-system, which momentarily is one of the most important diagnostic guidelines within the capacious psy-field.

The official absence of hysteria and hysterical madness in our opinion does not so much testify to a real disappearance of hysteria but rather to a blunt refusal to acknowledge them as yet. Furthermore, we are of the opinion that this refusal can refer to the same definition as the one Freud gives in his discussion of amentia. In both cases a piece of unbearable reality is rejected by veiling it with wish-fantasies that originate in the unconscious (desire). In this way, the rejection of hysteria and hysterical madness can be found in the various enlisted argumentations or justifications for no longer having to use these diagnoses—the veiling fantasies. The unbearable of hysterical reality is determined by the numerous detrimental encounters with hysteria in general, where there is certainly no lack of history. From this angle it then turns out that what in the first instance can be deduced from official historiography as a natural outfall of hysteria and hysterical madness, in the second instance is the masking of an unbearable reality—that of hysteria in general. This reality is unbearable since it brings to mind innumerable detrimental encounters from the past. In this connection Charcot can be put forward as the historical prototype of such an encounter with hysteria that ended noxiously.

Our interpretation leads on further—to the conclusion that the present absence of hysteria and the marginal acknowledgement of hysterical madness under the heading of hysterical psychosis are not just the absolute reproduction of an objective reality (every bit as little as the former heyday of hysteria and the recognition of hysterical madness were) but can also be understood as representing some part of the psychic reality of the researcher, the therapist, etc. This much was already in evidence from our resumption of the multi-layered structure of the material.

This view also implies that history, beyond the official account of the peregrinations of hysteria and hysterical madness, is just as much a chain of tales about encounters and thus bears both testimony to the subjective fascination of the respective researchers and clinicians as well as to a certain knowledge regarding the defined object of research, although the subjectivity does not surface in a superficial reading.

At this point we would like to introduce the Lacanian notion of the master discourse as the discourse which supports the official version of history, as it emerges from the factual material.[1] This discourse allows us to place our double reading of history within one and the same frame, thus bringing together both readings.

$$\uparrow \frac{S_1}{\$} \; \frac{\rightarrow}{//} \; \frac{S_2}{a} \downarrow$$

In this formula of the master discourse, we can indicate two levels which find themselves respectively above and under the fracture lines: that of objective and that of subjective historiography. Since the latter is in the bottom half of the formula, it emerges that the subjective story is veiled by the objective account. The objective historiography then can be set as follows: a master, S_1, makes something his research object that exists within his knowledge, S_2. In our case this is hysteria and hysterical madness. The subjective historiography takes into account the real engine of the discourse, as well as its product. The knowledge of the master reduces the hysterical subject into an object and procures the master with an overcoming (*plus-de-jouir*) which is linked to this knowledge: *a*.[2] He considers himself more than satisfied with the constructed theory or the established facts. However, he is not aware that the production of his knowledge is ultimately being directed and is therefore also colored by his own subjectivity, $\$$, which, at all times, is veiled under the cloak of objectivity or even veracity.

When we now read the objective historiography together with the subjective historiography, then every argument ceases to exist in order to conclude a priori, on the basis of the official historiography, that both hysteria and hysterical madness are temporary phenomena. With this, however, it has not yet been demonstrated how hysteria, beyond the subjectivity of every researcher (which concerns us, too, for that matter), actually can be grasped in its symbolic status. Lacan's discourse theory, more particularly his elaboration of the hysterical discourse, in our opinion proffers the possibility to define hysteria and hysterical madness in a positive fashion. With this a first guideline has been indicated.

The second history lesson ensues from the first and regards the function of the subject. This brings us to the other side of the relationship of the hysterical subject to the master, namely the manner in which the hysterical subject installs the master.

Official historiography tells of hysteria as an object of study, which leads to conceptions on hysteria as an illness, as a reaction or as a personality disorder. These constants disown the structural aspect of the hysterical subject, notably its division.

Those who wish to learn about hysteria and comprehend it with regard to its state of division as a subject, must approach it in its status of divided subject and not reduce it—as does the master—to an object. This implies allowing oneself to be instructed by listening to the hysteric speaking. History may well exemplify how easily hysteria lends itself to the confirmation of some or other theory, but also just how once-only and transient these proofs are when they have been acquired at the expense of an object. The theories turn out to be just as transitory as the masters, since the latter category abandons hysteria for what it is, once their theory is confirmed. At that point, the hysteric becomes waste matter. For, reduced to an abject object, the hysteric forfeits his or her claim to an individual, particular approach. This does not mean, however, that the hysterical subject is finished. On the contrary, the search for a next master and a new theory is continued all the more doggedly. The type of example of a similar, momentarily master is again Charcot.

For over forty years Freud let himself be taught, to his own bitter experience (he too at times was tempted enough to assume the role of the master), by his hysterical patients. By listening, he put the hysteric on center stage as a speaking subject and not as a visual object. His theory of hysteria, therefore, is neither an a priori, nor an established knowledge construction, but a theory which is permanently in a nascent state. Constituted on the basis of the speech of hysterical patients, Freud's theorizations are propelled by his quest for a truth regarding the unconscious. Furthermore, his theory is unremittingly tested by clinical experience. Hence, evolution plays a constant and preponderant role. At certain points, however, this evolution turns out to be a revolution in the original etymological sense of the word, i.e., a return to the point of departure. Put in Lacanian terms, this means that the real, i.e., what keeps appearing at the same place be it under various disguises, continues to play tricks on Freud and his hysterics.

After Freud there is Jacques Lacan. If Freud discovered the unconscious and psychoanalysis, Lacan is the one who further developed this discovery. This French psychiatrist-psychoanalyst initially defined his démarche as a counterweight for the degeneration of psychoanalysis in Anglo-American circles, with a return to the meaning of Freud, to the core of the Freudian line of thought. His resumption of crucial Freudian concepts and texts leads him to a working hypothesis which renders explicit what can already be read implicitly in Freud and which indicates the importance of language. According to Lacan, language as a structure precedes the subject (of the unconscious) and determines this subject. His basic thesis, therefore, is as follows: the unconscious is structured as a language. Gradually it becomes clear that Lacan's theory goes beyond and radicalizes that of Freud on several essential scores. Two of these points are of particular interest to us: (1) the radical distinction between the structure of neurosis and that of psychosis; (2) a theory on the subject which defines it as pertaining to the order of psychical causality and which makes a radical break with psychogenesis.

Both the oeuvre of Freud and that of Lacan are typified by a constant evolution. With Freud the interaction between theory and praxis is distinctly present. His theorizations can be pursued along the impasses to which his hypotheses time and again lead him. With Lacan clinical practice is not overtly present in the construction of his theory and his teachings, as is the case with Freud. Where clinical examples come to the fore, they are transposed onto the level of paradigms; abstract frames in which crucial concepts such as desire and the fundamental fantasy are grasped. One example of this is the dream of the beautiful butcher woman (a dream from Freud's *The Interpretation of Dreams*) which is made into the paradigm of the hysterical desire by Lacan. Insofar as Lacan's theory is not easily accessible, its evolution, too, is unmistakable.

The above elaboration should be read as a plea, both for centrally placing the hysterical subject as well as for a theory which radically distinguishes between hysteria and psychosis and in doing so establishes a respective appropriate clinical field. With this, next to the discourse theory, two additional courses have been set out which can direct a study that seeks to discover the distinction between hysteria and psychosis.

The Unsuccessful Encounter(s) Between Psychiatry and Psychoanalysis

In conclusion, in one hundred and thirty years of history it seems appropriate to focus on an encounter which turned out to be problematic. What we are aiming at is the encounter between psychiatry and psychoanalysis. Our intention is twofold: first we wish to indicate a certain shared misrecognition in order to grasp, in the second instance, the relation of psychoanalysis to psychiatry by means of two signifiers—singularity and acknowledgement.

First of all, there is the denial with which psychiatry has received psychoanalysis. Both nineteenth-century hysterical madness, a specific type of madness originating from or associated with hysteria, and the present hysterical psychosis, a so-called specific psychotic structure that separated itself from the schizophrenia group are products of psychiatry. They are governed by the medical model and are part of the descriptive psychiatric clinical field. In this, the setting with respect to psychoanalysis can be described as follows: hysterical madness, more exactly *folie hystérique* and *hysterisches Irresein* are Prefreudian notions while hysterical psychosis, a Postfreudian concept, is the product of a psychiatry which has assumed psychoanalytic theory as a nosology—a psychiatric pathology. The constant mention of "Freud's view of hysterical psychosis" as well as a certain usage of Freudian terms (which have been turned hollow over the years) are indications of this. The radical (epistemological) fracture, introduced by psychoanalysis, has been rendered innocuous by psychiatry and simultaneously made unserviceable by adopting it as an interesting body of knowledge which can be fragmentarily applied in order to confirm the own medical view of illness and normality. Chazaud, with his view of hysterical psychosis, presented us with a form of this tactic carried to its extreme—deactivation of the distinction between neurosis and psychosis, introduced by Freud and radicalized by Lacan, as well as the Freudian reference to the unconscious.

In a lecture from 1916 on psychiatry and psychoanalysis Freud asserts that in his view that they are neither incompatible, nor each other's opposite, "It is to be expected that in the not too distant future it will be realized that a scientifically-based psychiatry is not possible without a sound knowledge of the deeper-lying unconscious processes in mental life."[3] In his enthusiasm, Freud could not foresee the fact that psychiatry was to search for its singularity elsewhere and lose it.

In the time span demarcated by the two above indicated moments, an involution takes shape. This involution proceeds from the initial bloom of clinical psychiatry which did not rise to an actual synthesis between the distinct Schools or tendencies. It results in the hegemony of biological psychiatry and a clinical field that has been camouflaged and distorted by the pharmacon. This development can be typified as an involution, for it is characterized by a persisting search elsewhere, where the singularity of clinical psychiatry was more and more at risk. Clinical psychiatry initially concentrated on the sickbed and therefore around the concrete case. It had a final peak with Kraepelin. Since then, the singularity of clinical psychiatry has been gradually forfeited and replaced with high expectations towards psychology, sociology, psychopharmacology, biology, etc.[4] The result is that, beyond the stagnation, we get a degeneration of present-day psychiatry into a statistiatry (DSM) which is determined by a biological frame of reference where the pharmacon now determines the diagnosis. The promising past has passed into oblivion. The present disparate attempts to revert to earlier nosographical and nosological entities, apart from the tribute to and the nostalgia for the lost wealth, are to be considered as a temporary onrush of clinicians who, confronted with a certain uneasiness in the everyday clinical practice, look back to the good old days. Their efforts, however, do not exceed a furtive glance across the shoulder, from the present nosological frame of reference that is still dominated by schizophrenia. Not the early clinical descriptions, but their labels are resumed. The sporadic emergence of hysterical psychosis from the sixties onward lodges itself within this view and seems to be the answer to the question as to what is precisely located at the rim of the schizophrenic perspective. Whether one speaks in this respect of the rehabilitation of an old category (Follin) or of the introduction of a new category (Hirsch and Hollender), the commitment remains the same; rather than commence with the theoretical study of psychosis, one seeks to clinically recognize it at the earliest stage possible in order to salvage it by means of therapeutic sandbags. The first step, that of timely recognition, gives rise to categories such as pre-psychosis, latent schizophrenia and pseudoneurotic schizophrenia. The second step, which actually runs parallel to the first, concerns the fortification of the often fragmentarily existing neurotic dikes. One suddenly comes across certain phenotypes of hysteria, which one recognizes as a new miscellaneous form. With this, hysterical psychosis lodges itself in the line of the group of border states or borderlines.

Secondly, there is a certain development of the Freudian body of thought which, no matter how Freudian it labels itself, it implies a misrecognition, even denial of the fundamental discoveries of psychoanalysis, such as the primacy of the unconscious and the role of sexuality in the etiology of the neuroses, in particular of hysteria. Moreover, the representatives of this ego-tendency share in the sins of psychiatry. At best they assume a psychogenetic, deficiency view of psychopathology. Reality, of which the therapist makes up the representative, holds as the norm for the cure.

The development of the IPA-tendency within Freudian psychoanalysis voices a policy that is comparable to the involute line within psychiatry. Within this psychoanalysis, too, the bells of biology are chiming (sexuality becomes genitality), and the subject of the unconscious and with that also hysteria are disowned. Just as for the unconscious it holds for hysteria that it only speaks for the one who listens.

The above equalization of ego-psychology with psychiatry may sound harsh, but those who only follow the developments from a distance must perforce arrive at this conclusion. The fact that we put both in the same box does not mean that we identify them with each other. Perhaps not the only but certainly the essential dissimilarity between psychiatry and ego-psychology is the position with regard to the subject. Where psychiatry denies the subject as such, the ego-psychology will misunderstand the subject by putting it on a par with the ego. Ego-psychologists have at the very least worked out a coherent theory on the functioning of the ego that directs their analytic praxis and has created a clinical field of narcissistic disorders. Not the hysterical psychoses but the narcissistic disorders currently adorn the platform of the miscellaneous forms. And here is where we can take the comparison with the unconscious up again. Just as the unconscious appears in the crevices of the discourse, we must look for hysteria, as well as its mad variant (in particular during the periods when they have fallen from grace) in the slip-ups of nosology. We continue to exam the hiatuses of the theories on psychopathology and, in keeping with this, also the newly introduced screen-entities. We say in particular, because even in the heyday of hysteria and of hysterical madness, every knowledge with respect to their singularity only emerges in the fracture lines of the constituted scientific thought.

Both disciplines, psychiatry as well as psychoanalysis, have currently launched themselves into the borderlines. The manner in which this borderline group has created a distinct profile for itself, i.e., the history of the label is different. In psychiatry the borderline has emancipated itself from the study of psychosis; in ego-psychology it did so from the arduous approach of neurosis. In both, the study of psychosis, however, has been replaced by that of the borderline. Just how close borderline and psychosis actually lie was demonstrated to us by Frosch, who at the end of the sixties wanted to introduce the psychotic character as a substitute for the borderline.

But here the restriction must be made that the few exceptions, in fighting upstream, hardly do anything more than confirm and accentuate this rule since they can offer no alternative beyond the formulated criticism. With the (small-scale) overseas success of Lacan's theory we can expect some current movement in this domain.

How do we view the relationship between psychoanalysis and psychiatry? Throughout this entire work we used the view of Julien Quackelbeen who asserts that "psychoanalysis is faced with the paradoxical mission of being a radically different clinical field and at the same time assuming the past of clinical psychiatry in order to preserve it from further decline. Not only because present psychiatry no longer seems capable of doing so but also because it can improve itself from this."[5] We interpret this minimally as the acknowledgement of the fact that in past psychiatry a certain knowledge lurks, constituted on a descriptive clinical practice. The comprehensiveness we presented of the early contributions on hysterical madness is to be framed in this perspective. Furthermore, we should not neglect the fact that both Freud and Lacan proceeded from the impasses of psychiatric clinical practice, determined by the master discourse, in order to construct a radically different, psychoanalytic clinical field, defined by the analytic discourse.

Opposite the descriptive psychiatric clinical field the structural psychoanalytic clinical field places itself where we draw attention to the rigorous distinction between both. It is by no means our intention to propound psychoanalysis as something that might fill a lack in psychiatry, or might complement psychiatry. With this, we would lapse into the position what psychiatry assumes with regard to psychoanalysis. Neither do we consider psychoanalysis as a rediscoverer of clinical psychiatry—an idea that brings closer the danger of colonization. In our opinion, it is very much that same attitude as it is for the cure that is befitting here: language that discloses the history of psychiatry throws it open for elaboration.

Notes

1. This specific relation of the hysterical subject to the master figure has already been pointed out. The master discourse provides a formalization of this relationship.
2. Lacan introduced the concept of ***plus-de-jouir*** in his Seminar *L'envers de la psychanalyse* (1969-1970), in which he elaborates his discourse theory. The English translation "overcoming" expresses the ambiguity of the French ***plus***: both "end-of-coming/enjoying" and "excess-of-coming/enjoying". J. Lacan (1990[1974]), *Television*, trans. from the French by D. Hollier, R. Krauss & A. Michelson, edited by J.-A. Miller, New York, London, Norton, p. 32.
3. S. Freud (1916-1917[1915-1917]), *Introductory Lectures on Psychoanalysis*, Lecture 16: Psychoanalysis and Psychiatry, *S.E.*, 16, p. 255.
4. J. Quackelbeen (1987), De psychoanalyse tegenover het verleden van de klinische psychiatrie, in J. Quackelbeen (ed.), *Psychoanalyse en klinische psychiatrie: Een geschiedenis van eigenheid of verbondenheid?*, Pegasos series no. 2, Ghent, Idesça, pp. 18-21. Author's translation.
5. *Ibid.*, p. 21.

Bibliography

For the works of Sigmund Freud, we make use of the *Standard Edition* (shortened as *S.E.*) by James Strachey. We also mention the references to the *Gesammelte Werke* (shortened as *G.W.*).

Abraham, K. (1965[1908]), Die psychosexuellen Differenzen der Hysterie und der Dementia Praecox, *Zentralblatt für Nervenheilkunde und Psychiatrie*, 19, pp. 521-533; Les différences psychosexuelles entre l'hystérie et la démence précoce, trans. from the German, *Œuvres complètes 1*, Paris, Payot, pp. 36-47.

Abraham, K. (1965[1910]), Über hysterische Traumzustände, *Jahrbuch für psychoanalytische und psychopathologische Forschungen*, 2, pp. 1-32; Les états oniriques hystériques, trans. from the German, *Œuvres complètes 1*, Paris, Payot, pp. 63-90.

Abse, D. (1967), Hysteria, in Arieti, S. (ed.), *American Handbook of Psychiatry*, vol. 1, Basic Books, New York, pp. 272-292.

Aldridge-Morris, R. (1989), *Multiple Personality. An Exercise in Deception*, Lawrence Erlbaum Ass. Ltd. Publishers.

Alexander, F. (1950), *Psychosomatic Medicine: Its Principles and Applications*, New York, Norton.

Alves Garcia, J. (1959), Les formes pseudo-névrotiques des schizophrènies, *Annales médico-psychologiques*, 117, pp. 25-45.

American Psychiatric Association (1944), *One Hundred Years of American Psychiatry (1844-1944)*, New York, Columbia University Press.

American Psychiatric Association (1980), *Diagnostic and Statistical Manual of Mental Disorders. Third Edition*, Washington.

American Psychiatric Association (1987), *Diagnostic and Statistical Manual of Mental Disorders. Third Edition Revised*, Washington.

Anderssen, J. & Laerum, H. (1980), Psychogenic Psychoses, *Acta Psychiatrica Scandinavica*, 62, pp. 331-342.

Aragon, L. & Breton, A. (1928), Le cinquantenaire de l'hystérie (1878-1928), *La Révolution surréaliste*, 11, pp. 20-22.

Arieti, S. & Meth, J. (1967), Rare, Unclassifiable, Collective, and Exotic Psychotic Syndromes, in Arieti, S. (ed.), *American Handbook of Psychiatry*, vol. 1, Basic Books, New York, pp. 546-563.

Asaad, G. & Shapiro, B. (1986), Hallucinations: Theoretical and Clinical Overview, *American Journal of Psychiatry*, 143, 9, pp. 1088-1097.

Asaad G. & Shapiro, B. (1987), Hallucinations as Conversion Symptoms. Drs. Asaad and Shapiro Reply, letter to the editor, *American Journal of Psychiatry*, 144, pp. 696-697.

Attié, J. (1982), Billy Milligan, l'Homme aux 24 personnalités, *L'Ane*, 7, p. 26.

Aubin, B., Thiriat, J., de Montmarin, M., Tixier, G. & Vergé, J. (1977), Schizophrénie et/ou hystérie, *Etudes Psychothérapeutiques*, 28, pp. 81-90.

Azam, Ch. (1893), *Hypnotisme et double conscience. Origine de leur étude et divers travaux sur des sujets analogues*, Paris, Félix Alcan.

Bail, P. (1967), Les moments psychotiques de l'existence hystérique. Contribution à l'étude psychopathologique du cadre des bouffées délirantes, doctor's thesis, University of Paris.

Baillarger, J. (1869), *Des symptômes de la paralysie générale et des rapports de cette maladie avec la folie*, Appendix to «Traité des Maladies mentales» by prof. Griesinger, trans. from the German, Paris, Delahaye.

Bally, G. (1930), Zur Frage der Behandlung schizoider Neurotiker, *Internationale Zeitschrift für Psychoanalyse*, 16, pp. 253-260.

Barnes, M. & Berke, J. (1971), *Mary Barnes. Two Accounts of a Journey through Madness*, London, Mc Gibbon & Kee.

Baruk, H. (1947), *Psychoses et névroses*, Que sais-je?, Paris, PUF.

Baruk, H. (1956), Les fausses schizophrénies, *Evolution Psychiatrique*, 21, pp. 15-21.

Baruk, H. (1967), *La psychiatrie française de Pinel à nos jours*, Paris, PUF.

Basz, S., Chamorro, J. & Nepomiachi, R. (1986), Phénomènes psychotiques et pervers dans la cure de l'hystérique, in Fondation du Champ freudien, *Hystérie et obsession. Les structures cliniques de la névrose et la direction de la cure*, Proceedings of the Fourth International Meeting of the Freudian Field, 14-17 February 1986, Paris, Fondation du Champ freudien, pp. 415-425.

Benadiba, M., Adjedj J.-P., Horber, M. & Sichel J.-P. (1980), Quelques problèmes particuliers posés par la pathologie mentale des transplantés nord-africains, *Annales médico-psychologiques*, 138, 1, pp. 88-94.

Bercherie, P. (1980), *Les Fondements de la Clinique. Histoire et Structure du Savoir psychiatrique*, La Bibliothèque d'Ornicar?, Analytica no. 20-21, Paris.

Bercherie, P. (1988), *Géographie du champ psychanalytique*, Bibliothèque des Analytica, Paris, Navarin.

Bergeret, J. (1974), Limites des états analysables et états-limites analysables, *Nouvelle Revue de Psychanalyse*, 10, pp. 107-122.

Besso, L. (1969), Contribution à l'approche psychodynamique du problème des rapports entre l'hystérie et la schizophrénie. Etude clinique de cinq cas, *Archives Suisses de Neurologie, Neurochirurgie et de Psychiatrie*, 105, 1, pp. 115-144.

Billiet, L. (1988), Libido en Oedipuscomplex versus symbolisering en Naam-van-de-Vader. Freud en Lacan over de psychose (Libido and Oedipus complex vs. symbolization and Name-of-the-Father. Freud and Lacan on psychosis), Ph.D. dissertation, University of Ghent.

Binswanger, O. (1904), *Die Hysterie*, Specielle Pathologie und Therapie, edited by H. Nothnagel, vol. 12, part I.2., Vienna, Alfred Hölder.

Birnbaum, K. (1923), *Der Aufbau der Psychose*, Berlin, Springer

Verlag.

Bishop, E. & Holt, A. (1980), Pseudopsychosis: a Reexamination of the Concept of Hysterical Psychosis, *Comprehensive Psychiatry*, 21, 2, pp. 150-161.

Bleuler, E. (1950[1911]), *Dementia praecox oder Gruppe der Schizophrenien*; *Dementia praecox or the Group of Schizophrenias*, trans. from the German, New York, International Universities Press.

Bloch, J. (1991), *Assessment and Treatment of Multiple Personality and Dissociative Disorders*, Sarasota, Professional Resource Press.

Briquet, P. (1859), *Traité clinique et thérapeutique de l'hystérie*, Paris, Ballière.

Brunner, J. (1991), Psychiatry, Psychoanalysis, and Politics during the First World War, *Journal of the History of the Behavioral Sciences*, 27, pp. 352-365.

Bruno, M.-D. (1979), L'hystérique délirant, doctor's thesis, University of Paris.

Bruno, M.-D. & Maurey, G. (1979), L'hystérique délire toujours, *Etudes Psychothérapeutiques*, 38, pp. 287-292.

Bruno, P., Bautista, B., Bousseyroux, M., Lapeyre, M., Sauret M.J., Terrisse, C. & Vals, A. (1986), 1886-1986: l'hystérie masculine, in Fondation du Champ freudien, *Hystérie et obsession. Les structures cliniques de la névrose et la direction de la cure*, Proceedings of the Fourth International Meeting of the Freudian Field, 14-17 February 1986, Paris, Fondation du Champ freudien, pp. 183-195.

Caldwell, T. & Stewart, R. (1981), Hysterical Seizures and Hypnotherapy, *American Journal of Clinical Hypnosis*, 23, 4, pp. 294-298.

Capgras, Rouart & Dérombier (1953), Délire imaginatif. Hystérie ou schizophrénie, *Annales médico-psychologiques*, 93, 2, pp. 73-80.

Carroy-Thirard, J. (1979), Figures de femmes hystériques dans la psychiatrie au 19e siècle, *Psychanalyse à l'université*, 4, 14, pp. 313-324.

Carroy, J. (1993), *Les personnalités doubles et multiples. Entre science et fiction*, Psychopathologie-Epistémologie/Histoire, Paris, PUF.

Cattell, J. (1966), A Psychodynamic View of Pseudoneurotic Schizophrenia, in Hoch, P. & Zubin, J. (eds.), *Psychopathology of Schizophrenia*, New York, London, Grune & Stratton, pp. 19-36.

Cavenar, J., Sullivan, J. & Maltbie, A. (1979), A Clinical Note on Hysterical Psychosis, *American Journal of Psychiatry*, 136, 6, pp. 830-832.

Charcot, J.-M. (1882), Sur les divers états nerveux déterminés par l'hypnotisation chez les hystériques, *Comptes Rendues hebdomadaires Académie des sciences*, 44, pp. 403-405.

Charcot, J.-M. (1887), *Leçons sur les maladies du système nerveux faites à la Salpêtrière*, Paris, Delahaye & Lecrosnier.

Charcot, J.-M. (1892), La foi qui guérit, *Revue Hebdomadaire*, Dec., pp. 112-132.

Charcot, J.-M, Brissaud, E. & Bouchard (eds.) (1894), *Traité de médecine*, vol. 6, Paris, Masson.

Charcot, J.-M. & Richer, P. (1887), *Les démoniaques dans l'art*, Paris.

Chase, T. (1987), *When Rabbit howls*, New York, Dutton.

Chazaud, J. (1981), A propos du concept de «psychose hystérique», *Information Psychiatrique*, 57, 1, pp. 47-53.

Chazaud, J. (1983), *Hystérie, schizophrénie, paranoia. Chemins vers une psychiatrie psychoanalytique*, Domaines de la psychiatrie, Toulouse, Privat.

Chazaud, J. & De La Payonne-Lidbom, A. (1988), A propos d'une correspondance récemment découverte entre Freud et Bjerre, *Frénésie. Revue de la Société Internationale d'Histoire de la Psychiatrie et de la Psychanalyse*, 5, pp. 97-114.

Chertok, L. & Stengers, I. (1989), *Le cœur et la raison. L'hypnose en question de Lavoisier à Lacan*, Paris, Payot.

Claude, H. (1937), Rapports de l'hystérie avec la schizophrénie, *Annales médico-psychologiques*, 95, 2, pp. 241-264.

Claude, H., Dublineau, J. & Rubenovitch (1934), Troubles psychiques de type mystique. Etat oniroïde et confusionnel avec pouvoir de résurrection. Crises nerveuses avec émission d'urine. Possibilité d'un état comitial, *Annales médico-psychologiques*, 92, 1, pp. 103-109.

Clément, C. & Kakar, S. (1993), *La folle et le saint*, Paris, Seuil.

Colin, H. (1890), Essai sur l'état mental des hystériques, doctor's thesis, University of Paris.

Cordié, A. (1976), Névrose ou psychose: deux cas cliniques, *Lettres de l'Ecole Freudienne de Paris*, 18, pp. 104-128.

Cottraux, J., Reyss-Brion, M. & Massot, D. (1969), La notion de psychose hystérique. Discussion à propos de deux cas, *Journal de Médecine de Lyon*, 50, pp. 959-965.

Courbon, P. (1937), Hystérie, schizophrénie, pithiatisme et simulation, *Annales médico-psychologiques*, 95, 2, pp. 268-273.

Dalle, B. (1969), Syndrome hallucinatoire chronique et hystérie, *Evolution Psychiatrique*, 34, pp. 339-358.

De Boucaud, N. & Demangeat, T. (1962), Les psychoses hystériques: une tentative de réhabilitation, *Journal de médecine de Bordeaux*, 139, 8, p. 962.

De Boucaud, N., Hubert, L., Gachie, J. & Seze, M. (1971), Psychoses délirantes aiguës et structure hysterique, in *Comptes rendus du Congrès de Psychiatrie et de Neurologie de langue française, Caen, 5-10 juillet 1971*, Paris, Masson.

De Mijolla, A. (1986), Du prudent usage des notions d'«hystérie» et d'«hystérique» en psychanalyse, *Revue française de psychanalyse*, 3, pp. 891-904.

Demoulin, C. (1984a), Critique de la théorie de Jean Bergeret, *Quarto*, 15, pp. 57-60.

Demoulin, C. (1984b), Aux frontières de la psychose. Présentation clinique, *Quarto*, 17, pp. 65-68.

Deniker, P. & Quintard, J. (1961), Les signes pseudonévrotiques dans les formes limites de la schizophrénie, *Encéphale*, 50, 3, pp. 307-323.

Derksen, J. (1986), *Strukturele diagnostiek van psychische stoornissen: neurose, borderline, psychose* (Structural diagnosis of psychic disorders: Neurosis, borderline, psychosis), Baarn,

Nelissen.

Derksen, J. (1989), Over het ego en zelf bij borderline- en narcistische stoornissen (On the ego and self in borderline and narcissistic disorders), *Tijdschrift voor Psychiatrie*, 31, Books 2, pp. 8-13.

De Urtubey, L. (1985), Histoire d'Agar servante-épouse d'Abraham ou de la décompensation de l'hystéro-phobie en bouffée délirante, *Revue Française de Psychanalyse*, 49, 1, pp. 457-464.

Di Ciaccia, A. (1983), Bleuler ou la psychanalyse apprivoisée, *Quarto*, 9, pp. 56-58.

Didi-Huberman, G. (1982), *Invention de l'hystérie*, Scènes, Paris, Macula.

Eissler, K. (1986[1979]), *Freud as an Expert Witness. The Discussion of War Neuroses Between Freud and Wagner-Jauregg*, trans. from the German, Madison, Conn., International Universities Press.

Ellenberger, H. (1965), Charcot and the Salpêtrière School, *American Journal of Psychotherapy*, 19, pp. 253-267.

Ellenberger, H. (1968), La conférence de Freud sur l'hystérie masculine (15 octobre 1886). Etude critique, *Information Psychiatrique*, 44, 10, pp. 921-929.

Ellenberger, H. (1970), *The Discovery of the Unconscious. The History and Evolution of Dynamic Psychiatry*, New York, Basic Books.

Ellenberger, H. (1972), L'histoire d'«Anna O»: étude critique avec documents nouveaux, *Evolution Psychiatrique*, 37, 4, pp. 693-717.

Eskelinen de Folch, E. (1984), The Hysteric's Use and Misuse of Observation, *International Journal of Psycho-Analysis*, 65, pp. 399-410.

Evrard, E. (1958), Aux confins de la schizophrénie. Considérations sur certains états limitrophes, *Acta Neurologica Psychiatrica Belgica*, 58, 5, pp. 356-371.

Ey, H. (1973-1975), *Traité des hallucinations*, 2 vol., Paris, Masson.

Fairbairn, R. (1974), Les facteurs schizoïdes dans la personnalité, *Nouvelle Revue de Psychanalyse*, 10, pp. 35-55.

Falret, J. (1890), Folie raisonnante ou folie morale, *Etudes cliniques sur les maladies mentales et nerveuses*, Paris, Baillière & Fils.

Federn, P. (1952), *Ego Psychology and the Psychoses*, New York, Basic Books.

Fenichel, O. (1945), *The Psychoanalytic Theory of Neuroses*, New York, Norton.

Ferenczi, S. (1978[1916-1917]), Über zwei Typen der Kriegsneurose (Hysterie), *Internationale Zeitschrift für Psychoanalyse*, 4, pp. 131-145; Deux types de névrose de guerre (hystérie), trans. from the German, *Œuvres complètes. Psychanalyse 2*, Paris, Payot, pp. 238-252.

Ferenczi, S. (1982[1919], Die Psychoanalyse der Kriegsneurosen, in *Zur Psychoanalyse der Kriegsneurosen*, Vienna, Internationaler Psychoanalytischer Verlag; Psychanalyse et névroses de guerre, *Œuvres complètes. Psychanalyse 3*, trans. from the German, Paris, Payot, pp. 27-43.

Ferenczi, S. (1925), Charcot, *Internationale Zeitschrift für Psychoanalyse*, 11, 3, pp. 257-260.

Fischer-Homberger, E. (1975), *Die traumatische Neurose*, Bern, Stuttgart, Vienna, Hans Huber Verlag.

Flournoy, O. (1974), Les cas-limites: psychose ou névrose?, *Nouvelle Revue de Psychanalyse*, 10, pp. 123-124.

Follin, S. (1947), Une psychose oniroïde de culpabilité (aspects cliniques de la sociogenèse des troubles mentaux), *Evolution Psychiatrique*, 12, pp. 61-95.

Follin, S., Chazaud, P. & Pilon, L. (1961), Cas cliniques de psychoses hystériques, *Evolution Psychiatrique*, 26, pp. 257-286.

Foucault, M. (1972), *Histoire de la folie à l'âge classique*, Paris, Gallimard.

Freud, S. (1886), Über männliche Hysterie, *Wiener medizinische Wochenschrift*, 23 Oct., pp. 1444-1446.

Freud, S. (1886d), Beobachtung einer hochgradigen Hemianästhesie bei einem hysterischen Manne (Beiträge zur Kasuistik der Hysterie I), *G.W.*, Nachtragsband, pp. 57-64; Observation of a Severe Case of Hemi-Anaesthesia in a Hysterical Male, *S.E.*, 1, pp. 25-31.

Freud, S. (1886f), Vorwort des Übersetzers von J.-M. Charcot «Leçons sur les maladies du système nerveux, faites à la Salpêtrière (1860)», *G.W.*, Nachtragsband, pp. 52-53; Preface to the Translation of Charcot's 'Lectures on the diseases of the nervous system' (1860), *S.E.*, 1, pp. 21-22.

Freud, S. (1888b), Hysterie, *G.W.*, Nachtragsband, pp. 72-90; Hysteria, *S.E.*, 1, pp. 41-57.

Freud, S. (1892-1893), Ein Fall von hypnotischer Heilung nebst Bemerkungen über die Entstehung hysterischer Symptome durch den «Gegenwillen», *G.W.*, 1, pp. 3-17; A Case of Successful Treatment by Hypnotism, *S.E.*, 1, pp. 117-128.

Freud, S. (1892-1894), Vorwort und Anmerkungen zur Übersetzung von J.-M. Charcot «Leçons du mardi à la Salpêtrière (1887-1888)», *G.W.*, Nachtragsband, pp. 153-164; Preface and Footnotes to Charcot's 'Tuesday Lectures' (1887-88), *S.E.*, 1, pp. 133-136.

Freud, S. (1893c[1888-1893]), Quelques considérations pour une étude comparative des paralysies motrices organiques et hystériques, *G.W.*, 1, pp. 39-55; Some Points for a Comparative Study of Organic and Hysterical Motor Paralyses, *S.E.*, 1, pp. 160-172.

Freud, S. (1893f), Charcot, *G.W.*, 1, pp. 21-35; Charcot, *S.E.*, 3, pp. 11-23.

Freud, S. (1893h), Über den psychischen Mechanismus hysterischer Phänomene, *G.W.*, Nachtragsband, pp. 183-195; On the Psychical Mechanism of Hysterical Phenomena, *S.E.*, 3, pp. 27-39.

Freud, S. (1894a), Die Abwehr-neuropsychosen, *G.W.*, 1, pp. 59-74; The Neuro-Psychoses of Defense, *S.E.*, 3, pp. 45-61.

Freud, S. (1895g), Über Hysterie, *G.W.*, Nachtragsband, pp. 328-351.

Freud, S. (1896a), L'hérédité et l'étiologie des névroses, *G.W.*, 1, pp. 407-422; Heredity and the Aetiology of the Neuroses,

S.E., 3, pp. 143-156.

Freud, S. (1896b), Weitere Bemerkungen über die Abwehrneuropsychosen, *G.W.*, 1, pp. 379-403; Further Remarks on the Neuro-Psychoses of Defense, *S.E.*, 3, pp. 162-185.

Freud, S. (1896c), Zur Ätiologie der Hysterie, *G.W.*, 1, pp. 425-459; The Aetiology of Hysteria, *S.E.*, 3, pp. 191-219.

Freud, S. (1900a), *Die Traumdeutung*, *G.W.*, 2 and 3; *The Interpretation of Dreams*, *S.E.*, 4 and 5.

Freud, S. (1905d), *Drei Abhandlungen zur Sexualtheorie*, *G.W.*, 5, pp. 29-145; *Three Essays on the Theory of Sexuality*, *S.E.*, 7, pp. 125-243.

Freud, S. (1905e[1901]), Bruchstück einer Hysterie-Analyse, *G.W.*, 5, pp. 163-286; Fragment of an Analysis of a Case of Hysteria, *S.E.*, 7, pp. 7-122.

Freud, S. (1906a[1905]), Meine Ansichten über die Rolle der Sexualität in der Ätiologie der Neurosen, *G.W.*, 5, pp. 149-159; My Views on the Part Played by Sexuality in the Aetiology of the Neuroses, *S.E.*, 7, pp. 271-279.

Freud, S. (1907a[1906]), Der Wahn und die Träume in W. Jensens «Gradiva», *G.W.*, 7, pp. 31-125; Delusions and Dreams in Jensen's 'Gradiva', *S.E.*, 9, pp. 7-95.

Freud, S. (1908a), Hysterische Phantasien und ihre Beziehung zur Bisexualität, *G.W.*, 7, pp. 191-199; Hysterical Fantasies and their Relation to Bisexuality, *S.E.*, 9, pp. 159-166.

Freud, S. (1909a[1908]), Allgemeines über den hysterischen Anfall, *G.W.*, 7, pp. 235-240; General Remarks on Hysterical Attacks, *S.E.*, 9, pp. 229-234.

Freud, S. (1910i), Die psychogene Sehstörung in psychoanalytischer Auffassung, *G.W.*, 8, pp. 94-102; The Psycho-Analytic View of Psychogenic Disturbance of Vision, *S.E.*, 11, pp. 211-218.

Freud, S. (1911c[1910]), Psychoanalytische Bemerkungen über einen autobiographisch beschriebenen Fall von Paranoia (Dementia Paranoides), *G.W.*, 8, pp. 240-320; Psycho-Analytic Notes Upon an Autobiographical Account of a Case of Paranoia (Dementia Paranoides), *S.E.*, 12, pp. 9-82.

Freud, S. (1913j), Das Interesse an der Psychoanalyse, *G.W.*, 8, pp. 390-420; The Claims of Psycho-Analysis to Scientific Interest, *S.E.*, 13, pp. 165-190.

Freud, S. (1914d), Zur Geschichte der psychoanalytischen Bewegung, *G.W.*, 10, pp. 44-113; On the History of the Psycho-Analytic Movement, *S.E.*, 14, pp. 7-66.

Freud, S. (1915d), Die Verdrängung, *G.W.*, 10, pp. 248-261; Repression, *S.E.*, 14, pp. 146-158.

Freud, S. (1916-1917[1915-1917]), *Vorlesungen zur Einführung in die Psychoanalyse*, *G.W.*, 11; *Introductory Lectures on Psycho-Analysis*, *S.E.*, 15 and 16.

Freud, S. (1917a[1916]), Eine Schwierigkeit der Psychoanalyse, *G.W.*, 12, pp. 3-12; A Difficulty in the Path of Psycho-Analysis, *S.E.*, 17, pp. 137-144.

Freud, S. (1917d[1915]), Metapsychologische Ergänzung zur Traumlehre, *G.W.*, 10, pp. 412-426; Metapsychological Supplement to the Theory of Dreams, *S.E.*, 14, pp. 222-235.

Freud, S. (1920a), Über die Psychogenese eines Falles von weiblicher Homosexualität, *G.W.*, 12, pp. 271-302; The Psychogenesis of a Case of Homosexuality in a Woman, *S.E.*, 18, pp. 147-172.

Freud, S. (1921[1919d]), Einleitung zu *Zur Psychoanalyse der Kriegsneurosen*, *G.W.*, 12, pp. 321-324; Introduction, in Jones, E. (ed.), *Psycho-Analysis and the War Neuroses*, The International Psychoanalytical Library no. 2, The International Psycho-Analytical Press, London, Vienna, New York, pp. 1-4.

Freud, S. (1921c), *Massenpsychologie und Ich-Analyse*, *G.W.*, 13, pp. 71-161; *Group Psychology and the Analysis of the Ego*, *S.E.*, 18, pp. 69-143.

Freud, S. (1923b), *Das Ich und das Es*, *G.W.*, 13, pp. 237-289; *The Ego and the Id*, *S.E.*, 19, pp. 12-66.

Freud, S. (1923d[1922]), Eine Teufelsneurose im siebzehnten Jahrhundert, *G.W.*, 13, pp. 317-353; A Seventeenth-Century Demonological Neurosis, *S.E.*, 19, pp. 72-105.

Freud, S. (1924b[1923]), Neurose und Psychose, *G.W.*, 13, pp. 387-391; Neurosis and Psychosis, *S.E.*, 19, pp. 149-153.

Freud, S. (1924e), Der Realitätsverlust bei Neurose und Psychose, *G.W.*, 13, pp. 363-368; The Loss of Reality in Neurosis and Psychosis, *S.E.*, 19, pp. 183-187.
Freud, S. (1925d[1924]), *Selbstdarstellung*, *G.W.*, 14, pp. 33-96; *An Autobiographical Study*, *S.E.*, 20, pp. 7-74.
Freud, S. (1927e), Fetischismus, *G.W.*, 14, pp. 311-317; Fetishism, *S.E.*, 21, pp. 152-157.
Freud, S. (1928b[1927]), Dostoevski und die Vatertötung, *G.W.*, 14, pp. 399-418; Dostoevski and Parricide, *S.E.*, 21, pp. 177-194.
Freud, S. (1950[1895]), *Entwurf einer Psychologie*, *G.W.*, Nachtragsband, pp. 387-477; *Project for a Scientific Psychology*, *S.E.*, 1, pp. 295-391.
Freud, S. (1955c[1920]), Gutachten über die elektrische Behandlung der Kriegsneurotiker, *G.W.*, Nachtragsband, pp. 704-710; Memorandum on the Electrical Treatment of War Neurotics, *S.E.*, 17, pp. 211-215.
Freud, S. & Breuer, J. (1893a), Über den psychischen Mechanismus hysterischer Phänomene. Vorlaüfige Mitteilung, *G.W.*, 1, pp. 81-98; On the Psychical Mechanism of Hysterical Phenomena: Preliminary Communication, *S.E.*, 2, pp. 3-17.
Freud, S. & Breuer, J. (1895d), *Studien über Hysterie*, Frankfurt-am-Main, Fischer Verlag; *Studies on Hysteria*, *S.E.*, 2.
Freud, S. & Breuer J. (1940d[1892]), Zur Theorie des hysterischen Anfalls, *G.W.*, 17, pp. 9-13.
Frosch, J. (1988), Psychotic Character versus Borderline, *International Journal of Psycho-Analysis*, 69, 3, pp. 347-357 and 4, pp. 445-456.
Ganser, J. (1898), Über einen eigenartigen hysterischen Dämmerzustand, *Archiv für Psychiatrie und Nervenkrankheiten*, 30, pp. 633-640.
Garrabé, J. (1981), Monopsychose?, *Information Psychiatrique*, 57, 1, pp. 39-46.
Garrabé, J. (1992) *Histoire de la schizophrénie*, collection Médecine et Histoire, Paris, Seghers.
Geerardyn, F. (1993), *Freuds psychologie van het oordeel. Over*

het begin van de psychoanalyse (Freud's psychology of judgment. On the beginnings of psychoanalysis), Pegasos series no. 10, Ghent, Idesça.

Gelder, M., Gath, D. & Mayon, R. (1989), *Oxford Textbook of Psychiatry*, 2nd edition, Oxford Medical Publications, Oxford, New York, Melbourne, Oxford University Press.

Gift, T. & Strauss, J. (1986), Drs. Gift and Strauss Reply, letter to the editor, *American Journal of Psychiatry*, 143, 8, p. 1071.

Gift, T., Strauss, J. & Young, Y. (1985), Hysterical psychosis: An Empirical Approach, *American Journal of Psychiatry*, 142, 3, pp. 345-347.

Gilles de la Tourette, G. (1891), *Traité clinique et thérapeutique de l'hystérie d'après l'Enseignement de la Salpêtrière. Première Partie: Hystérie normale ou interparoxystique*, Paris, Plon, Nourrit & Co.

Gilles de la Tourette, G. (1895), *Traité clinique et thérapeutique de l'hystérie d'après l'Enseignement de la Salpêtrière. Seconde Partie: Hystérie paroxystique I et II*, Paris, Plon, Nourrit & Co.

Gilman, S.L., King, H., Porter, R., Rousseau, G.S. & Showalter, E. (1993), *Hysteria Beyond Freud*, Berkeley, Los Angeles, London, University of California Press.

Giudicelli, S. (1986), Hystéries et psychoses, *Evolution Psychiatrique*, 51, 3, pp. 639-669.

Gold, S. & Mallett, B. (1964), A Pseudoschizophrenic Hysterical Syndrome, *British Journal of Medical Psychology*, 37, pp. 59-70.

Green, A. (1974), L'analyste, la symbolisation et l'absence dans le cadre analytique, *Nouvelle Revue de Psychanalyse*, 10, pp. 225-258.

Gregory, I. & Smeltzer, D. (1977), *Psychiatry. Essentials of Clinical Practice*, Boston, Little, Brown & Co.

Griesinger, W. (1865[1845]), *Pathologie und Therapie der psychischen Krankheiten*; *Traité des maladies mentales, pathologie et thérapeutique*, Paris, Delahaye.

Grosskurth, Ph. (1987[1986]), *Melanie Klein. Her World and her*

Work, Cambridge, Mass., Harvard University Press.
Guillain, G. (1955), *J.-M. Charcot (1825-1893). Sa vie, son œuvre*, Paris, Masson.
Guir, J. (1983), *Psychosomatique et cancer*, Paris, Point hors ligne.
Gutheil, E. (ed.) (1950), *The Autobiography of Wilhelm Stekel*, New York, Liveright.
Hirsch, S. & Hollender, M. (1964), Hysterical Psychosis, *American Journal of Psychiatry*, 120, pp. 1066-1074.
Hirsch, S. & Hollender, M. (1969), Hysterical Psychosis: Clarification of the Concept, *American Journal of Psychiatry*, 127, 7, pp. 909-915.
Hirschmüller, A. (1989[1978]), *The Life and Work of Josef Breuer. Physiology and Psychoanalysis*, trans. from the German, New York, London, New York University Press.
Hoch, P. (1967), Pharmacologically Induced Psychoses, in Arieti, S. (ed.), *American Handbook of Psychiatry*, vol. 2, Basic Books, New York, pp. 1697-1708.
Hoch, P. & Cattell, J. (1959), The Diagnosis of Pseudoneurotic Schizophrenia, *Psychiatric Quarterly*, 33, pp. 17 et seq.
Hoch, P., et al. (1954), The Course and Outcome of Pseudoneurotic Schizophrenia, *American Journal of Psychiatry*, 111, pp. 337 et seq.
Hoch, P. & Polatin, P. (1949), Pseudoneurotic Forms of Schizophrenia, *Psychiatric Quarterly*, 23, pp. 248-276.
Hoch, P. & Zubin, J. (eds.) (1966), *Psychopathology of Schizophrenia*, New York, London, Grune & Stratton.
Hollender, M. & Pattison, E.(1986), Why no cases of Hysterical Psychosis?, letter to the editor, *American Journal of Psychiatry*, 143, 8, p. 1070-1071.
Hollender, M. & Welles, Ch. (1972), Hysterical Psychosis, *Journal of the National Association of Private Psychiatric Hospitals*, 4, 3, pp. 36-38.
Hoogduin, C., Van Dyck, R. & De Haan, E. (1990), Behandeling van conversies met hypnose (Hypnotic treatment of conversions), *Tijdschrift voor Psychiatrie*, 32, 7, pp. 450-461.

Hummelen, J. (1990), De bruikbaarheid van de diagnose borderline (The usefulness of the diagnosis of borderline), *Tijdschrift voor Psychiatrie*, 3, pp. 147-160.

Israël, L. (1976), *L'Hystérique, le sexe et le médecin*, Paris, Masson.

Jaccard, R. (ed.) (1982), *Histoire de la psychanalyse*, vol. 2, Paris, Hachette.

Janet, P. (1889), *Automatisme psychologique*, Paris, Félix Alcan.

Janet, P. (1893), Contribution à l'étude des accidents mentaux chez les hystériques, doctor's thesis, University of Paris.

Janet, P. (1910[1909]), *Les névroses*, Paris, Flammarion.

Janet, P. (1911[1892-1894]), *L'état mental des hystériques*, 2nd edition, Paris, Félix Alcan.

Janet, P. (1914), *Névroses et idées fixes*, 3rd edition, vol. 2, Paris, Félix Alcan.

Janet, P. (1919), *Les Médications psychologiques (Etudes historiques, psychologiques et cliniques sur les méthodes de la psychothérapie)*, Paris, Félix Alcan.

Janet, P. (1926-1928), *De l'angoisse à l'extase I & II*, Paris, Félix Alcan.

Janet, P. (1927), A propos de la schizophrénie, *Journal de Psychologie*, 24, pp. 477-492.

Janet, P. (1980[1923]), *La médecine psychologique*, Paris, La société Pierre Janet et le laboratoire de psychologie pathologique de la Sorbonne.

Jaspers, K. (1922), *Strindberg und Van Gogh. Versuch einer pathographischen Analyse unter vergleichender Herabziehung von Swedenborg und Hölderlin*, Bern, Ernst Bucher.

Jaspers, K. (1923[1913]), *Allgemeine Pyschopathologie*, 3rd edition, revised and enlarged, Berlin, Heidelberg, Springer Verlag.

Jeanneau, A. (1974), Le délire n'est pas un rêve, *Revue Française de Psychanalyse* 38, 5-6, pp. 1137-1140.

Jeanneau, A. (1985), L'hystérie. Unité et diversité, *Revue Française de Psychanalyse*, 49, 1, pp. 107-326.

Jeanneau, A. (1990), *Les délires non psychotiques*, Le fait Psy-

chanalytique, Paris, PUF.
Jones, E. (1921), War Shock and Freud's Theory of the Neuroses, in Jones, E. (ed.), *Psycho-Analysis and the War Neuroses*, introduction by S. Freud, The International Psychoanalytical Library no. 2, The International Psycho-Analytical Press, London, Vienna, New York, pp. 44-59.
Jones, E. (ed.) (1921), *Psycho-Analysis and the War Neuroses*, introduction by S. Freud, The International Psychoanalytical Library no. 2, The International Psychoanalytical Press, London, Vienna, New York.
Jones, E. (1980[1954-1957]), *Sigmund Freud. Life and work*, 4th edition, 3 volumes, London, Hogarth Press.
Jung, C. (1902), Zur Psychologie und Pathologie sogenannter occulte Phänomene, doctor's thesis, University of Leipzig.
Jung, C. (1903), Über Simulation von Geistesstörung, *Journal für Psychologie und Neurologie*, 2, pp. 181-201.
Jung, C. (1979[1907]), *Über die Psychologie der Dementia praecox: Ein Versuch*, Halle a. S.; *The Psychology of Dementia Praecox*, trans. from the German, *C.G. Jung. The Collected Works*, vol. 3, London, Routledge & Kegan, pp. 70-98.
Kalhbaum, K. (1874), *Die Katatonie oder die Spannungsirresein*, Berlin.
Kammerer, Th. & Wartel, R. (1986), Dialogue sur les diagnostics, in Gori, R., Miller, J.-A. & Wartel, R. (eds.) (1986), *La Querelle des diagnostics*, Collection Cliniques, Paris, Navarin, pp. 68-71.
Kaplan, J. & Deabler, H. (1975), Hypnotherapy with a Severe Dissociative Hysterical Disorder, *American Journal of Clinical Hypnosis*, 18, 2, pp. 83-89.
Kaufmann, P. (ed.) (1993), *L'apport freudien. Eléments pour une encyclopédie de la psychanalyse*, Paris, Bordas.
Kendell, R. (1988), Other Functional Psychoses, in Kendell, R. & Zealy, A. (eds.), *Companion to Psychiatric Studies*, 4th edition, Edinburgh, Churchill Livingstone, pp. 362-371.
Kernberg, O. (1975), *Borderline Conditions and Pathological Narcissism*, New York, Jason Aronson.

Keyes, D. (1982), *Billy Milligan, l'Homme aux 24 personnalités*, trans. from the English, Paris, Balland.

Klein, Melanie (1946), Notes on some Schizoid Mechanisms, *International Journal of Psycho-Analysis*, 27, pp. 99-111.

Klein, Milton (1983), Freud's Drive Theory and Ego Psychology: A Critical Evaluation of the Blancks, *Psychoanalytic Review*, 70, 4, pp. 505-517.

Kohon, G. (1984), Reflections on Dora: the Case of Hysteria, *International Journal of Psycho-Analysis*, 65, pp. 73-84.

Kortmann, F. (1981), Van neurose naar borderline pathologie (From neurosis to borderline pathology), *Tijdschrift voor Psychiatrie*, 3, pp. 151-162.

Kovess, V. (1982), Le diagnostic de l'hystérie: enquête auprès de psychiatres français, *Information Psychiatrique*, 58, 10, pp. 1239-1250.

Kraepelin, E. (1899), *Psychiatrie. Ein Lehrbuch für Studierende und Ärzte*, 6th edition, vol. 2, Leipzig, Barth.

Kraepelin, E. (1909), *Psychiatrie. Ein Lehrbuch für Studierende und Ärzte*, 8th edition, vol. 3, Leipzig, Barth.

Kraepelin, E. (1980[1912-1913]), *Les paraphrénies*, trans. from the German, presented by P. Bercherie and with a study of F. Bridgman, La Bibliothèque d'Ornicar?, Analytica no. 19, Paris.

Kraepelin, E. (1984[1905]), *Introduction à la psychiatrie clinique*, trans. from the German, Bibliothèque des Analytica, Paris, Navarin.

Kretschmer, E. (1923), *Über Hysterie*, Leipzig, Georg Thieme.

Lacan, J. (1977[1957-1958]), On a Question Preliminary to any Possible Treatment of Psychosis, *Ecrits. A Selection*, trans. from the French by A. Sheridan, New York, Norton, pp. 179-225.

Lacan, J. (1966[1958]), Remarque sur le rapport de Daniel Lagache: «Psychanalyse et structure de la personnalité», *Ecrits*, Paris, Seuil, pp. 647-684.

Lacan, J. (1990[1974]), *Television*, trans. from the French by D. Hollier, R. Krauss & A. Michelson, edited by J.-A. Miller,

New York, London, Norton.

Lacan, J. (1991[1969-1970]), *Le Séminaire, Livre XVII, L'envers de la psychanalyse*, edited by J.-A. Miller, Paris, Seuil.

Langness, L. (1967), Hysterical Psychosis: The Cross-Cultural Evidence, *American Journal of Psychiatry*, 124, 2, pp. 143-152.

Laplanche, J. & Pontalis, J.-B. (1973), *Vocabulaire de la psychanalyse*, Paris, PUF.

Laruelle, L. (1908a), Les psychoses hystériques (étude clinique), *Bulletin de la Société de Médecine Mentale de Belgique*, 140, pp. 245-307 and 141, pp. 346-401.

Laruelle, L. (1908b), Les psychoses hystériques, Psychiatric Report of the Belgian Conference of Neurology and Psychiatry, 26-27 September 1908, *Encéphale*, 2, 3, pp. 606-612.

Lasègue, E. (1881), Les hystériques, leur perversité, leurs mensonges, *Annales médico-psychologiques*, 6, 6, pp. 111-118.

Laurent, E. (1988), Limites de la psychose, in GRAPP, *Les psychiatres et la psychanalyse aujourd'hui*, Paris, Navarin, pp. 88-93.

Le Goe-Diaz, I. (1988) La dépersonalisation, in *Encyclopédie Médico-Chirurgicale, Psychiatrie*, 37125 A10, 6, pp. 4-5.

Le Roux, A. & Rochard, L. (1984), Contribution à l'étude des rapports entre névrose hystérique et psychose schizophrénique, *Annales médico-psychologiques*, 142, 7, pp. 975-988.

Léger, C. (1984), La «tierce personne», *Ornicar?*, 31, pp. 149-157.

Legrand du Saulle, H. (1885), Cas insolite de névrose convulsive, *Annales médico-psychologiques*, 1885, 7, 1, pp. 499-500.

Legrand du Saulle, H. (1883), *L'état mental des hystériques*, Paris.

Legué, G. & Gilles de la Tourette, G. (eds.) (1985[1886]), *Sœur Jeanne des Anges, Supérieure de couvent des Ursulines de Loudun (XVIIe). Autobiographie d'une hystérique possédée*, Montbonnot St. Martin, Jerôme Millon.

Leguil, F. (1979), Etats limites et naufrages de la clinique, *Actualités Psychiatriques*, 8, pp. 75-78.

Lemoine, P. (1973), Sur la place occupée par un délire au cours d'une cure psychanalytique, *Lettres de l'Ecole Freudienne de Paris*, 11, pp. 146-156.
Leroux-Hugon, V. (1987), L'évasion manquée de Geneviève, ou des aléas de la traduction, *Frénésie. Revue de la Société Internationale d'Histoire de la Psychiatrie et de la Psychanalyse*, 4, pp. 103-112.
Lévy-Friesacher, Ch. (1983), *Meynert-Freud. «L'Amentia»*, Psychiatrie ouverte, Paris, PUF.
Lewis, N. (1967), American Psychiatry from its Beginnings to World War II, in Arieti, S. (ed.), *American Handbook of Psychiatry*, vol. 1, Basic Books, New York, pp. 3-17.
Libbrecht, K. (1989), *Hysterische waan. Symptoom of structuur?* (Hysterical delusion: Symptom or structure?), introductory study by J. Quackelbeen, Pegasos series no. 3, Gent, Idesça.
Libbrecht, K. (1989), L'usage imitatif du symptôme: le mimétisme hystérique, *Quarto*, 37-38, pp. 75-79.
Libbrecht, K. (1992), La possession de Loudun: les deux scénarios religieux de Sœur Jeanne de Anges, *Quarto*, 48-49, pp. 53-58.
Liberini, P., Faglia, L. & Salvi F. (1993), What is the Incidence of Conversion Pseudodementia, letter to the editor, *British Journal of Psychiatry*, 162, pp. 124-125.
Lidz, Th. (1967), General Concepts of Psychosomatic Medicine, in Arieti, S. (ed.), *American Handbook of Psychiatry*, vol. 1, Basic Books, New York, pp. 647-658.
Lotterman, A. (1985), Prolonged Psychotic States in Borderline Personality Disorder, *Psychiatric Quarterly*, 57, 1, pp. 33-46.
Macalpine, I. & Hunter, R. (1956), *Schizophrenia 1677. A Psychiatric Study of an Illustrated Autobiographical Record of Demoniacal Possession*, London, Dawson.
Mairet, A. (1908), *La simulation de la folie*, Montpellier, Coulet & fils.
Mairet, A. & Salager, E. (1910), *La folie hystérique*, Paris, Masson & Co.
Maître, J. (1993), *Une inconnue célèbre. La Madeleine Lebouc*

de Janet, foreword by G. Lantéri-Laura, collection Psychanalyse, Paris, Anthropos-Economica.
Maleval, J.-C. (1979), A propos de la symptomatologie «limite» de l'homme aux loups, *Etudes psychothérapeutiques*, 38, 4, pp. 261-271.
Maleval, J.-C. (1981), *Folies hystériques et psychoses dissociatives*, Paris, Payot.
Maleval, J.-C. (1983), Les illusions verbales hystériques, *Cahiers de lectures freudiennes*, 2, pp. 53-72.
Maleval, J.-C. (1985a), Postface aux éditions en langues espagnole et portugaise de 'Folies hystériques et psychoses dissociatives', *Cahiers de lectures freudiennes*, 6, pp. 87-91.
Maleval, J.-C. (1985b), Les hystéries crépusculaires, *Confrontations Psychiatriques*, 25, pp. 63-97.
Marie, P. (1925), Discours à l'occasion du centenaire de Charcot, *Revue neurologique*, 1, 6, pp. 731-745.
Martin, P. (1971), Dynamic Considerations of the Hysterical Psychosis, *American Journal of Psychiatry*, 128, 6, pp. 745-748.
Masson, J. (ed.) (1985), *The Complete Letters of Sigmund Freud to Wilhelm Fliess, 1887-1904*, Cambridge, Mass. and London, Belknap Press.
Maurey, G. (1977), A propos de ce qui suit, *Etudes Psychothérapeutiques*, 28, pp. 77-79.
Mc Guire, W. (ed.) (1974), *The Freud-Jung Letters. The Correspondence between Sigmund Freud and Carl Gustav Jung*, Princeton, N.J., Princeton University Press.
Mc Kegney, F. (1967), Auditory Hallucinations as a Conversion Symptom: A Theoretical Proposal with Two Case Illustrations, *Comprehensive Psychiatry*, 8, pp. 80-89.
Mc Kegney, F. (1987), Hallucinations as Conversion Symptoms, letter to the editor, *American Journal of Psychiatry*, 144, 5, p. 696.
Megens, J. (1985), De multipele persoonlijkheid, een literatuuroverzicht (Multiple personality. A review of the literature), *Tijdschrift voor Psychiatrie*, 27, 5, pp. 301-310.

Meynert, T. (1884), *Psychiatrie. Klinik der Erkrankungen des Vorderhirns begründet auf dessen Bau, Leistungen und Ernährung*, Vienna, Braumüller.
Mikhail, A. (1973), Exotic Syndromes. A Review, *Foreign Psychiatry*, 2, 3, pp. 55-84.
Miller, J.-A. (1981), Encyclopédie, *Ornicar?*, 24, pp. 35-44.
Miller, J.-A. (1983), Schizophrénie et paranoia, *Quarto*, 10, pp. 18-38.
Miller, J.-A. (1984), Liminaire, *Ornicar?*, 29, pp. 5-6.
Milner, M. (1969) *The Hands of the Living God. An account of a Psycho-Analytic Treatment*, London, Hogarth Press.
Mitchell, S. Weir (1885), *Lectures on the Diseases of the Nervous System, especially in Woman*, Philadelphia, Lea Brothers & Co.
Modestin, J. & Bachmann, K. (1992), Is the Diagnosis of Hysterical Psychosis Justified?, *Comprehensive Psychiatry*, 33, 1, pp. 17-24.
Möbius, P. (1888), Über den Begriff der Hysterie (1888), *Zentralblatt für Nervenheilkunde*, 11, pp. 66-71.
Möbius, P. (1894[1890]), Über Astasie-Abasie, *Neurologische Beiträge*, vol. 1, Leipzig, Ambrosius Abel, pp. 8-19.
Möbius, P. (1908[1901]), *Über den physiologischen Schwachsinn des Weibes*, 8th edition, revised and enlarged, Halle a. S., Marhold.
Möbius, P. (1895), Über die gegenwärtige Auffassung der Hysterie, *Monatschrift Geburtsheilkundige Gynäkologie*, 1.
Moreau de Tours, J. (1865), *De la folie hystérique et de quelques phénomènes nerveux propres à l'hystérie convulsive, à l'hystéro-épilepsie et à l'épilepsie. Etudes cliniques*, Union médicale.
Moreau de Tours, J. (1869), *Traité pratique de la folie névropathique (vulgo hystérique)*, Paris.
Morel, B. (1860), *Traité des maladies mentales*, Paris.
Müller, C., Burner, M. & Villa, J.-L. (1956), Hystérie ou schizophrénie. Contribution au diagnostic différentiel, *Encéphale*, 45, pp. 256-266.

Munthe, A. (1930), *The story of San Michele*, New York, Dutton.

Nicholi, A. (ed.) (1988), *The New Harvard Guide to Psychiatry*, Cambridge, Mass. and London, The Belknap Press of Harvard University Press.

Noble, D. (1951), Hysterical Manifestations in Schizophrenic Illness, *Psychiatry*, 14, pp. 153-160.

Nobus, D. (1993), In de schaduw van het fetisjisme (In the shadow of fetishism), review, *Psychoanalytische Perspektieven*, 19-20, pp. 200-203.

Oberndorf, C. (1953), Autobiography of Josef Breuer (1842-1925), *International Journal of Psycho-Analysis*, 34, pp. 64-67.

Pankow, G. (1969), *L'homme et sa psychose*, Paris, Aubier-Montaigne.

Pankow, G. (1972), Image du corps et structures familiales chez les psychotiques, *Information Psychiatrique*, 48, 2, pp. 157-164.

Pankow, G. (1973), L'image du corps dans la psychose hystérique, *Revue Française de Psychanalyse*, 37, 3, pp. 415-438.

Pankow, G. (1977), *Structure familiale et psychose*, Paris, Aubier-Montaigne.

Pankow, G. (1981[1956]), *L'être-là du schizophrène*, Paris, Aubier-Montaigne.

Perrier, F. (1968), Structure hystérique et dialogue analytique, *Confrontations Psychiatriques*, 1, pp. 101-117.

Perry, J. & Klerman, G. (1978), The Borderline Patient. A Comparative Analysis of Four Sets of Diagnostic Criteria, *Archives of General Psychiatry*, 35, pp. 141-150.

Perry, J. & Klerman, G. (1980), Clinical Features of the Borderline Personality Disorder, *American Journal of Psychiatry*, 137, 2, pp. 165-173.

Peters, U. (1984), *Wörterbuch der Psychiatrie und medizinischen Psychologie*, München, Vienna, Baltimore, Urban & Schwarzenberg.

Pontalis, J.-B. (1974), Bornes ou confins?, *Nouvelle Revue de*

Psychanalyse, 10, pp. 5-16.

Porot, A. (ed.) (1975), *Manuel Alphabétique de Psychiatrie clinique et thérapeutique*, Paris, PUF.

Postel, J. (ed.) (1993), *Dictionnaire de psychiatrie et de psychopathologie clinique*, Références Larousse, Paris, Larousse.

Postel, J. & Quétel, C. (eds.) (1983), *Nouvelle histoire de la psychiatrie*, Toulouse, Privat.

Prince, M. (1913[1906]), *The Dissociation of a Personality*, London, Longmans Green.

Putnam, F. (1989), *Diagnosis and Treatment of Multiple Personality Disorder*, London, Guilford Press.

Quackelbeen, J. (ed) (1987), *Psychoanalyse en klinische psychiatrie: Een geschiedenis van eigenheid of verbondenheid?* (Psychoanalysis and clinical psychiatry: A history of singularity or alliance?), Pegasos series no. 2, Ghent, Idesça.

Quackelbeen, J. (1987), Uit de geschiedenis van de gekheid: een gekke geschiedenis. Ten geleide (From the history of madness: A mad history. Introduction), in Quackelbeen, J. (ed.), *Psychoanalyse en klinische psychiatrie: Een geschiedenis van eigenheid of verbondenheid?*, Pegasos series no. 2, Ghent, Idesça, pp. 5-11.

Quackelbeen, J. (1988), Eduquer contre le passage à l'acte, analyser l'acting out?, *Scientia Paedagogica Experimentalis*, 25, 2, pp. 29-41.

Quackelbeen, J. (1989), Hysterische psychose? Een probleem! (Hysterical psychosis? A problem!), in Libbrecht, K., *Hysterische waan. Symptoom of structuur?*, Pegasos series no. 3, Ghent, Idesça, pp. 7-61.

Quackelbeen, J. & Libbrecht, K. (1991), Over mannelijke hysterie (On male hysteria), *Rondzendbrief uit het Freudiaanse Veld*, 49, pp. 29-41.

Racamier, P. (1958), A propos de «Schizophrenia 1677» de I. Macalpine et R. Hunter, *Evolution Psychiatrique*, pp. 669-674.

Refsum, H. & Astrup, C. (1982), Hysteric Reactive Psychoses: A Follow-up, *Neuropsychobiology*, 8, pp. 172-181.

Reich, W. (1927[1925]), Eine hysterische Psychose in «statu

nascendi», *Internationale Zeitschrift für Psychoanalyse*, 11, pp. 211-222; A Hysterical Psychosis in «statu nascendi», *International Journal of Psycho-Analysis*, 8, pp. 159-173.
Richer, P. (1881), *Etudes cliniques sur l'hystéro-épilepsie ou grande hystérie*, Paris, A. Delahaye & Lecrosnier.
Richman, J. & White, H. (1970), A Family Review of Hysterical Psychosis, *American Journal of Psychiatry*, 127, 3, pp. 280-285.
Rosen, J. (1953), *Direct Analysis*, New York, Grune & Stratton.
Rosenfeld, H. (1947), Analysis of a Schizophrenic State with Depersonalization, *International Journal of Psycho-Analysis*, 28, pp. 130-139.
Rosenfeld, H. (1965), *Psychotic States*, London, Hogarth Press.
Ross, C. (1989), *Multiple Personality Disorder. Diagnosis, Clinical Features and Treatment*, New York, John Wiley & Sons.
Rouanduano de Maeso, M. (1986), Hystérie et psychose, *Ornicar?*, 39, pp. 91-109.
Roudinesco, E. (1986), *Histoire de la psychanalyse en France*, 2 vol., Paris, Seuil.
Rümke, H. (1973[1967]), *Psychiatrie III. Tussen psychose en normaliteit* (Psychiatry III. Between psychosis and normality), Amsterdam, Scheltema & Holkema.
Sakheim, D. & Devine, S. (eds.) (1992), *Out of Darkness: Exploring Satanism and Ritual Abuse*, New York, Lexington Books, Macmillan.
Satow, R. (1979), Where has all the Hysteria gone?, *Psychoanalytic Review*, 66, 4, pp. 463-477.
Scharbach, H. (ed.) (1983), *Les états limites. Approche compréhensive chez l'adulte et chez l'enfant*, Conference of Psychiatry and Neurology of French Speaking Countries, Psychiatric Report, 27 June-2 July 1983, Paris, Masson.
Schreber, D. (1973[1903]), *Denkwürtigkeiten eines Nervenkranken*, Frankfurt-am-Main, Berlin, Vienna, Ullstein.
Schreiber, F. (1973), *Sybil*, New York, Warner.
Schüle, H. (1886[1878]), *Klinische Psychiatrie. Specielle Pathologie und Therapie der Geisteskrankheiten*, 3rd edition, Leip-

zig, F.C.W. Vogel.

Sechehaye, M. (1947), *La réalisation symbolique (Nouvelle méthode de psychothérapie appliquée à un cas de schizophrénie)*, supplement to the *Revue suisse de psychologie et de la psychologie appliquée* no. 12, Bern, Hans Huber Verlag.

Sechehaye, M. (1950), *Journal d'une schizophrène*, Paris, PUF.

Seeman, K., Widrow, L. & Yesavage, J. (1984), Fantasized Companions and Suicidal Depressions: Two Case Reports, *American Journal of Psychotherapy*, 38, 4, pp. 541-557.

Simmel, E. (1946), Obituary Otto Fenichel, *International Journal of Psycho-Analysis*, 27, pp. 67-71.

Siomopoulos, V. (1971), Hysterical Psychosis: Psychopathological Aspects, *British Journal of Medical Psychology*, 44, pp. 95-100.

Sirois, F. (1977), La psychose hystérique, *Acta Psychiatrica Belgica*, 77, pp. 216-227.

Smith-Rosenberg, C. (1972), The Hysterical Woman: Sex Roles and Role Conflict in 19th Century America, *Social Research. An International Quarterly of the Social Sciences*, 39, pp. 652-678.

Souques, A., Peige, H. (1939), J.-M. Charcot (1825-1893), *Les Biographies médicales*, Paris, Baillière, pp. 329-352.

Spiegel, D. (1991), Dissociation and Trauma, in Tasman, A. & Goldfinger, S. (eds.), *American Psychiatric Press Review of Psychiatry*, vol. 10, Washington, American Psychiatric Press, pp. 261-275;

Spiegel, D. & Fink, R. (1979), Hysterical Psychosis and Hypnotizability, *American Journal of Psychiatry*, 136, 6, pp. 777-781.

Steingard, S. & Frankel, F. (1985), Dissociation and Psychotic Symptoms, *American Journal of Psychiatry*, 142, 8, pp. 953-955.

Sternbach, O. (1983), Critical Comments on Object Relation Theory, *Psychoanalytic Review*, 70, 3, pp. 403-421.

Stewart, H. (1977), Problems of Management in the Analysis of a Hallucinating Hysteric, *International Journal of Psycho-*

Analysis, 58, pp. 67-76.

Steyaert, M. (1992), *Hystérie, folie et psychose*, Paris, Les Empêcheurs de penser en rond.

Steyerthal, A. (1908), *Was ist Hysterie?*, Sammlung zwangloser Abhandlungen aus dem Gebiete der Nerven- und Geisteskrankheiten, edited by A. Hoche, vol. 8, part 5, Halle a. S., C. Marhold Verlag.

Strachey, J. (1934), The Nature of the Therapeutic Action of Psychoanalysis, *International Journal of Psycho-Analysis*, 15, pp. 127-159.

Strachey, J. (1966), Editor's Introduction to Freud's Papers on Hypnotism and Suggestion, *S.E.*, 1, pp. 63-69.

Strachey, J. (1955), Editor's Introduction to Freud's Studies on Hysteria, *S.E.*, 2, pp. ix-xxviii.

Tachon, J.-P. & Raffaitin, F. (1983), A la recherche d'un langage commun. A propos du D.S.M. III, *Information Psychiatrique*, 59, 6, pp. 789-802.

Tausk, V. (1916a), Diagnostische Erörterungen auf Grund der Zustandsbilder der sogenannten Kriegspsychosen, *Wiener medizinische Wochenschrift*, 66, pp. 1427-1433 and pp. 1456-1463.

Tausk, V. (1975[1916b]), Zur Psychologie des Deserteurs, *Internationale Zeitschrift für Psychoanalyse*, 4, pp. 193-204 and 229-240; Contribution à la psychologie du déserteur, *Œuvres psychanalytiques*, Paris, Payot, pp. 129-156.

Tilleskjor, C. & Watson, C. (1983), Interrelationships of Conversion, Psychogenic Pain and Dissociative Disorder Symptoms, *Journal of Consulting and Clinical Psychology*, 51, 5, pp. 788-789.

Trillat, E. (1986), *Histoire de l'hystérie*, Collection Médecine et Histoire, Paris, Seghers.

Tsoi, W. (1973), The Ganser Syndrome in Singapore: A Report on Ten Cases, *British Journal of Psychiatry*, 123, pp. 567-572.

Tsuang, M., Faraone, S. & Day, M. (1988), Schizophrenic Disorders, in Nicholi, A. (ed.), *The New Harvard Guide to Psychiatry*, Cambridge, Mass. and London, The Belknap Press of

Harvard University Press, pp. 259-295.
Tuckett, D. (1989), A brief View of Herbert Rosenfeld's Contribution to the Theory of Psychoanalytical Technique, *International Journal of Psycho-Analysis*, 70, pp. 619-625.
Tyrer, P. (1989), *Classification of Neurosis*, Chichester, New York, John Wiley & Sons.
Vandereycken, W. (1989), review, *Tijdschrift voor Psychiatrie*, 31, Books 2, pp. 18-19.
Van der Hart, O. (1991), review, *Tijdschrift voor Psychiatrie*, 33, Books 1, pp. 21-22.
Van der Hart, O. & Boon, S. (1990), Het Münchhausen-syndroom «by proxy» en de relatie met de dissociatieve stoornissen (The Münchhausen syndrome «by proxy» in relation to dissociative disorders), *Tijdschrift voor Psychiatrie*, 1, pp. 54-56.
Van der Hart, O & Spiegel, D. (1993), Hypnotic Assessment and Treatment of Trauma-induced Psychoses, *International Journal of Clinical and Experimental Hypnosis*, 41, 3, pp. 191-209.
Van der Hart, O., Witztum, E. & Friedman, B. (1993), From Hysterical Psychosis to Reactive Dissociative Psychosis, *Journal of Traumatic Stress*, 6, 1, pp. 43-64.
Van Hoorde, H. (1984), De hysterische psychose, nosologische struikelsteen en eerherstel? (Hysterical psychosis: nosological obstacle and rehabilitation?), *Psychoanalytische Perspektieven*, 6, pp. 45-57.
Van Hoorde, H. (1988), Psychosomatiek. Veel vragen onder het mom van een bevestiging (Psychosomatics. Many questions under the guise of a confirmation), *Rondzendbrief uit het Freudiaanse Veld*, 33, pp. 3-20.
Van Hoorde, H. (1992), *Psychiatrie en Psychoanalyse: Scheiding van Tafel en Bank?* (Psychiatry and psychoanalysis: Separation of table and sofa?), Pegasos series no. 9, Ghent, Idesça.
Veith, I. (1965), *Hysteria. The History of a Disease*, Chicago and London, The University of Chicago Press.
Verhaeghe, P. (1987), *Tussen hysterie en vrouw—een weg door-*

heen honderd jaar psychoanalyse (Between hysteria and woman—a way through 100 years of psychoanalysis), Medusa series no. 2, Leuven, Amersfoort, Acco.

Verhulst, F. (1981), Diagnostiek van borderline patiënten (Diagnosis of borderline patients), *Tijdschrift voor Psychiatrie*, 1, pp. 21-33.

Villaret, A. (ed.) (1898-1900), *Handwörterbuch der gesamten Medizin*, 2nd edition, 2 vol., Stuttgart, Ferdinand Enke.

Villechenoux, C. (1968), Le cadre de la folie hystérique de 1870 à 1918 (Contribution à l'histoire de la psychiatrie; aspects de l'évolution des idées sur la frontière entre la névrose et la psychose), doctor's thesis, University of Paris.

Von Endts, A. (1924), Über Träume von Schizophrenen, *Internationale Zeitschrift für Psychoanalyse*, 10, pp. 292-295.

Von Krafft-Ebing, R. (1886), *Psychopathia Sexualis*, Stuttgart, Ferdinand Enke.

Von Krafft-Ebing, R. (1893[1879-18880]), *Lehrbuch der Psychiatrie auf klinischer Grundlage für praktische Ärzte und Studirende*, 5th edition, Stuttgart, Ferdinand Enke.

Vowinckel, E. (1930), Der heutige Stand der psychiatrischen Schizophrenieforschung, *Internationale Zeitschrift für Psychoanalyse*, 16, pp. 471-492.

Wajeman, G. (1982), *Le Maître et l'Hystérique*, Paris, Seuil/Navarin.

Ward, C. (1989), *Altered States of Consciousness and Mental Health, a Cross-Cultural Perspective*, London, Sage Publications.

Weiss, J. & Rhoads, J. (1979), Brief Reactive Psychosis: A Psychodynamic Interpretation, *Journal of Clinical Psychiatry*, 40, 10, pp. 440-443.

Weller, M. (1988), Hysterical Behavior in Patriarchal Communities: Four Cases, *British Journal of Psychiatry*, 152, pp. 687-695.

Williams, T. (1910), The Simulation of Hysteria, *American Journal of Insanity*, 67, 2, pp. 287-297.

World Health Organization (1975), *Schizophrenia: a Multinatio-*

nal Study, Public Health Papers no. 63, Geneva, World Health Organization.

Zarifian, E. (1986), Un diagnostic en psychiatrie: pour quoi faire?, in Gori, R., Miller, J.-A. & Wartel, R. (eds.), *La Querelle des diagnostics*, Collection Cliniques, Paris, Navarin, pp. 75-87.

Zetzel, E. (1968), The so-called Good Hysteric, *International Journal of Psycho-Analysis*, 49, pp. 256-260.

Index

FSC
www.fsc.org
MIX
Papier | Fördert
gute Waldnutzung
FSC® C083411

Kolibri 360 GmbH
Ferdinand-Jühlke-Straße 7
99095 Erfurt, Deutschland
produktsicherheit@kolibri360.de